A WAR OF CHAOS AND FURY - PART 2

THE LEVANTHRIA SERIES
BOOK SIX

A.P BESWICK

A.P BESWICK PUBLICATIONS

Editing - Quinn Nichols at Quill & Bone Editing

Cover Design - Rafido Design

ISBN

Paperback: 978-1-916671-34-8

Hardback: 978-1-916671-35-5

THE MERRY MEN.... AND WOMEN

Seth (The Little) Alexander
Joshua (The Scarlett) Gray
Daniel (The Friar) Dorman
Robin (The Hood) Hill

The Legendary Pieces Of Eight

Seth (Blackbeard) Alexander
Z (The Sparrow)

THE DRAGON

Louis Jay Dombroski
Jen Smith
Zaakir (The Archer) Patel
Sunny Side Up
Señor Neo
Jacob Salm
Rhonda K Koenning
Brandon H Beers
Jeremiah Silva
Seth Alexander
Christopher Simard
Matthew Schaaff
Armin Enjoyer of Well Written Books
Damien Troutman
Meredith Carstens
Tanya Hagel
Michael William
Alexander Gonser

THE DRAGON

Andrew Sheridan

Ian White

Geoff Seutter

R. S. Howell

Brian R Knoblich

Kevin Camps

Benjamin Powell

Oliver Stegmann

Lauren O'Connor

Travis Hawkins

Joshua Gray

Troy Hauck, RN

Kat Holder

Christian Mays

Dominic Jones

Charlotte Lotte de Reuver Valerie Wiechmann and Shane
Libihoul

THE LEGENDS OF LEVANTHRIA

NeonPixxius
Trevor "TJ" Meeds
Heather Dangerfeld
Louis Dombroski
Oleg
Samuel Bellis
Joe Wright
Samuel Silveira
Steven Hessing
Nathanial Landreville
Johnathon VandenHeuvel
Brandon Beers
Philip J. Harley
Alexander Edwards
Brandon Blayney
Bonnielee Radford

This book is for every single one of you who has supported me throughout this series. From the bottom of my heart Thank You.

Levanthria

iterian plains

Uster

Antar

Yugo's Tears

Rivah

N

Voraz

Zakron Keep

BOOK FIVE OF
THE LEVANTHRIA SERIES

A WAR OF CHAOS AND FURY

PART 2

A.P BESWICK

FOREWORD

We made it, this is the conclusion of a series that has taken years to bring to you. In the final battle there are scenes that run concurrently as you are reading a battle from multiple point of views. As with the last story I have tried my best to organise chapters to the best of my ability to follow the correct timeline.

I hope you enjoy this final instalment

I
VIREO

Some spellcasters, namely those who delve in necromancy believe that on the night where the moon casts a red shadow, the spirits of the dead are free to roam the lands. It is on this night where a necromancers magic is considered most potent and one that they often celebrate until the sun rises once again.

Liana Veck, Volume VII of The History of Levanthria - 205 KR

I find myself questioning my choices from the day past as I stand on the deck of what looks like an abandoned pirate ship. I still have daylight on my side, but not for too much longer. The boat rocks gently where it has dropped anchor, the gulls above sing loudly as they scream out for food, taking refuge on the ship's mast as they taunt and goad me.

The sound of the ocean is somewhat calming. Having not been on a ship for so long, I have spent more time on ships recently than I would have liked. I am surprised by the memories that come flooding back to me just from the smell of the sea salt in the air coinciding with the motion of being on a ship. Long journeys alongside Gillam, alongside Lek, both no longer of this earth, and my heart fractures at the suppressed memories of them.

My emotions catch me by surprise as I picture both their faces. We were all so naive to the world, to the cruelty it can bring, to the cruelty we were part of for so many years. Grief turns to shame as quickly as the rising tide, and I look out at the vast expanse of water beyond the horizon, feeling a lump form in my throat.

"I will always do my best," I say, as if Gillam can hear me. Lek can rot in the afterlife for all I care.

I turn to examine the ship that continues to sway eerily. What would cause its crew to abandon it so freely? I look up at the ship's mast where the flag hangs limply. Its black and blue colours are unmistakable, as is the ornate carving of a girl at the front of the ship, her face contorted with anger and rage. *Esara's Revenge* is the most feared pirate ship on the seas. Why would they not leave anybody here to at least guard it?

Unless they left in haste.

But there is no sign of a struggle. The ship bears the marks of battle but not recent. It is in pristine condition, the dark wood well looked after even after all these years. I have heard so many stories of this ship, of its crew, stories that contradict what Jordell told me all those years ago in the Forest of Opiya. He was adamant that they could be trusted, that behind the stories were decent people, ones who wanted to make the world better. The two versions of the same crew could not be more polarising, however if there is a man whose judgement I trust more than anyone, it is Jordell's.

My footsteps drum loudly on the ship's deck as I look around, my hand resting on the hilt of my blade, just in case. When I reach the centre of the ship, a noise catches my attention, a noise that is not in tandem with the ocean or the light groaning of the ship as it rocks in the ocean.

I stifle a breath and close my eyes to try and focus on the sound that is in my periphery, blending in with the ambience.

A knock, ever so light.

Then, three knocks follow, one after another. It could be that something has fallen below deck and the motion of the ship is causing it to catch against something, but none-theless, it is something I need to investigate.

There is a latch on the door that leads to below deck, and I reach down and grab hold of it. The metal is cold and the latch is heavy, but I heave it up to reveal a set of stairs descending into a darkened void. I remove my sword and begin a slow descent down the steps. They are wet, and it takes my best effort not to slip on my arse as I make my way to the bottom.

The ship's creaking and groaning echoes loudly down here as the boat rocks, and I can't see anything beyond the light that is cast from above.

Then the knocking happens again.

To my right, I see an old lamp hanging up. I rest my sword on the floor, then remove some flint from the inside of my tunic and light the lamp. With sword and lamp in hand, I continue further into the ship. There is definitely no crew here.

Whether it is against my better judgement or not, I call out, "Hello?" I wait for a moment before continuing, "Is anybody there?"

Only a few seconds pass before another knock calls to me, this time faster and louder.

My heart spikes. "I mean you no harm. Can you knock if you need help?"

No sooner have I spoken than another rapid knocking greets me, and I move quickly towards the sound.

"Keep knocking," I call out.

They do. The knock becomes constant and more energised. I pass through the crew quarters and soon find myself at another set of stairs which take me into the cargo hold. The knocks get louder and louder as I draw closer.

Barrels, fruit, bread, and other supplies are still piled up down here, meaning they did leave in haste – but why?

Another knock draws my attention to the back of the cargo hold, where I see some metal bars. It looks like some form of cell. Most ships have them, mainly for prisoners or mutineering shipmates. As I approach, I raise my lantern to see something in the corner of the cell.

Or should I say someone.

A woman with long, cascading black hair is curled up on her side. She is bound, her mouth gagged. Her skin is almost as white as snow, and there is a wildness in her eyes. Muffled shouts escape her as she tries to speak to me, but I can't make out her words.

I sheathe my sword and place the lantern beside us, then take hold of the rusted iron bars between us and pull on them. It is locked, with no sign of a key.

"Try and get close to the bars," I say.

She does what she can to shuffle along the ground towards me with her arms bound behind her back. Even her ankles are tied tightly together. She builds up some momentum before I can finally reach her, and I take hold of the gag and pull it from her mouth.

She gasps for breath, gulping in air. I have no clue how long she has been here.

"That motherfucker!" Her accent is soft, her voice gentle despite the aggression that she shows. I don't blame her; I would be the same had I been tied up and left like this.

When I see the sheen of her jet-black hair, I make a bold assumption based on information that Jordell had told me.

"Zerina?" I ask, sure that it is her, despite only being able to see her features by lamplight.

"Who are you?" she asks, a wary, untrusting look in her eyes, one that I do not blame her for.

"I assure you I am a friend," I say as I yank on the bars once more, but there is no chance that I can pull them free. "I don't suppose you happen to know where the key is?"

"Can you do me a favour?" she asks. "The amulet around my neck, can you remove it? Ulrik placed it there purposely to suppress my magic."

That makes sense. Jordell told me that she was a powerful witch.

Sure enough, I see a thin, black cord hanging loosely from her neck, attached to a green jewel that sits delicately at the base of her collarbone.

"Is he not an ally?" I ask, leaning through the bars again and grabbing hold of the amulet. It is warm to the touch as if charged by fire, and when I lift it, I notice it is deceivingly weighty. "Why would he place this on you?"

Zerina leans her head forward so that I can lift the amulet over her head, freeing her from it.

"Because they are a scoundrel," she says. Then, with a flare of magic, the ropes bound around her wrists and ankles ignite into flames, disintegrating in an instant without so much as a flick of her finger. I didn't realise that magic use could be so refined, so controlled. She stands up, rubbing her wrists and looking at the metal bars that still encase her. "Stand back," she says.

Obliging, I give us some distance and watch in awe as Zerina grabs the bars and her hands begin to glow with an intense brightness emitting from under her palms. A powerful heat pushes against me as the bars start to drip with molten metal, Zerina's focus maintained on the cell. In moments, the lock mechanism is glowing white-hot, sizzling as she disintegrates it. With a gentle push, the door swings open, and she steps out from inside the cell.

"I need to go," she says. "What Ulrik plans on doing is madness, I need to stop them."

"Wait, what happened here?" I ask, still confused. Zerina walks past me and starts making her way to the main deck of the ship, so I quickly follow, calling from behind her. "Why did he lock you away? How long have you been here?"

Zerina's steps are staggered and she stumbles several times. She is clearly in need of food and drink. "I've been here for days," she says with a shamed tongue. "That bastard would have left me here to die. They have been planning this for so long, to have an amulet to suppress my magic without me knowing. Well, it just makes me wonder if I ever knew them at all. I have been so naive to look past all the warning signs all these years, I should have acted sooner."

I cannot tell if Zerina is talking to me or herself as she rambles without making any eye contact with me.

"That still doesn't answer why he locked you in that cell," I call after her as I follow from behind. When we reach the main deck, the fresh air brings a welcome reprieve from the dank dampness from below. Zerina raises her hand to shield her eyes from the setting sun and I see how pale her skin is, how malnourished she is.

"Because they know I will stop them, that I won't –" she pauses for a moment. "I can't let them go through with this." Her legs buckle and I quickly rush to her side to help keep her upright.

"I am no damsel in distress," she says, shrugging from my clutches.

"I wouldn't be bold enough to make that assumption," I say, stepping away to give her the space that she desires. "You do, however, need to eat and drink before you do anything else. You won't be able to stop anyone in your current state."

"I don't have time to stop, they are already ahead of me. I am days behind!"

"You will eat and drink, then I will take you to wherever it is you need to go," I say, an assertive tone to my voice. "Just do me a favour though. Don't try and steal my horse. It is the only way I have of getting back to the Forest of Opiya."

"You would do this for me? A stranger? Tell me, who exactly are you and why are you here?" Zerina grows suspicious of me now that she has had chance to get a grip on her surroundings and the current situation.

Instinctively I raise my hands while saying, "I assure you, I am a friend. Someone just happened to tell me about your ship when I was nearby, and I knew in that instant that I needed to speak with you. My name is Vireo," I say, lowering my hood for the first time. "We have a mutual friend, Jordell."

"Jordell?" she says, her hostility calming. "How is the old mage? I haven't seen him for years."

"He isn't great," I start. "It didn't sit well with him what happened to Laith, when Rhagor took control of his body. He has lived in exile for such a long time in Zakron that I fear madness has taken him. I tried to get him to come back, to help take back Levanthria and end Rhagor's reign, but he sent me away. I thought his magic could help us. After all, Rhagor is a god. We need all the strength we can get."

"Which is why you are here," Zerina is quick to deduce that I would want to recruit her to my cause.

I raise my shoulders and give her a softened look. I am not in as bad condition as she is, but I am tired, and my body aches as an age that I ignored for so long creeps up on me.

"I have my own agenda, yes, but I am more than happy to help you if you will allow me." I walk to the side of the ship's deck and ready myself to climb down the ladder to the longboat I used to get here. "I have supplies with my horse." I point down to the shoreline where my horse is luckily still tied to a tree. "Eat and drink, at least. If you want to go it alone, that's fine."

Zerina rolls her eyes, knowing that I am right. "Lead the way, then," she says.

I smile before climbing down and getting onto the boat. I almost lose my footing as I take a seat by the oars to steer us back to shore, nearly falling into the water as the boat rocks wildly underneath my boots.

Zerina lets out a laugh as she climbs in easily and settles into the longboat. "You're not used to the ocean," she says. For the first time, I see her smile, and light sparkles in her eyes.

"I am more versed in the forest than the ocean," I say. "It is only through desperation that I find myself exploring Levanthria once more."

"Tell me, what is your story, Vireo?" Zerina asks as I start to steer us ashore.

We spend the subsequent time setting up a makeshift fire, which is so much easier when you have someone with you that can wield fire magic. As we eat, I tell her everything that has brought me to this point, to this moment.

"So you want to stop Rhagor, who is a god, that possessed your friend to take control of these lands? And to do this, you want to create an army by uniting the most powerful people across the lands?" She drinks from a flask before wiping her lips with the cuff of her sleeve.

"All I want is for Levanthria to be free from tyranny, to be truly free for the first time in so long."

Zerina eyes me up before taking a bite of the stale bread she clutches in her hand. "That's all well and good, but from where I am sitting, all I can see is you on your own, with limited resources." She looks around us mockingly. "And no army in sight."

"Do not be mistaken, we have men and women a plenty in our ranks. My mission is to find those powerful enough to give us the slightest chance in battle. I need people to lead, to command the battlefield. Are the stories of the King's Keep true?" I ask.

Zerina stares into the campfire, seemingly finding herself lost for a fleeting moment. "It is not a day I am proud of, but yes, it is true," she sighs. "Many lives were lost that day."

"It's been over eight years since King Athos Almerion was killed. I, like many others, celebrated the day that news broke of his killing. I thought that it would bring stability to Levanthria, that it could be the start of a new dawn, but I was wrong. That blasted sword, that blasted god." I feel the anger and frustration building within me and my jaw clenches tightly as I try to gather myself. "So many lives were taken because of King Almerion's foolish wars, but he thought he was benefitting Levanthria. I refuse to call Rhagor king. He is not, and he's not a deity, either. I don't believe the gods would cause so much suffering simply for the sake of it. He is something else, something far worse. And we need to stop him."

"We?" Zerina looks up. "That is a little presumptuous."

"If the stories are true – if you really held the line against the Zarubians on your own – then you could help us in the battle that is to come."

Zerina thinks on this for a moment longer before raising her head and saying, "I have spent so many years sailing the seas with Ulrik, all over a foolish promise to keep them safe. I fear they are lost. For too long have I been complicit or turned to look the other way as they gradually became more and more twisted, more corrupted." Zerina looks up to the stars, her tears sparkling with their reflections. "If only I had done something different, I wouldn't be in this position, and neither would they. The fact that after all this time, they left me bound without a way of escape, even Darmour . . ." Her voice breaks at the mention of the name. "I understand his decision, I respect his decision to follow Ulrik. After all, he is first mate of *Esara's Revenge*, and he is bound by code. But that doesn't mean it didn't hurt me when he also left me, no matter how conflicted he may have been."

Zerina's gaze meets my own once again and she says, "If you help me with stopping Ulrik, with stopping this madness, then I will swear a new oath to you and this impending battle. Help me stop them, and I will help you defeat Rhagor."

2

MORGANA

I walk through the rocky terrain of the Gondoron Pass with heavy, tired legs, and my body hurts in ways that I didn't know was possible. Bloodied and broken, I drag my right leg behind me as I hobble slowly, desperately searching for my sister. I am still in shock from what happened during the night, and I continue to draw on my magic to test it, but each time I try to home in on my core, my magic feels further away from me.

It is not even as if my fingertips are on the edge of my power, striving to stretch just that little bit further so that I can be reunited with it. There are simply no traces of it at all. There is nothing there, and I have never felt so empty.

Those spectres, those ghastly spirits – whatever it is that they have done, they have drained me completely of my power and left me here to die. They said it was a result of my actions, that they were stuck between this world and the afterlife because of me. Because of the lives I had taken from them.

Aside from me losing my magic, the worst part was that I did not recognise any of their faces, although it was difficult because of their translucent energy. It shames me to know I have ended so many lives. Young and old. Men, women, and children. I have done the most despicable things in order to attain what I have.

But in this state, in this broken and deprived body, what do I have to show for it? When everything is peeled back to the bare bones, what is being queen really worth? The more my mind searches, the harder I find it to really think of anything I have achieved in this life.

My ankle rolls on a rock as I step forward, causing excruciating pain, and I scream out at the top of my lungs until nothing but a rasp escapes me. My eyes sting with anger and hatred, not for the situation, but for the consequences that I have brought upon myself.

More than anything, I am angry that these spirits chose to exact their revenge on me when I was heading somewhere to do good, to do the right thing. All I want is to find my sister and my niece, to help them get to safety, to get as far away as possible from Rhagor. After that, I will gladly meet the afterlife, it is no less than what I deserve.

I laugh to myself at the visions I once had about my death at Zakron's Keep, and how far removed this situation was. That vision was clearly created by Rhagor from afar, to manipulate me into granting his freedom from his stone prison where he had been held for so long. In cruelty and desperation, he manipulated me through these visions, causing me to engage in all these unspeakable acts, each time chipping away at my soul until nothing but stone remained. And now I find that stone being weathered away by the spirits that torment me, and I imagine that they will continue to do so until that stone is eroded into sand.

The air is still and the sun sits harshly above me, hammering down on the last of my resolve as I continue through the pass. The cliffs on either side of me rise high, and everywhere I look is barren of life. It will be a miracle if I am not attacked by another wyvern or some other creature soon. I am perfect prey, an easy meal for anything else that might be lurking here.

My body may be broken, but I still have my resolve. I will use this to move forward, to keep going, and when I have found them, I can finally rest. I only hope they have not been met with any danger in the time it took me to get here.

The sound of my scream of pain and frustration continues to echo down the pass, causing some nearby birds to take flight from the clifftops. At least that means it isn't completely barren of life. My flask is near enough empty of water and I have no rations of food in the groya skin bag strapped to my back. I question if I should just toss the bag, but decide to keep it in case I find anything that I can forage like berries or mushrooms.

I stop for a moment, taking in the sight of the pass as I perch against a boulder, pulling my bag around and removing my flask to drink.

When I tip it towards my mouth, I am disheartened as the last of the water pours down my throat, the moisture it provides not lasting long.

"Fuck!" I curse as I throw the flask onto the ground. Something I instantly regret as I know I will need to pick it back up.

Why now? Why is it now that these spirits seek to torture me, why could it not be in a few days' time when I was done? They could have done whatever they wanted with me then.

Instead of looking up at the skies to curse the gods, I lower my eyes to the ground, towards the afterlife. It is a good job they have taken my magic away, because given the chance, I would smite them with the foulest of curses.

There's no sign of anyone at all, let alone my sister or niece. Whether alive or dead, I can only assume they are no longer here, and that means this whole journey has been pointless. Had I stayed in Askela, would this have happened to me? Would Rhagor have protected me from those vengeful spirits, would he have protected me from losing my magic?

Rhagor is a cruel king, a cruel god. Would he be smiling if he could see the state that I am in? I imagine so. Given the haste with which I left, he must have figured out by now that I have been secretly scheming behind his back for such a long time. Needs must, and I do not regret hiding Gillam from him. I am all but sure that if he knew of her existence, he would have had her executed long ago.

I lean forward to pick up my discarded flask once again, losing balance in the process. I stumble forward, falling flat against the dirt-covered stones underneath. My legs instantly feel numb as my knees bounce off the stone before my hands slap down on the ground. This time I don't cry out. Instead, I begin to sob, simply unable to carry on.

Then movement catches my eye.

My eyes sting as I look up. In the distance, I see the birds that took flight earlier have landed on the ground, and they seem to be pecking at something.

Fear grips me. I drag myself up from the floor and continue to stumble through the centre of the pass with a newfound determination. I continue to shuffle along slowly and painfully towards the birds, fearful of what they may have found. Perhaps if they are simply scavenging an animal carcass, it will not be too far rotten, and I could at least feast on its meats should I be able to start a fire. Something that I haven't done in years without magic. I wonder if I'd even remember how.

As I draw closer, the birds cackle as though they are mocking me, goading me. Their squawks grow louder with every step that I take towards them.

It feels like an age, but when I eventually reach them, they take flight in a flurry, scattering for safety as if I was hunting them.

In their wake, a man is lying face-down in the dirt. His hands and the back of his head are covered with marks from the birds pecking at him as they feasted on his skin. I breathe a sigh of relief; it's not Yaelor or Gillam. But I'm disappointed it is human, because this means I'll have to find food some other way, or face dying in this destitute place.

The sun feels as though it is intentionally shining brighter, forcing down even harsher rays of heat which cause my skin to prickle and blister. I'm drowning in sweat, and I do not know whether it is the weather conditions or an infection of my wounds that draws this temperature from me – or worse, both. I desperately need water, and the pounding in my head is becoming unbearable. My body throbs from the cuts that coat my body, burning as though I have been pressed with red-hot pokers.

And suddenly I find myself struggling to remain standing as the terrain around me begins to blur into one. The world spins so fast that I fear I will spill my empty stomach. I find myself falling once again, but this time, I am unable to break the fall. I slam down hard into the dirt, my head ricocheting off the ground. A ringing noise vibrates in my head, so loud and shrill that I wonder whether it will cause my ears to bleed. The temptation to close my eyes and simply drift away becomes too much. Should I just let my injuries ravage my body, drift off to the afterlife? That is, if those vengeful spirits will let me.

I close my eyes, waiting for the darkness to consume me, for the pain to stop. At least I will pass with the knowledge that I tried.

"Who's that over there?" the voice of a young man calls out.

A glimmer of hope forces me to open my eyes, but the bright light above me causes them to blur and sting. I raise my head as best as I can, but I'm unable to make out the figures that approach me.

"Help me," I groan, barely able to speak and feeling as though I'm clinging on to the very edges of life.

"Rior, go check them, but make it quick. We don't know if there are any more bandits around." There is a familiarity to the voice that commands the other, but in this confused state, I cannot decipher it, yet it brings me comfort somehow.

I feel hands rest on my shoulders as someone checks over me. They are surprisingly cold.

"It can't be," the man says. "It must be a trick."

"What do you mean?" his companion says, his tone frustrated. "We don't have time for this, we need to get this woman to a healer. Looks like we have two to take care of, now. We are at least a full day's ride to Eltera."

"This isn't just anyone, Orjan," the voice says.

My eyes bolt open. As the young man watching over me comes slowly into focus, I am shocked to find that I recognise him.

"Morgana?" Orjan's young squire asks, peering into my face.

"You must be mistaken," the other voice snaps, and

now I know by his accent that it is him. "Why would she be out here?"

"I know what I see, and I am telling you, it is her."

"Here, take hold of this woman so I can check."

The two of them fumble around, and again I try and raise my head, but I struggle to form words.

"How can this be?" Orjan says as he leans over me.

But now it is my turn to be confused, because the face that I see is not that of a lizard man, but that of an attractive, olive-skinned man with a dark grey stubbled beard and grey matted hair, his face slightly aged with tinges of grey that line the side of his head.

"Orjan?" I attempt to speak his name but barely a whisper leaves my lips.

If I am to meet the afterlife on this day, I do so in front of the man who sent me on my path for redemption.

3

ULRIK

Everything I've done for the last ten years of my life has brought me to this moment.

My breath trembles as I push myself to take the final steps. I am beyond redemption. No one would do the things I have done, and because of that, I know that one day I will meet my maker and face the consequences of my actions. As long as this plan works, then it will have all been worth it. After all, I would do anything for my brother. And now here I stand, ready to instigate his resurrection.

Even though it does not sit well with me what I did to Zerina, abandoning her like that, there was no way in this world, no possible scenario, where she would have been willing to assist me with this plan.

That was why I secretly bartered for the amulet, knowing that it was imbued with magic capable of suppressing hers. How else was I meant to stop her?

It would never have been my intention to physically hurt her. But I saw the hurt in her eyes when I forced my crew to take her and hold her in the cell of my ship. I cannot see how she can ever forgive me for what I have done.

That is a consequence that I'm prepared to live with if it means that I can bring my brother back to this world.

I look around my old bedroom. The house is decrepit with age, rot, and mould, and there are gaps in the walls where the planks of wood have simply fallen away. The windows have broken beyond repair, and the ceiling has collapsed in places. There is a musk in the air, and with every breath I take, it feels like the mould latches on to my lungs. I haven't been here for so long, and even though time has passed, it has not made it any easier. This place holds so many long-suppressed memories that I fear it may break down the boundaries of the fortress I've built around my heart.

In the corner of the room sits a rocking chair, perfectly still under a patchwork cushion that I remember being cream and red. It now sits with blackened dirt creeping in from the edges, and in front of it is a small teddy bear that I find myself drawn to.

It is a chair where my mother would have nursed me as a babe, soothing me, reassuring me before placing me back into my bed. What I would give to see her one last time, to let her hold me and tell me that no matter what I have done, everything will be okay. Even if those words are not true. There is a sense of safety that only a parent can give their child, and given that I was just a babe when my father passed, all I know is the unconditional love my mother had for me, and I for her.

The crew are outside in the street, waiting. Darmour has taken up guard duty with a couple of others, while I have sent the rest of the crew down to the local tavern to blow off some steam. I've told them that they better be on their best behaviour or face my wrath. After all, this is the town of my birth. This is where my mother raised me and where I left the remains of my brother.

True, it is strange being back in Osar, for being here makes me feel close to him once more. He sacrificed himself for the rest of us. He did so much for me when he returned from the King's Fleet, and even though he wasn't here for much of my upbringing, I know that everything he did was for me and for my mother.

Reaching into the pocket of my jacket, I take hold of the Resurrection Stone and squeeze it tightly in my hand. I have sacrificed so much to get to this point, my soul now shattered into a thousand pieces.

Swallowing down my feelings and feeling at risk of being overwhelmed, I turn on my heels and exit my room, walking across the rickety hallway towards what was my brother's room. A room that my mother left exactly as it was even after he left to join the navy. There were so many times I had asked her for the space given that the room was far bigger than my own. She always declined, and I never understood why.

But now I have lived with this grief for so long, I fully understand her reasoning. If only I had my mother's remains, I could bring her back from the dead, too, and with that, our family would be reunited. My father, too.

I gently push open the door to my brother's room, letting it move back slowly on its creaking hinges. The room is filled with darkened shadows. The curtains are drawn, still hanging on despite being ravaged by moths. As I pull the curtains back, I'm greeted by a plume of dust and the culprits of the small holes in the fabric as moths fly out to get to cover. I find myself drawn to the way they move as they make their bid for safety.

It is bright outside, and a light breeze creeps in through

the broken glass. I look down past the garden to see Darmour and two others stood watching down the road. The two newer members of the crew seem restless, fidgeting while they stand watch. I don't blame them. If Zerina were to turn up, they wouldn't stand a chance, and I have no doubt that she would let free her fury for what we have done to her.

She knows our plan. She knows what we intend to do, and she knows where we'll be. After my brother died, she and Darmour were the only members of the crew that were around to help me bury him.

Darmour stands to attention with his hooked hand by his side, his good hand resting on the hilt of his blade, ready for combat. He's a good man, a good pirate. One I'm proud to have served alongside and who has fulfilled his duty to me as my first mate.

I turn to leave, knowing that it is time.

I stop in my tracks, however, when I am greeted by the full-length dressing room mirror. In its reflection, I see my brother's image looking back at me. He hasn't aged a day since the day that I lost him, and although I know that it is me glamoured to look like him, it still catches me off guard and my heart breaks. For years I have avoided this, avoided seeing my reflection, for I found it too painful to see his eyes looking back at me.

"Ulrik," I say through stifled breath. I stand for a further moment looking over him in the mirror. He wears a long, waxy black coat with a dirty white shirt underneath – all the attire you'd expect a pirate captain to wear, including the tricorn hat that was my brother's. His face is coated with grime and muck. I am in dire need of a bath after all the travelling we have done.

The only thing that has changed in his appearance is

the thick, black beard that clings to his face. It's kind of ironic that this black beard is how most people would remember him by, instead of the bravery that he was capable of.

"You are doing what you have to," the reflection says, eyes deep, dark, and unmoving. There is a coldness to them.

"I know," I say in return, my usual frosty demeanour thawing like snow in the shadows gradually touched by the creeping sun.

"Remember why you do this, what you have been working for."

"We're so close," I say, my voice starting to tremble. "It is not long now, brother. We will be together again."

"Tell me your name."

"Ulrik," I say, struggling to keep eye contact with the reflection. My voice is gravelly, and I can't bear to see the image of my brother that looks back at me.

"Tell me your real name."

"Ulrik," I repeat in defiance, my voice just as stern.

"Is that what you're going back to when I have returned? Do not be so foolish."

It's true, it is something that I had not thought about in my haste to resurrect my brother. Mine is an identity that I have long hidden, that I have suppressed in my quest for absolution.

"I can't," I protest, still unable to make eye contact with Ulrik's reflection.

"You can."

"I can't."

"Look at me," he commands assertively, "look at me as the true you, and tell me your name." Anger spills from his tongue as though he's disappointed in me, and it breaks my heart.

"No," I say, "I will not." I hold too much shame. I do not want to look at myself. I can't do it, I'm not strong enough. A lump forms in my throat, my voice breaking. What is happening to me? What is wrong with me?

"LOOK AT ME!"

With a snap, I quickly raise my head and breathe heavily as I stare at the stranger that looks back at me. I've borne Ulrik's image for half of my life, and I'm not prepared for the person that now stands opposite.

It is a stranger, a face I barely recognise, one that has changed so much over the years. After all, it has aged, matured into adulthood. Long, wavy blond hair cascades from underneath my hat, sitting far beyond my shoulders and resting just above my chest. I struggle to breathe with the weight that sits heavy on my chest. Deep green eyes blink back at me from above a row of light freckles that are speckled across my cheeks and the bridge of my nose. The knot in my throat threatens to stop my breathing, and my legs feel so heavy that they might collapse underneath me at any moment.

After all the time that has passed since I have remained in Ulrik's form, nothing can prepare me for the sight of the young woman that hides behind his glamour.

I try to form words, but a torrent of emotion slams into me like a crashing wave, consuming me and threatening to drown me. Before I have a chance to breathe, her cries leave my throat, followed by uncontrollable sobs as my chest heaves. All I long for in this moment is for my brother to wrap his strong arms around me and comfort me.

For so long I have hidden in plain sight. If I were to walk out to my crew in this form, only one man would recognise me, but even Darmour has not seen this face in years. I was a child when I started wearing my mask, pretending to be something that I am not.

I look down in shame, staring at my boots. I can't bring myself to look at my own reflection.

"That wasn't hard, was it?" I hear his voice.

When I raise my head, it is his reflection that greets me once again. Tears continue to pour down my face like a cascading waterfall. I wipe them away, then reach into my pocket. From it, I pull out the Resurrection Stone.

Its hard, polished surface is ice-cold to touch, and my fingers and palm tingle with the magic that is stored within it.

"It is time," I say, looking one last time in the reflection. If this magic works, then the next time I see that face, it will be my actual brother standing before me, not a reflection in a mirror. My heart starts pounding in my chest like a battle drum as I slowly make my way down the rickety stairs, each step I take causing them to groan as if they are ready to collapse underneath my weight. I make my way into the kitchen and out of the back door where a large jarjoba tree stands.

It stands tall, its trunk thick and aged. The large leaves billow out from the cascade of branches that intertwine with one another above. It was the tree that my great-great-grandfather planted when he first claimed this land. I had often played at its base as a child, and it is here where I buried Ulrik.

I walk towards the tree tentatively. The long grass is wild and untamed after all these years, reaching as high as my knees. There is a calmness around me, which counteracts the storm that has raged inside me since I lost him. The sky is clear and blue with not a cloud in sight, as though the gods themselves have intervened to make it possible for them to watch over us on this day.

But I stopped believing in the gods long ago.

When I reach the tree, I grab hold of the shovel that had been perched against the rough bark. My hands tremble so much that I struggle to hold on to the instrument. I take a deep breath and remind myself why I am doing this. A glimmer of excitement overcomes me as I start to dig.

It is not long now until we will be reunited.

Hopefully then I can find some semblance of peace.

4

JORDELL

The Kraken is a legend and nothing more, hidden in the oceans far beyond Levanthria. It is believed to be as old as the ocean itself. Sailors claim its tentacles can crush entire ships, that said as far as I am aware there have never been any actual sightings, only tales and whispers amongst ship mates. There are ships a plenty though that have simply vanished.

Savorgia Wielstrom, Leviathans of the Deep, 214 KR

I t has been two days since we left the shores of Voraz. We were there only long enough to resupply for the rest of the journey to the mainland; I did not wish to stay in Voraz longer than necessary, as there were one or two sets of eyes paying particular attention to Elara when we landed at the docks.

After all, a growlite is most unusual in these parts, and would fetch a nice price for someone looking for a more exotic acquisition. This was reason enough not to stay longer than we needed to. Elara has chosen to follow me for some reason, but she is a wild beast that, in my opinion, cannot and should not be tamed. Should she wish to leave me at any time, she is free to do so.

Nareen, as I have since come to know him by, sits at the rear of the small fishing boat. It is dangerously thin, like a miniature version of the longboats that the Barbaraqs use. Initially I had patched the sail with cloth from my cloak, but the one thing we did manage to get in Voraz was material to fix the sail and a small amount of supplies for the journey back to the mainland. Although I am not quite sure what Nareen used to barter with, given that I had no coin to offer.

His hand is fixed to the rudder, steering us through the calm waters. There is a light mist around us but nothing that is obscuring our view too much, and nothing more than what I would expect when the sun has not long since risen. Is it possible that the fog that Nareen found himself lost in when we first crossed paths was an intervention from the gods?

I sit with my back against the mast, facing out at the vast expanse of water ahead of us. It would not surprise me if we had been sailing around in circles.

"Land ahead," Nareen says, his loud, deep voice startling me from my thoughts.

I raise my head and lo and behold, I can see the land that he speaks of, yet it is a strange feeling that I am greeted with. I left these lands in shame as I blamed myself for everything that passed all that time ago, and therefore the things that have passed since.

Now is the time though. If I can make amends, I will do what I can. If that means protecting Laith's child, then so be it.

I can't see any discernible landmarks ahead, so I am not too sure where we are, but as we draw closer to the shore, my heart thunders just that little bit faster, and I look up at the skies above.

I don't know if I will ever trust a god and their words fully again, but where this child is concerned, I feel drawn to get involved.

"That's the mountain ranges of the Gondoron Pass," Nareen says, staring ahead as he studies the vast mountain ranges I can see in the distance. "It is to the east where Osar lies."

Elara squawks as she glide above us, her wing near full health following the intervention of my healing magic. I have been studying her biology as best I can, making mental notes of how her wings work, her behaviours as she skulks around the boat looking for fish to feed on. She is truly fascinating. I watch her as she elegantly glides, albeit with a bit of a wobble, letting the sea breeze guide her.

Osar is where Vireo told me the child was, so this is where I shall head. It won't be long, now.

I lean forward from my seat and let out a sigh. When I get to Osar, I have no clue what I will say. My thoughts drift back to when I left. I could barely look Yaelor in the eye when I told her my plans to leave. Yaelor had protested, insisting that I should stay. Now I see why she argued with me so much. She must have known she was with child when I left. But if that was the case, why didn't she tell me? Losing Laith was too much, and through the darkness, it became even darker. At times I wondered if I should end my life, end the pain and heartache that I was feeling, that was consuming me.

I hadn't wanted a big send-off. I didn't want the awkwardness of that, so I left in the dead of night, ensuring that no one saw me leave. For that alone, I do not think

Yaelor will ever forgive me. This isn't about me, however. This is about the child.

When we reach the shore, I help Nareen pull the boat to the embankment. The rope bites into my shoulder, and I am not sure if my frail frame actually offers him any help as he does the bulk of the strong work. Elara is padding around in the sand, pecking the ground before she lets out a squawk and flies at some rocks. She taps on them over and over, then tosses a small crab into the air which she catches in her mouth, crunching the hard shell. Satisfied, she flaps her purple-scaled wings and runs around in a circle as if she is delighted. I find her behaviour fascinating.

"What about the boat?" I ask Nareen as he starts to walk away.

"The gods can have it," he says. "I tell you now, I am never going back out to sea again after this. I just want to be back with my family. I thank the gods that I came across you in Zakron."

"They do move in strange ways," I say under my breath. Was it the gods that intervened or was it fate? Or even a mere coincidence. I suppose that we will never know. What I can be thankful for is being able to barter safe passage back to the mainland.

Taking a step forward, I bed my staff into the ground to brace myself. As I do, the ground starts to shake.

Elara gives a confused chitter before skipping up from the floor and taking to the skies. The ground begins to rumble around me and if I was not holding on to my staff, I am sure I would have fallen to the ground.

"What's going on?" Nareen asks, panic in his voice, and understandably so.

"I don't know," I reply as I look around. Then I notice an indentation in the sand around where I stand, as if the quake is centred around me.

"What are you doing?" Nareen says.

"Nothing," I say, shocked myself at what is happening. "Not intentionally, anyway," I add. Have I accidentally triggered a spell?

When the tip of my staff glows an ice-blue colour, it confirms that it is responsible, but I know for certain I am not controlling it.

Ahead of me, a blue orb that matches the glow of my staff hangs suspended in the air, spinning and crackling as if a storm surges in the very centre of it. The air around us starts to flow as if it is a whirlwind that surrounds us, spraying sand up in the air. I raise my arm to shield my face as the blue orb ahead of us continues to grow in size.

"It can't be!" I gasp as the orb grows about the same size of myself, if not bigger. Within it, I can see thick, brown tree trunks with the odd splash of green, but a strange smell greets me. I sniff up again to confirm it.

"Something's burning." As I mutter the words, smoke starts to billow out from the orb. "What is this?"

"Jordell," I hear the words faintly. It is a woman's voice, and she's in pain.

I stare into the orb, confused.

"Jordell," the voice says again, and I am drawn to it. As I move towards the orb, I am confused by what is happening.

Then I see someone beyond the smoke, lying on the ground. Blood has pooled around her. Her soft blue skin confirms to me who it is, and I dart towards the orb.

"Jordell, no!" I hear Nareen's words behind me, but the sound of him vanishes as I run towards Zariah.

As I jump through the air, the sound of the ocean is

quickly replaced with the sound of flames, and I am greeted with an intense heat. I am in the Forest of Opiya, as if I have walked from one room to the next. I look up to see the Elder Tree engulfed in flames, reaching high into the sky, spewing up thick, black smoke that clings to the air. Instantly I start coughing, but my attention switches to Zariah. The fae queen is badly injured, lying on her back with her hands clasped around her stomach.

With a squawk, Elara flies past me, barely stopping herself before she clatters into a tree. The wind from the orb stops as it begins to dissipate behind me. Nareen is quick enough to pass through. In an instant, he and the beach we were on vanish from sight. I pray that he makes it back to his family.

"Zariah," I say as I trace my hands over her. "What happened? Who did this to you?"

"Rha-gor," she says. There isn't much life remaining in her as she clings to her breaths. Smoke and flames are spreading out, surrounding us. A fire this intense could take the entire forest with it.

Just what on earth has Rhagor done? How has he done this and why? My mind races for answers to questions that I just simply cannot keep up with. All I know in this moment is that if I do not act fast, Zariah will lose her life, leaving her kingdom without a queen.

Grabbing hold of my staff, I start to mutter a healing incantation under my breath. I have not cast a spell this powerful for a long time, and never with anyone so close to death. My magic has come such a long way since the days where healing potions and remedies were the only way that I could help people.

My staff glows brightly as I feel its power reverberate through me. I will need to draw on heavy amounts of

31

power, but this staff is like nothing else in this world. It allows me to use my magic without suffering the consequences, my body unchanged from using the ancient power.

Zariah's breathing stabilises as a yellowish, golden glow courses over her as if water is being splashed onto her. It covers her body in its entirety before pooling round her stomach and intensifying. Her tired eyes widen as new life moves through her. She sits bolt upright, gasping for air and coughing from the thick smoke. I have saved her. For now, at least.

"Can you stand?" I ask as I turn to face the burning Elder Tree. "The flames are going to destroy everything!"

"There's nothing we can do," Zariah says, pulling on my arm. "The Elder Tree is lost. We must warn my people to give them chance of evacuating."

"Go," I say, "I will follow shortly. I must try and contain this." I raise my staff high into the air, my body feeling energised and invigorated as if a newfound strength courses through me. The ice-blue light at the end of my staff intensifies as I start to wave my staff around in the air in a circular motion, my voice echoing loudly as if it is amplified as I start an incantation. I search for the connection within the staff, like a tipping point, as if it is intrinsically connected to me in some way. Then at the core of my stomach I feel it tug, and I know I have found the point that I was searching for. Then I slam my staff into the ground.

My magic shakes the ground violently, but the spell I need to cast is more powerful than anything I have ever tried, especially at this scale. The flames licking out from the Elder Tree look as though they have hit a translucent wall, stopping them in their tracks as my barrier spell starts to take effect, tracking around the outer edge of the tree. I can see the shimmer it reflects as it continues to trace the skies high above, as far as I can see and into the thick cloud of blackened smoke. It doesn't do anything with the burning trees around us, but hopefully it will be enough to stop the fire from spreading. I bed my staff into the ground when I feel the barrier connect and know it to have taken hold around the tree.

Such magic should break my body, but it doesn't. The magic within my staff grows brighter than ever. It vibrates in my hand but shows no sign of breaking despite being pushed to its limits. I step away, letting go of the staff. It is at a point of self-sustaining. I have no clue how it works, only that it does.

Zariah is stood awestruck at what she sees, and I grab hold of her hand, pulling her away. "Come, you must get back to your people."

Tears stream down Zariah's face. "You have no idea what Rhagor has done," she says, her words trembling with grief. "Or what he plans to do next."

5

ORJAN

We return to Eltera with haste, and all the while I question how the gods work in such mysterious ways for us to have stumbled across Morgana hanging on to her life in the middle of nowhere.

Luckily we have three horses between us, and the child proves to be somewhat skilled at riding. I travel with Morgana on the back of my horse and Rior with the Barbaraq woman, Yaelor, who is drifting in and out of consciousness due to the wounds she sustained from the slave traders. What are the chances of fate bringing these two to one place in the middle of nowhere? I question what games it is that the gods themselves are playing. It has been years since I last saw Yaelor in the Forest of Opiya, but there is no mistaking that it is her.

The ride is fast and hard, and once we have returned, I find myself pacing outside of my chamber, hoping that the healers are able to save Morgana. She has taken ill and is being treated in my bed. Somehow, she is still alive, and I dread to think what would have happened to her had our paths not crossed when they did.

The castle walls whisper with the hushed words between the chambermaids and the footmen as word spreads of the queen's presence in Eltera and the grave state she is in. As much as we left things on a frustrated turn last we spoke, I would never want her to be on the end of such harm. We have been through too much together.

The servants give me strange looks as they pass; they have never seen me in my true form, free from my curse.

Rior remains with Yaelor and Gillam in the healers' wing. The child has shown dedication to her mother, refusing to leave for even the slightest bit of rest, or so Rior tells me. For now, I have told him to remain by her side and let me know when the healers are done with her. Having not seen her for so many years, I think it is too much of a coincidence that we have met again. And thanks to the gods that blight us, I do not believe in coincidences.

I find myself muttering under my breath as I pace around the top end of the corridor over and over again. It's not even that I'm lost in my thoughts; I'm just worried and fear for Morgana's well-being. I know her reputation all too well, as do the people of this kingdom. However, after what she did to help liberate Eltera from the Wyverns and the Barbaraq incursion, the vast majority of Elterans have pledged allegiance to her willingly.

The door to my chamber opens and closes, and I turn to face it at once, spinning on my heels. Eltera's head healer, Nora, greets me with a solemn bow of her head, something that I have repeatedly told her she need not do, yet she continues to all the same. She is the most powerful healer that we have in Eltera, and one that I am glad that we have in our ranks.

She's a portly woman of older age and her wisdom is far beyond mine. She wears a long, white dress with golden embroidery on it, which she says is to honour her patron god, Ayaz. She has often told me that Ayaz is the god of healing and wisdom who grants powerful healing charms to those she deems worthy.

After the things I know Morgana has done throughout her life, I can't help but feel apprehensive that on this occasion, Nora will remain ignorant to her plight and the aid that she so desperately needs. After all, Morgana may be queen, but she has many enemies in these lands.

"How is she?" I ask in haste. All I wish in this moment is for her to confirm that Morgana has survived. I care not how long it will take her to recover, just as long as she is still here. Some would dance on her grave and celebrate the dawn of a new queen if she were to pass, but I would not be one of them, for I feel that I am one of the few that has seen Morgana for who she truly is and what she is capable of.

"She is alive," Nora says. Her tone is calm, but I can't help but notice the air of surprise in her own voice. "She is lucky to still be of this world," she says, walking over to me. She stops in front of me and looks up at my face, examining me. It is a bit strange for her to see me this way, to no longer be a lizard man. She reaches down and takes hold of my hands, then closes her eyes as if focusing on something.

I feel relief at her words. My heartbeat is elevated but it is as though the largest of weights has been lifted from my chest, and I let out a huge gasp of air as I finally breathe and stop holding my breath.

"Thank you," I say, "for all that you and your healers have done. You have saved the queen, and I have no doubt that you will be greatly rewarded."

Nora does not open her eyes as she continues to

squeeze my hands. "Strange magic courses through you, Orjan. Magic that I've never come across before." Then her eyes open, and she reaches up and grabs the collar of my tunic, then lowers it to reveal the amulet that is embedded in my skin.

She gasps at what she sees. "It's fused to your – your bones," she stammers. "Where did you come across this amulet?"

"I happened upon it in the ruins of Hora," I tell her. "When I picked it up, it seemed to connect with me in a way that I cannot describe. I tried to fight it, but the temptation was too much, and before I knew it, it had fused with my body. And when I turned to face Rior, my curse was broken."

Nora gives me a solemn smile, continuing to hold my hands delicately as if she was speaking to an elder. "There's something different about this magic. I've never heard or read of any kind of magical artefact that is able to do this, to break curses. I . . . I think you should remove it, Orjan. It may be dangerous."

"I cannot remove it. I've already tried. This artefact has fused with my body, but it has freed me from the burden of my curse. For too long I was forced to walk these lands in the form of the lizard man, and I do not intend to ever go back that way. As long as I can keep it out of the attention of Rhagor."

I instantly regret the words as soon as I speak them, because Nora's expression turns from one of concern to outright fear. "King Rhagor?" she says as though merely saying his name epitomises terror. "What has he got to do with all this?"

"I've already said too much. You do not need to concern yourself with my affairs, Nora. All I need you to focus on is making sure that Morgana is okay." I pull my hands from her grasp.

"But Orjan," she protests, "if you cross him, you will put the entire fate of Eltera in his hands. Curse or no curse, is that really what you want? I fear your actions will already have grave consequences for us all."

I understand her fear and her concern, but what am I supposed to do? It's not like I asked for this. Yes, I was curious as to what they were searching for underneath Hora, but I had no clue what this amulet was or what magic it was imbued with.

"Please concern yourself only with Morgana and leave me to worry about Rhagor," I say. "I will not allow anything to happen to this kingdom or its people." I make my words dismissive and abrupt, cold even. I feel as though I have been ravaged by a fierce storm these last two days, and I'm still processing everything that has happened, not only to me but also to the Barbaraq woman and Morgana.

"Can I see her yet?" I ask, changing the subject.

I can see the disappointment in Nora's eyes as her shoulders drop, but she says no more of the amulet. "Yes. She's still weak though, so please do not press her too hard. We will not lose the queen on my watch. Not after everything she has done for us."

I give Nora a polite bow of my head. "Thank you," I say, and then I head to the door of my chambers. The mahogany door is large, thick, and heavy, and I push it open as delicately as I can so as to not make too much noise.

In the centre of my room sits a large wooden bed with thick quilts lying on top, accompanied by a red throw that covers the bottom half. Morgana is set up on stacks of pillows behind her. Her long red curls contrast against the white of the cotton. She is ashen-faced, and her cheeks are brown and purple with large bruises, her face decorated with a large scratch down her cheek that has been stitched together. Her arms lie on top of the covers, littered with stitched-up gashes that vary in size. It is horrible to see her in this state, to see her so vulnerable, to have succumbed to such injuries. Her eyes are closed as I approach, and in this moment, she looks peaceful.

Other healers are bustling around her. Two are chanting an incantation, while a young man clad in black-embroidered apprentice's attire is busy mixing a hazy tonic. He pauses with his next ingredient in hand when he notices my puzzled look.

"It's turmeric, my lord," he says, clearly nervous in my presence. "It will help hold off infection, which she is vulnerable to in this state."

The other two healers are waving their hands around in the air, channelling magic and incantations under their breaths. One is focusing on the air, the other on the ground surrounding my bed. They wear the same uniform as Nora and the apprentice, but the thread of their tunics is green, denoting a lower rank.

"What are you doing?" I ask them. "What kind of magic is this?"

"We are creating wards, my lord," one of the healers says. She doesn't look happy that I have disrupted her incantation.

"Why do we need wards? Is there something I should be concerned about?"

"N–Nora instructed us to place them around the room," the apprentice answers. "When the queen arrived, she was close to death. She was rambling, as if madness had taken hold of her. She was talking about things, my lord. Dark things. Nora wants the wards, just in case."

I huff as the healer does not answer my question entirely. I am not as well-versed as others in magic, but even I know that when wards are being cast, they are done so to protect.

"So what is Morgana being protected against?" I ask as I study the two healers casting the spells around the room. What look to be Elvish hieroglyphs are lit up on the ground in varying sizes, a soft glow emanating from them that gives a calming, pulsating hum through the stone floor.

"Spirits," the apprentice answers, "vengeful spirits."

I look over the intricate runes glowing inside the room and then across to Morgana. Just what has she gotten herself into?

I take a seat in a large, dark wood chair. It is plain to look at, but does have a velvet cushion fastened to it, offering some semblance of comfort.

I watch over Morgana for the rest of the morning while the healers finish tending to her and mapping the wards around the room. When they are done, they pack up their effects and exit my chamber, leaving me and Morgana alone.

Her breathing is so soft that you would be forgiven for questioning if she was in fact drawing breath at all. Every now and then she takes a stronger intake of breath, reassuring me that she is still alive.

I find myself examining my hands, over and over again, as if expecting them to develop harsh scales once again, as if all of this is just a dream. I have no clue what to do next, what move to make. I have been naive in taking this amulet. It is only a matter of time before Rhagor figures out it was me that took it. Codrin is not the brightest, but even he would know of my involvement given the altercation we had the night that we took it. In my haste, I fear I have put this kingdom at risk, just as Nora said.

The air between Morgana and myself feels like a void as I find myself focusing on her dangerously shallow breaths, often wondering whether she is still with us. As close as I sit, I feel as though I could not be further away from her.

Hours pass without so much as a murmur from her, and I feel powerless to help her. The healers come back into my chambers at various points throughout the day to tend to Morgana as well as check on the runes that have been cast around her. Each time they enter, I assure them that there has been no sign of whatever spirits they're seeking to protect her from.

While I sit in quiet reflection, my thoughts drift from the amulet that is now fused to my bones to Rhagor's response when he learns I have what he is looking for. And yet despite the risk to myself and this kingdom, mostly I dwell on Morgana's health.

I have never seen her looking so vulnerable. She is usually so well dressed, so well kept and confident in herself and her abilities. When we found her in the Gondoron Pass, there was a fear in her eyes that I have never seen before. Whatever it is that she has experienced, whatever it is that has done this to her, it must be bad. I can only hope that she wakes soon so that I can finally expel the breath of air that I feel I have been holding for so long.

One of the healers is about to leave again when I raise my hand to stop them. "Thank you," I say.

The young woman gives me a nervous smile, not wanting to keep her eyes on me for longer than necessary. I have seen her eyeing me, and it is clear she is intrigued to see me sitting here in my human form, no longer the cursed beast that she and everyone else have become accustomed to after all this time.

"My lord." She bows her head and averts her gaze, but I do not mind her looking. In fact, it is something I have avoided since being back.

"Could I ask that you fetch me a mirror?" I ask. I have not had need of one for the last decade, as I could not bear to lay eyes on my own hideous appearance.

"Of course, my lord," she says while hurriedly heading for the door, "I will fetch one straight away."

She is only gone for a few moments before returning with a medium-sized vanity mirror, which she places on my desk. She bows once more and makes her leave.

I stare at it for a few moments before exhaling deeply, afraid of what I'll see, afraid the mirror will show my lizard skin once again and all of this will have just been a surreal dream, or even a nightmare.

My legs feel as though they are made of metal when I stand and take a step forward. When I reach my desk, I pull out the wooden chair and it scrapes against the floor. Then I close my eyes and sit down in front of the mirror.

At first, I cannot lift my gaze from the mahogany wood of my desk. It takes a few moments to prepare myself. Finally, slowly, I raise my head until I can see the stranger that is looking back at me.

My skin is an olive colour, and my hair is dark, longer than I would like, with streaks of grey down the sides. A black and grey stubble has formed on my face, and cracked wrinkles reach outwards from my eyes, showing me the ageing warrior that sits opposite me now. It is as though I am looking at someone that I no longer recognise as I raise my hands to my face and trace my fingers over my skin, feeling each wrinkle, each grain of stubble, half-expecting to feel scales.

And I sob.

"I am free," I say to myself as my tears splash on the surface of my desk. A indescribable weight lifts from me, a weight I didn't know I carried.

Then I sit up straight and stretch my neck upwards to look at the amulet. My skin feels restricted, similar to having a noose around it. My neck itself looks scarred, the skin damaged from where the amulet has fused with my body. The edges appear slightly blackened, and I lower my hands to touch the surface of the magical amulet. It feels like I am touching a part of me. I can feel my fingers against the surface as clear as a hand running over my own skin.

Whatever it is, this thing is part of me now, and I do not see how it can possibly be removed. Not that I would want it to be; I have no intention of ever being back in that cursed form.

"Orjan?"

The dry, tired voice makes me jump. I turn to see Morgana sitting up in my bed. Weary and exhausted, her eyes are wide with confusion and surprise. I give her a smile, grateful that she is awake, that she has survived her ordeal.

"Yes, Morgana," I say, "it's me."

6

YAELOR

In the mist-shrouded frost lands to the north. I encountered a Krampus, a dream-eater that matched my every skill and trapped me in a realm of nightmares for weeks. This shadow-stalker remains my most formidable foe, I barely survived and to this day its location remains unknown despite us facing off more times than I care to remember.

Gregor Yerald, Journal Entry, 189 KR

The healers have been great at numbing my pain, but none of my injuries are grave, aside from a cut that needed stitching on my upper right arm. I just need time to recover from the bruising and the exhaustion that comes with fleeing from our home.

I appreciate the kindness that people have shown me, but it is not my intention for us to stay here longer than needed. Last time I was in Eltera, it was to lead an attack against its people. Staying is a risk that I cannot take. They may be an ally at the moment, but if they were to know who I was, who Gillam truly was, I can only assume that Rhagor would find out.

"Are you finished?" I ask as a healer checks over some of her stitching. She is a plump lady with a blotched, blemished face, much older than the other healers.

She gives me a polite nod and stands. "You just need to rest for a few days. You have been through a lot," she says with a concerned tone. "However, you seem to be in a rush, and we will not keep you here against your will." The healer reaches into a small pouch that hangs over her shoulder and pulls out a vial. "I believe you should be best resting for another few days, but if there is something urgent you need to attend to, please take this ointment with you. It will stop that wound becoming infected. The last thing you want when you are travelling on the road is to come down with a fever." Her tone is off, and I wonder if I am getting a scolding.

"Especially with a child," the healer says with raised eyebrows, confirming my suspicion.

I muster a laugh. "What is your name?" I ask her. "It would be nice to know the person who has offered me such kindness." I stand up from the stool where I have been sitting, my body reminding me that I am nowhere near ready for travel. I wince and raise my hand to my ribcage, knowing I have at least one broken rib. The last couple of days are hazy like a fog. I do not remember much of our rescue or our journey to Eltera. I simply recall waking up feeling like I had been trampled by a wild herd with the healers tending to me.

"I can give you some more tea to help you with that pain, but other than that, there is nothing more we can do. That kind of healing would take from our life essence and I can't ask my healers to do that, not for something that isn't life threatening. My name is Nora, by the way," she adds before passing me a cloth jacket. "I would suggest wearing this too if you are walking around the castle and the grounds. The people here do not take kindly to Barbaraqs."

Shame fills me with how many lives were needlessly lost that day, on both sides. Would Nora offer me such kindness if she knew that it was I that led the incursion that day?

"Thank you, Nora," I say. "Do you happen to know where my daughter is?"

"She is with Rior in the courtyard," Nora says with a smile. "She certainly is a spirited one." A chuckle escapes her, and I can't quite tell whether she means that as a good thing or a bad thing. "Just follow the hall to the end and take a right."

I gingerly exit the healers' quarters, keen to find Gillam and make sure that she is okay. This is the longest I have been away from her, and I do not like not having her by my side, especially given the circumstances.

The castle is unlike anything I have ever seen. The corridor is large and spacious, and the ground is lined with white and grey stone so pristinely polished that I feel like I could slip on the surface. There are gold lamps protruding from the walls at intervals, the light helping keep the natural darkness that comes with these buildings at bay. Blue cloth banners hang in the spaces between them. The golden embroidery on the flags seems to depict a dragon head, with runes stitched underneath. I am not familiar with the language that has been used. Above, the stone has been carved into large archways which amplifies the space surrounding me, allowing a gentle breeze to pass through the building that brings this place a positive, vibrant freshness. I head towards the large wooden door that is also painted blue, sitting at the top of the corridor. I pass a few whispering maids and several guards who walk in tandem, their tunics the same blue that lines the walls. They barely seem to notice me as I step aside to allow them to pass.

When I push open the large doors, a forceful breeze hits me. The air tastes fresh, as though I have just taken a dip in a crisp brook, cold but not uncomfortable.

It doesn't take me long to reach the castle courtyard, and there I am met with a swell of noise as I find myself in the midst of a market square. In the centre sits a grey stone well protruding out of the ground, surrounded by chattering water collectors. A young girl is smiling as she pulls on a rope beside it, fetching a bucket filled with water while others wait their turn.

To the right-hand side of the courtyard, a herd of men and women are busy carrying supplies from the backs of carts and into the castle, while scores of guards take up position, some stationary, some moving around on a patrol. A group of five move together out of the main gate and into the city of Eltera, each of them carrying crates overflowing with fruit, vegetables, and freshly baked bread. A wagon filled with more produce follows closely behind.

It looks like Orjan has created a sustainable kingdom, one that sees to the needs of everyone, not just those who can afford it. It is something I am not used to seeing in these lands that are so often fuelled by poverty and greed. As I continue to survey the courtyard, I see the training ground to the left: a small circular patch of dried soil with mannequins sitting on wooden pillars, perfect for testing archery and skill with a blade.

In front of them, Gillam is sparring with Rior, the young man who helped Orjan rescue me from the slave traders. He is holding two wooden swords in his hands, while Gillam clings tightly to a wooden sword of her own. It's too large for her, and I muster a laugh at the sight of it threatening to tip her over before wincing with the sharp sting that greets me in my side.

Raising my hand to my ribs, I walk towards the two of them as they continue to spar, blissfully unaware of my advance. Both of them are lost in the moment, smiling and laughing as Gillam desperately tries to best Rior. He feigns falling backwards, only just keeping his feet.

There is an innocence to the interaction that brings me joy as I watch the smile on Gilliam's face, one that I rarely see. I slow my walk so I can enjoy the scene just a little bit longer.

"Take that, Rior!" Gillam squeals with glee as she takes a wild swing at the young soldier.

He raises his two wooden swords side by side just in time to block Gillam's heavy swing, and dare I say it, I see a bead of sweat on Rior's head, which tells me he is needing to try harder than he is letting on.

"That's good, Gillam," he says with conviction, a hint of pride in his voice as he lightly pushes back against her. He steps away to provide some distance between the two of them, then whirls his swords around in each hand, showing off his swords skills. Gillam laps it up, her eyes widening with sheer joy. She tries to copy him, but the sword is too big for her and it hits the ground.

"Keep practicing, you will get better," Rior says. "One day, you will be the finest warrior Levanthria has ever seen." His smile is genuine, and I can see by his demeanour that he has a natural way with children. He doesn't look too far into adulthood himself. His hair is short, but he has a slender, athletic build. He wears a blue tunic like the guards, along with silver-looking chainmail underneath.

Such armour does not come cheap, and I can't help but wonder what rank he holds here, especially at such a young age.

I start clapping as I approach, capturing both of their attentions. Gillam's eyes fill with happiness at seeing me and her smile brings me a comfort that I know only she can provide. She drops her sword and runs towards me at speed. "Mama!" she calls, a dust cloud forming beneath her feat as she hurtles across the dirt. She launches herself into me, wrapping her arms tightly around me.

It hurts and I wince again, which causes her to stop the embrace and step away from me, a panicked look on her face as though she has done something wrong. "I'm sorry, I didn't mean to, are you okay?" She speaks quickly, and I have to remind myself that I have been resting in and out of sleep for the last two days. Knowing Gillam, she will have two days of stories to tell me as quickly as possible.

"It's okay, I am fine. Just a little bruised." I rest my hands on her shoulders and look into her big, sparkling eyes. "All thanks to you and the bravery that you showed in finding me help."

"It was Orjan and Rior," Gillam says proudly. "They are the bravest warriors I have ever met." She smiles as she runs over to Rior and takes him by the hand, dragging him over to me. He looks bashful as he approaches.

"Why do I get the feeling we are the only warriors you have ever met," he laughs before stopping in front of me.

"One day I will be able to fight like them," says Gillam. "That way I will be able to keep you safe, Mama, like you did with me in the fire."

Involuntarily, I cast Gillam a stern look. She wouldn't have meant to, but she has already said too much, and fear consumes me. Has she already told them about the fire back home, that we had to flee in the dead of night? My mind takes over and dread consumes the pits of my stomach. What if they assume the wrong thing, what if word reaches the wrong ears and the King's Guards are already on their way here to have us arrested?

"It's okay," Rior says, "children have the wildest of imaginations."

I can't help but feel he is humouring me, but I appreciate it nonetheless. "So, this is the man who I owe my life to," I say, trying to quickly change the subject.

"I was only doing what a squire should," he says dutifully, nodding to me. "If not for the actions of your daughter, I fear we would not have been able to find you in time." He reaches down and ruffles Gillam's hair which falls onto her face. "And because of your bravery, not only was your mother saved, but five other people." He then looks back at me and says, "Your mother must be so proud of you, Gillam, as are we all."

The news of the others being safe brings me a welcoming, warm sensation that counteracts my worry.

"I am so grateful that they are safe," I say. "Thank you."

"Just thank the gods that we happened to be passing by when we crossed paths with Gillam." And then Rior picks her up into the air, and she squeals with delight as he starts to tickle her.

"Put me down, Rior!" she says before he tosses her into the air and onto his shoulder.

"This is the real champion of Eltera, Gillam the Great," he cheers as he beams with happiness.

Gillam raises her hands in the air in mock celebration and I smile like I never have before. To see her so happy, to see her so comfortable and at peace – it is all I have ever wanted.

Then the guilt creeps in again in the knowledge that this moment cannot last, that when the opportunity arrives, we must make our leave, and more than likely never return. We need to get to the Forest of Opiya, for that is the only place where I feel Gillam will truly be safe.

7
ULRIK

Sweat pools on my head as I stare at the consecrated remains of my brother, the surface of the casket finally exposed. It has taken me an age to dig down deep enough to reach him, and I stand at the foot of his grave, breathing heavily and covered in dirt. Above me, clouds have begun to form for the sun to hide behind, giving me welcome reprieve from its warmth.

My coat hangs from one of the branches of the jarjoba tree, and I walk over to it, reaching into one of the deep pockets to fetch the Resurrection Stone. Its magical properties fizz in my hand as I turn to look over my brother's dug-up grave, soil piled high on either side of it. I reach down and pull the lid of the casket loose, the shake in my hands getting even worse. I do not remove the lid fully; I simply leave it cracked, for now.

For a fleeting moment, I question whether or not I am doing the right thing, but I quickly bury these thoughts as deep as I can inside myself.

The stench that leaves his casket is nauseating. Stale death grips hold of me, causing my stomach to wrench. It is a smell that naively I was not expecting, and I turn to my side before heaving what little contents sit in my stomach until my throat burns as though I have drunk acid.

"What am I doing?" I shake my head. This is my brother's body. I hope he forgives me for what I am about to do.

I reach into the dark leather satchel that sits beside the mound of dirt and pull from it a rolled-up piece of parchment, delicately. After all, it contains a spell that, as far as I know, could be as old as time itself. A weighted metal ring clasps the parchment, and I pull it free, allowing the scroll to unfurl.

My chest continues to pound and my breath quickens as I kneel at the foot of my brother's grave, leaning down to rest the Resurrection Stone on top of the wooden casket.

I then take hold of the parchment top and bottom and open it up to reveal the spell that I must cast. The spellcaster must be a magic user, and given that magic courses through my body, I know I have the power to wield it. I am all too aware of the effects that powerful spells can have on the caster, and I have a flask containing the waters from the Fountain of Youth, ready to combat this. But I know I must prepare myself for the crippling pain I will likely endure at first. I am not even sure if I will be able to cast the spell fully, given that I have only ever wielded glamour magic. I have found no need to summon any other kind. Until now.

Taking a deep breath, I start to read from the scroll aloud, projecting my voice as clearly as possible. As far as I know, the words are Elvish, and I have transcribed them as best I can on my own. Had I asked Zerina for help, she would have figured out my plans and I know she would have tried to stop me.

"Horua, Gireya, Heyshaa, Livernum!" No sooner do I utter the words than a bolt of forked lightning ignites in the sky, accompanied by a low grumble of thunder. If ever there was a sign that the gods are unhappy, that would be it.

"Horua, Gireya, Heyshaa, Livernum!" I repeat, unsure if the words I am saying are fully correct. Another bolt of lightning darts across the sky above me and a gust of wind blows against me.

"HORUA, GIREYA, HEYSHAA, LIVERNUM!" I cry loudly as the scroll starts to vibrate aggressively in my hand. The power is intense as an ache crawls up my arms and the muscles in my hands tighten. Even if I wanted to let go of the scroll, I couldn't. I cry out with the pain that begins to course through my body. My voice cracks and breaks as the magic takes hold and the skies above me begin to turn into a fierce storm, turning a deep-purple colour imbued with a strange, greenish haze. Seeing my opportunity, I command the stone as my transcription instructs, my hands feeling as though molten fire courses through them.

"Ulrik Thatch, I want you to resurrect Ulrik Thatch!"

The parchment whips up into flames, disintegrating in an instant. I can only pray this works, because try as I might, I can already feel the words I have uttered disappearing into the darkened corners of my mind.

Dropping to my knees, I clench my hands into tight fists and try to focus on anything other than the pain I must endure as a consequence of the magic. I reach for my satchel and remove the flask, hastily taking a drink to stem the pain. I manage to pour as much down my shirt as I manage to drink, and I curse myself for being so wasteful.

The sky above grows even fiercer as a strong wind now blows around me, sending the dug-up dirt swirling into the air.

The green energy in the sky seems to drift down to me like a moth to a flame. I know the kind of energy this magic holds. It is necromancy, truly forbidden magic. As it wraps around me, my bones feel as though an unseen entity strokes their fingers beneath my flesh, and it knocks me sick.

It doesn't take long for the green mist to settle on the ground and pour over the side of Ulrik's grave, filling the void with a plume of magical smoke that makes the air feel thick and dense. Meanwhile, the lightning that forks above me becomes more frequent, with multiple bolts lighting up the now darkened sky adjoined by the continued rumbles of thunder.

It feels like I hold my breath forever as I wait for the magic to take hold of him, as I wait to see if it actually works. The green haze continues to billow into the grave, and I stare into it, just hoping and praying that he climbs out.

Time seems to stand still. I become oblivious to the storm, my chest thundering as fiercely as the thunder that rages above me like the fiercest of battles.

A croaking sound is what I hear first.

It sounds like the death rattle that I have often heard in people taking their final breaths, and it reminds me of the moment when I actually lost my brother. My cheeks become wet with tears as I listen to the strange croak coming out from within the grave, rasping and prolonged. What follows is a rasped inhale of breath, and my heart skips.

The magic must have worked.

I hear his rattled breathing. It sounds pained, and choking, and again I fear that I have made the wrong choice. Surely he's been dead for so long that it makes sense his first breaths would be riddled with pain.

It will all be worth it in the end.

"Ulrik?" I say. "Ulrik, it's me, your sister. Can you hear me? Tap on the wood if you can hear me."

After a moment's pause, a light knock sounds against the wooden casket, followed by another prolonged, rasping breath. The scraping noise fills my heart with hope as I realise the casket lid is moving, and I step back from the grave to give my brother space to climb out. I wait in anticipation, the green mist still sitting over the top of the grave. It is thick and viscous, as if you could swim or bathe in it, not that you would want to.

"It's okay, I am here," I say. "Just follow the sound of my voice, you must be so confused."

Further moments pass with nothing, but his rattled inhales comfort me, confirming that he is still there. Another crack of lightning followed by thunder that feels closer than ever shakes me to my core. Then a hand reaches out of the mist, grabbing hold of the edge of the casket from within.

"Ulrik," I stay again, desperate to hear him speak, to know that he's okay.

A second hand reaches out and I step back again, eagerly awaiting to see him in all his glory, desperate to embrace him once more.

Rain lashes down as if the skies have truly opened up, with thick, heavy droplets quickly soaking me to my core. They bounce off the ground, washing away the magical mist that continues to hide my brother.

Then the top of his head comes into view, followed by his confused face, and I can't help but gasp at what I see crawling out from the grave.

"What have I done?" I splutter.

Something has gone wrong with this spell. Did I mutter the incantation correctly? It is Ulrik that I see climbing from the dirt, wheezing with a rattled chest as though he has some form of breathing condition – but it is not his slightly olive skin that greets me.

Instead, his skin is pale, with portions missing that leave nothing but hollowed-out holes in his face. Skin and sinew desperately cling to his body as if trying to fuse back together.

Why does he still look as though he is dead? Is it that he is neither dead nor alive?

"Ulrik," I say once again, doing as best I can to hide my horror. "Are you able to talk?"

Ulrik raises his eyes to meet my own. They look shocked, fearful, and confused, but they look like his eyes. Within them, I can see his soul, and in this moment, I know that he has returned to me, regardless of the state of his body.

"Wh-wh-who?" His breath staggers as he struggles to form words, sounding as though he is drowning.

"It's okay," I say, "I can help you. Take a moment." I rush forward and grab hold of his hands, which are as cold as ice. I pull him towards me, dragging him free from the grave.

I fall back into the pile of dirt behind me and find myself coated in a thick layer of mud. I frantically climb back to my feet to help Ulrik up.

"Get away!" he cries.

"Let me help you," I say, taking another step towards him. The rain continues to lash against us both.

"Wh-what have you done?" Each word he utters sounds as though it is agonising. He raises his head and his eyes meet mine again. "Who are you? What magic has done this to me?" Realisation appears to dawn upon him as his eyes widen and his face turns into an expression as wild as the storm.

It is only then that I realise I'm still glamoured to look like him.

"How is it that I find myself staring back at me?" he says with another painful croak, grasping for air as if he clings on to his newfound life with every breath that he takes.

Before I have a chance to utter another word, he reaches for the sword that we buried him with. The metal is rusted and scrapes as he frees it from his belt.

For someone who was moving so slowly, his sudden speed catches me off guard as he takes a swing, nearly cleaving my head clean from my body.

"Shit," I say, "Ulrik, don't do this!"

He takes another wild swing, this time bringing his sword down on me. With nowhere else to go, I raise my hands and grab hold of his hand and hilt just in time.

His strength surprises me. I lock my arms straight as he pushes down and then grabs me around the throat with his free hand. I try to speak, but he squeezes so tightly that I fight to breathe. As his face draws close to mine, I can smell death. It clings to me, sending a chill down my spine.

"What witchcraft is this?" he says, staring at his own dead hand.

I wrap my hands around his wrist as I desperately try to pull his hand free so that I can breathe, but his strength is like nothing I have ever met, and it terrifies me to see that rage in his eyes.

Realising that I do not have the strength to pull myself free, I slam my fists against his chest and the side of his head, something which breaks my heart to do. But if I don't act fast, he quite simply is going to kill me.

It doesn't work. The world around me begins to darken

as rain continues to pour over us, making it difficult for me to move in the thickened mud. My arms fall by my side as I struggle to remain conscious. Then my right knuckle lands on the back of a stone.

I turn my hand over, digging my fingers through the mud until I can grip the stone tightly. With a wild swing, I bring it up and crash it into the side of Ulrik's skull. His hand snaps to the side and he falls from me, letting go of my throat and allowing me to breathe once more.

I desperately cough and gasp for every choking breath that I can muster as I desperately try to get to my feet.

"Ulrik, don't, it's not what you think," I say in sheer desperation.

He doesn't give me opportunity to explain any further. He runs at me again, sword raised.

"It's me, Esara!" I cry. It is a name I have not spoken since the day that he died.

He stops dead in his tracks, breathing heavily. The rain starts to calm as the magic that resurrected him fades away, leaving only him stood in front of me. He's angry and confused, his body language aggressive as he stares me down, clearly contemplating his next move.

Not taking any chances, I raise my hands to the hilt of my sword, bracing myself in case he decides to take another swing in an attempt to remove my head.

"Esara?" he asks as though tracing a memory. "Esara?" he says again, clearly confused.

Taking a deep breath, I allow my glamour to fade. His appearance has been my armour for so long, and without it, I feel vulnerable, exposed.

His breathing slows as my magic fades. The painful thrums in my body pale in comparison to what I had to endure when casting the spell that resurrected him, and yet I wince all the same.

"It is me, Esara," I say, my name hanging around in the back of my throat as if it threatens to choke me. "Do you see me?" I say. "Please tell me you recognise me?" My heart aches for him to understand as my magical glamour completely fades, leaving me standing there in my true form. Leaving me the most vulnerable that I have ever felt in my life. As angry as I feel at the world, as frustrated as I am at the things I've had to do to get to this point, it is this vulnerability the triggers the tidal wave of emotion that threatens to consume me.

"Esara?" Ulrik repeats once again, still not fully trusting. "How can this be? My sister was but a child last time I laid eyes on her." His eyes dart from side to side as his confusion continues to unsettle him, and I'm still not sure whether or not he will attack me once again.

"I am sorry, brother, I truly am. I assure you, this is me. I am your sister, it's just –" I struggle to form the next part of my sentence. "It's just, you died. Ten years ago, you were taken from me, and I've done everything I can to bring you back. I am so sorry for what I have done to you."

"Died?" Ulrik questions. "Ten years? You – you are a woman."

My heart fractures further when I see the anguish grabbing hold of him. "Ulrik, I am so sorry. I just needed to see you. I needed to let you know how much you mean to me, how much I love you."

Without a care and without warning, I run at my brother, reaching out and wrapping my arms around him. I burst into tears as my head slams against his chest. If he sends me to the afterlife, it is no more than what I deserve for what I have done, and if that was his choice, I would go there knowing that I have had this moment, knowing that I have had the opportunity to help him one last time.

The sound of his rusted blade bouncing off the ground is a welcome noise, and his arms wrap around me as he hugs me back.

"It's okay, Esara," he says, and although his voice is pained, it is so much more reassuring than his angered tone a few moments earlier. "I've got you, I am here."

I hear his heart begin to beat with new life with my head pressed against his chest. I can feel it beating quickly against my blemished cheeks.

Even after all of this, he only seeks to reassure me, to make sure that I am okay. It is in this moment that I raise my head to look up at his eyes. I smile at him, then bury my face and begin sobbing in a way that I have not done since I grieved his death. He continues to hug me just as tightly, patting my back as he shushes me and attempts to ease my pain.

He is here. My brother Ulrik has returned, and I realise that I no longer need to use his face as my armour to cope with my grief.

8

JORDELL

The charred ruins of the Elder Tree are still glowing with embers, but the flames and the thick, black smoke are now extinguished, at least.

I have no idea what the consequences of this will be, but I am sure that Zariah will explain everything. I find myself standing in an ornate room, large and unassuming. If this was a great hall in one of our castles, there would be artwork lining the walls – grotesquely pompous portraits, vases, trinkets, trophies of a value that I dare not think about. Here, though, the intricate carvings in the walls are the only craftsmanship on display.

The walls are lined with some form of mud that looks as though it has been baked on and hardened. Pillars and columns stand around the room, intricately carved into spires that spiral up to the ceiling. The room is large, and sound within it echoes. It is a room I have not seen before. I am fascinated with the work and skill that the fae have when it comes to how they have built not only the palace but their entire kingdom, much of which is suspended in the trees.

Elara stands by my feet, her usually purple scales blackened from the soot of the fire. My own clothes are charred and frayed, and a nasty, lingering burning smell tinges the air. My chest feels tight, too; I have inhaled more smoke than I would have liked, and I cough loudly to clear my throat, the sound of which skips around the walls as it echoes through the chamber.

"I'll have my maids take you to the baths shortly, Jordell," Zariah's softly spoken voice garners my attention from behind.

Elara shakes her body as she tries to dust herself free of the soot that clings to her.

"Zariah? Are you okay?" I ask, spinning to greet her.

Zariah wears a fearful expression on her bruised face as she walks slowly towards me, clearly still in pain. She rests her hands delicately on her stomach as she walks, and despite her weakened appearance, I have to stop myself from staring at her, for her fae appearance mesmerises me as she approaches. Her skin shimmers in the beams of light that cascade through the large windows onto the perfectly polished marble-like floor.

"I will live," she says, her expression still one of worry, "as will my people. All thanks to you." She offers her hand to me, which I accept, and her soft skin rests in my palm. It surprises me how cold her skin is to the touch. She gives my hands a light squeeze. "Thank you, Jordell. If not for your arrival, I fear what would have happened, how far the fire would have spread." She smiles and steps away from me, bowing her head. "It is as if the gods themselves willed this to happen. Perhaps Opiya continues to watch over us."

"I have been hearing those words a lot lately," I tell her. I must admit that with how things have happened recently, even I would be a fool to ignore that perhaps the gods are intervening here. "Tell me everything that happened. But then I must be on my way. I have to get to Osar."

"To see the child?" Zariah says.

"How do you know of the child?" I ask, confused that she would say such a thing.

"There is much that you have not been told, Jordell. Your visit here last time was brief."

"You mean the time when you did not send aid when we needed you?" I say, sudden frustration in my voice as I draw on the painful memory of the Battle of Opiya. "We were ambushed and attacked. We lost many of our own. I lost my son." The memory draws pain from my voice as it cracks. "The day that Rhagor returned to this world. I stood at the top of the battlefield that day, searching through the trees, praying to the gods that your forces would emerge to help us when we needed you most. But you did not come."

"It is forbidden for me to intervene in the battles drawn between man, even when it falls within the boundaries of the forest. Our people have their limitations and we cannot risk the ire of the gods. We are governed by the rules they cast down on us long ago. I cannot risk the fate of my people by interfering with the actions and decisions of man."

"You seem to forget that we also risked our own people rescuing your people from Askela. I seem to recall you caring little for the rules when it was your daughter who we were rescuing, at the cost of our kin. A good friend's life was lost."

"And I will be eternally grateful for all that you have done, Jordell, despite your grief, despite your frustration, for our inaction hasn't stopped you from lending us aid when we needed it the most." Zariah looks at my staff which is perched against a nearby pillar. "If I had not given you that staff, crafted from a fallen branch of the Elder Tree, I do not know how we would have stopped that fire. The gods must have willed it."

I feel the anger rising inside me and although she is a queen, although she is beautiful, although she shows me gratitude in this moment, I am powerless to stop the swell of emotion that pours out from me.

"How dare you thank the gods. They are cowards. Do they care that little for us that they would let all this suffering continue across Levanthria? The gods I worshipped, the ones that I dedicated most of my life to serving . . . When I needed them most, when I looked into the skies and begged them for aid, to grant us courage on the battlefield to defeat our enemies, I was greeted with nothing but silence. Why is it that the only time they seem to make any form of contact is when it is something that will benefit them? I spit at the ground before those gods. I am done with them."

Zariah is visibly taken aback by my anger. She looks awkward and uncomfortable as she studies me in silence, as if searching for a response. The silence hangs in the air between us, the good grace that she granted me when she entered the room more than likely eviscerated by my flared temper.

"There is so much more at play here, Jordell," she says. "There is so much more that you do not know."

I notice the tear that runs from her left eye. She quickly wipes this away with the back of her hand and straightens herself. "I am sorry for the trials you have faced in this life, I truly am, but what has passed before us was meant to be. As bad as this situation is, as catastrophic as the Elder Tree being destroyed is, there is reason for it."

I stand in disbelief as Zariah speaks. How can she be so

blinkered, how can she still show such faith with everything that has happened? Taking a breath, I allow myself to calm as I exhale. My voice is even when I say, "No more hidden truths. I need you to tell me everything."

"Last time you were here, I told you Rhagor's story, how he murdered his sister, that at her grave, the goddess Opiya planted a tree. The Elder Tree. Then, after capturing Rhagor, she imprisoned him in stone for the atrocities he had committed in this world." She takes a small step towards me, almost hesitantly. "I did not tell you all of the story. You see, the newly planted Elder Tree brought new life into the Forest of Opiya as we know it. It is why it is named after the goddess who gave that life, that in turn created the fae people of this kingdom –"

"What is it you need to tell me?" I cut her off. I do not have time for over-exaggerated stories. I need to get to Osar, to Yaelor and the child.

"That new life from the tree was poured into me, resurrecting me from my death." She pauses, as if the next words are that heavy that she dares not speak them. "A death that was given to me by my twin brother, Rhagor."

It takes a few moments for me to process what she says. "But that would mean that you are –"

"The daughter of Opiya."

"You told me your name was given to you in honour of her, not that you *were* her," I say. It is too much to take in. If what Zariah is saying is true, then I am in the presence of a goddess.

"Rhagor knew nothing of my resurrection. It happened after our mother imprisoned him. Since he has been back in this world, however, he has been limited with what he can do as he is bound to the body of a mortal." Zariah's concern falls on her as she continues, "He must have found out though, through the libraries of man. Because he came here, he stabbed me and left me to die. He burned the Elder Tree down, he knew that my life and my resurrection is intrinsically linked to that tree. In destroying it, he could truly end my life. He nearly succeeded, too. He would have, had you not appeared."

"Why didn't you tell me when I was here?"

"I did not know you. I felt indebted to you for rescuing my daughter, which is why I gave you a staff carved from the wood of the Elder Tree. I have never done that before. But I am so glad that I did, for now, that staff is the only remnants of the tree. Of the power that is tied to this forest, this kingdom."

"Do you need it back?" I ask. "Take it, it is from these lands, it is not mine to be owned."

"It is though, Jordell," Zariah says, and I am confused. If it truly is the only thing that remains of the Elder Tree, then surely she could have use of it. "Do you still not see? If I had not given you the staff on that day, both myself and the Elder Tree would be gone. But the magic of the tree lives on, through you." There is a conviction in her voice that tells me she truly believes the words she is speaking.

Suddenly I feel a weight of the situation that is so much bigger than I am, bigger than I could even begin to comprehend. "What does this mean for you?"

"It means that I am no longer bound to the tree. If I lose this life, I will be truly gone this time."

"What do you mean, this life? Just how many have you had?"

"How many lives can you live in two thousand years?" There is a simplicity to her answer that I still cannot fully comprehend.

"And why would Rhagor do all this? What is he trying to achieve?"

"That is something that I have spent the last eight years trying to figure out since his return. It is something that, until he tried to kill me again, I had no clue. He destroyed the Elder Tree so that he could destroy me. I am just one person he harbours disgust towards. But there is one who he hates more than anyone else in this world."

"Your mother," I say.

Zariah nods. "Opiya. I have not seen her for two millennia. She has kept away. After all, I still hold my own contempt for everything that she has done. She played such a big part in it all. Rhagor's revenge is against her. It is why he killed me in the first place. He was jealous of the love our mother held for me and bereft from the disdain and disappointment she always held for him. I often wonder if things would have turned out the same had she shown him the same love she showed me. Only now we are left with a demi-god who is driven by hatred and revenge. And now he has a way of exacting that revenge."

Her words weigh heavy on me. I am but a simple man, a spellcaster who used to help others in the names of gods who I've since deemed false. Now I am in the centre of a war between them. "What is his plan, Zariah?"

"When he came to kill me, he mentioned an amulet. Something he had buried before he was imprisoned by our mother. It is only now that I understand what he intends to do with it. That amulet is charged with magic, much like the sword that he carries, in which he managed to keep the essence of his soul dormant, despite his body being destroyed. One item, the sword, filled with the power and destruction of the gods, and the other imbued with a power to break magic. Opposite forces that, when combined, will have catastrophic consequences for the gods. It is why they fear him."

"And what is it he plans to do with this amulet, Zariah?" I ask. I can't help but feel that there is more that she is going to ask of me.

"Rhagor's plan is to imprison all of the gods, in the same way he was. I know my brother. He will not stop until he has had his revenge." She turns away from me and walks towards the large oval window on the far side of the room, casting her gaze over her kingdom. Then she looks over her shoulder at me. "He intends to drag the gods to this world and bind them here as mortals so he can kill them all, one by one. Starting with our mother."

He wants to destroy the gods? That is madness to think he is capable of doing such a thing, but he has managed all of this so far. What if Zariah's words are true? How do we even begin with stopping a god who is fuelled with so much hatred for all others?

"Why have you decided to tell me all of this?" I ask.

"Because I know the part you will play in what is to come. You hold the Elder Staff, and with that power, you alone can stop Rhagor." Zariah takes a sharp intake of breath and turns to face me once more.

"How do you know this?" I ask.

"Because I have had visions of the great battle to come. Jordell, I need you to help me stop my brother, to defeat Rhagor. Only then will Levanthria be truly free of the shadow he has cast over these lands for so long."

9

ZERINA

The ageless Lady Elara of Rosewood Manor is rumoured to possess a hidden portrait that ages in her stead. While she remains eternally youthful, the painting reportedly transforms into a horrific visage, reflecting the toll of her sins. These are of course whispers and never actually proven to be true.

Madame Klara, Myths And Magic, 210 KR

It has been odd to travel with someone other than my crew after all these years. All I have come to know is them. And yet, riding with a stranger has been somewhat nice, especially when they are so friendly and easy on the eye. I certainly could have found a worse person to be sat on the back of a horse with.

I rest my hands on Vireo's lower back, holding on to his tunic as best I can so that I do not fall from the horse as we ride. This is most definitely a better option than wrapping my arms around him like I am in desperate need for him to keep me safe. In fact, you could argue that he is the one who is safer for having my company.

Vireo seems to be noble, kind, and more than happy to

help others in need. I could have taken his horse from him if I had wanted, but choosing to ride with him has proved to have some benefits. It has been nice to hold a conversation with someone so knowledgeable, even if his recent past is limited to that of Levanthria and the Forest of Opiya. He isn't as well travelled as me; after all, I have sailed the seas in search of lost artefacts for the majority of my adult life. A far cry from the sheltered life that I used to live with my sisters at the top of the Pendaran Hills.

Oh how I miss them. How I long to be able to hold a conversation with them one last time. But I have drunk from the Fountain of Youth, and I was submerged under the waters long enough to absorb the index of magic that Elves have allowed. Therefore, I know the repercussions of such magic to attain such a wish. I understand the dangers of such forbidden magic, not to those we have lost, but to ourselves, to our souls.

It is why we race to Osar. I have used my magic to keep the horse replenished of energy, to ensure it can maintain a decent speed while we cross the plains of Levanthria with lesser need to stop and rest. The fact that Ulrik left me my flask suggests there's still an ounce of humanity in them, and this thought spurs me on. They have no idea what consequences they'll face if they proceed with their plan to awaken their brother from the dead.

I am tired from the journey, but I know that I can rest once my task is done, once I have stopped Ulrik with their plan. I can only pray that we are not too late. If so, I dread to think what we will find when we arrive.

"I see Osar," Vireo says, maintaining a steady pace, "it shouldn't take us much longer to reach them."

I lean around to look ahead and sure enough, I can see the small village of Osar, and in the backdrop, the Pendaran

Hills that I once called home. Perhaps when all this is done, I can go and visit my sisters' graves once again. It is here where I have found to have the best conversations with them, or so it feels. It fares better than their communications to me through visions when I am near death or heavily submerged underwater.

This is the first time that I have truly felt in conflict with Ulrik, and it pains me to be heading to his village with the knowledge that this may result with us doing battle. Still, I know on this occasion that it is I who hold the moral high ground, that actually Ulrik is getting beyond redemption, which is a dangerous place to be. I don't want to see them cause any more harm to others, especially by bringing their brother back to life with the Resurrection Stone. I know more than most that magic comes at a price, no matter how sweet the temptation may be. And with resurrection, the price is simply not worth paying.

"Hurry," I say, "we don't have long." My eyes turn to the sky above Osar, which has slowly changed from a clear blue to purple. Given the time of day, this is not a good sign, and I know that Ulrik has already set their plan into motion. We may already be too late.

Vireo kicks his heels into his horse and it goes from a steady trot to a gallop. I lean into him as best I can, tensing my core so that I do not fall off the back. We cover ground quickly as the light starts to flash with forked lightning, becoming more frequent and closer to the ground. Thunder roars loudly, a warning in itself, followed by rising winds. All things I would come to expect when casting this kind of magic.

When we reach Osar, we cannot afford to wait any longer. Ulrik has already taken things too far. I have made my peace with the fight we likely will end up having.

However, I have not made peace with the possibility of having to end their life.

"If you ride through town and pass the tavern, you will see a tavern on your right. Head down the road there. Ulrik's home is towards the bottom," I say, watching as villagers move indoors to avoid the storm that has seemingly come from nowhere. If only they knew the dark magic that has been summoned here. It is the kind that would have them leaving the village as fast as their legs could carry them.

When we pass the tavern, I instantly see a face or two that I recognise and I know even though we travel at speed, that they have recognised me. It is only a matter of time until they give chase.

"When we get there, I want you to take cover if you can," I say as Vireo takes a sharp right towards Ulrik's house. "This is not your fight, and I need you to respect that. I cannot have your blood on my hands."

"I understand," he says, "just know that if you need me, I will be there."

"Up there," I say, "that ramshackle house that looks as though the roof is about to collapse, that is where we are heading."

"The one with a few men outside?"

I lean out from the side again and sure enough, I see Darmour standing on guard, his attention on Vireo. He is more than likely unaware that I am sat behind him. Darmour's face is tired, as if he hasn't slept for days. He is wearing a bandana and his eye patch looks ready to slip down his face.

When he does spot me, he doesn't even look surprised. "I'm sorry, Zerina," he says, "I truly am."

"What is done is done." I climb down from the horse

where Vireo remains seated. "You know why I am here, and what I must do. I can't allow Ulrik to go through with using the Resurrection Stone. They are not thinking clearly."

Darmour grimaces as if my words cause him physical pain, pursing his dry, cracked lips. "I can't let you past, Zerina. Ulrik has demanded we stand guard, not to let anyone past." He can barely look me in the eyes as he speaks. I don't know if it is because he is conflicted or because he is a coward. "Especially you."

"I need to get to Ulrik's grave," I say, noticing Vireo looking down at me puzzlingly. I have not explained the full extent of our story. After all, he is a stranger. I take a step forward to find my path blocked by the two other crew members.

Both are better built than our usual recruits. They may be inexperienced seamen, but they are certainly hired swords, which means I can't be too lax with how I approach this.

"As the first mate said, it's captain's orders," says the man on the right. He's clearly more confident in his abilities with a blade, albeit naive in his approach. Surely he knows what I am capable of with my magic.

The man on the left looks a little more apprehensive, like he does know exactly what I am capable of. I give them all a wry smile, mainly out of my frustration.

"Zerina, please stop, we don't have to do this. Please don't force us," Darmour pleads, desperation in his voice. His good hand remains rested on top of his sword.

"Then move out of my way," I say. Darmour knows me better than anyone else in this world. He knows all my deepest, darkest secrets. I have confided in him, trusted him. He is my lover and holds my heart.

"What Ulrik is doing is bigger than any of us. I can't

allow that to happen, no matter who it is that stands in my way. The magic he is using is forbidden for a reason, surely you understand that." I let out an exasperated sigh. "Gods, Darmour, have I not taught you enough about the fabric of magic all this time?"

Darmour pauses for a moment before his eye meets my own. I can see how tormented he is as he draws his sword and raises it in a defensive position. "I can't let you past, Zerina. I am out bound to Ulrik. To break that oath would break the very fabrics of the code that I follow."

Although I know he is tormented, the fact he has drawn his sword on me is a new low, and my heart sinks. Even though I can rationalise his though process, it is what he stands for. This just cements that I can never get in the way of that.

"I swore an oath, too. Esara's soul will be truly lost if she follows through with her plan. I will do what I must to stop her from crossing a road that she cannot return from. Some things are simply bigger than us!" My voice cracks with pain. This whole situation is simply too much. Rain continues to pour down heavily, pooling in the folds of my hat, trickling over the sides. The forked lightning becomes more aggressive and frequent, splintering in the sky, and I can feel the rumble of the thunder in the ground where I stand. The gods are not happy, and I do not blame them.

"Please, Zerina, we don't have to do this," Darmour pleads one last time, his own voice breaking and pained at his own decision. If only he wasn't so stubborn, so duty bound.

"You have made it clear, Darmour, and as much as I don't want to do this" – I reach for the cutlass hanging at my waist and draw it – "I need to get to the other side of this house, and you all stand in my way."

I can see the hesitation, but Darmour lowers his head. "Seize them," he says.

He can't even do it himself.

"Do not harm them," I say to Vireo, who quickly drops from his horse and pulls out his sword without hesitation, standing by my side. "So much for me hiding," he says with a dry smile. "You okay with these three? There are four more heading our way from the tavern. I can deal with them."

"Just don't kill any of them," I reiterate. These are my crewmates. I could disintegrate them all in an instant with my magic, but that is not what I want, even if they did betray me.

"Maim, not kill. Got it," he says, and then he runs off behind me to meet the others, his footsteps splashing against the mud and pooled water.

The larger of the two men reaches me first, and I meet him with my blade, deflecting his strike. He is strong, and the impact reverberates down my forearm. I don't have time to waste though, as the second, less confident man comes at me with his blade. I parry his sword away easily, then use my momentum to turn and plant my boot into the chest of the stronger man. Air escapes him, and with a thud, he lands on his back in the mud. I flick a blast of fire at his feet and he cowers, scrambling away from it on the floor as flames lick up into the air between us.

"Wise choice," I say, and then I turn to stare at the other man. He wisely raises his hands and drops his sword, which beds into the mud. "Step aside."

He obliges, and moves out of my way as I take a step towards the house.

Darmour slowly walks in front of me, blocking my path. "Please stop," he says.

"You have made your choice, Darmour. I don't agree with it, but I will respect it." I start walking towards him, hoping – praying – that he will move out of my way. I do not want to have to cross blades with him, but I will if I must.

He swings a warning shot at me and I hop backwards, raising my blade and pressing it against his. Then I push, and my blade slides down the side of his.

Darmour raises his hooked hand behind him, adopting an offensive stance. I would be foolish to think I was better at sword combat than him. Everything I know is what he has taught me; my speciality is magic, not swordplay.

I strike quickly, then again and again, but Darmour is quick to each strike. I do not put much into them. He then returns the favour, and we go back and forth, testing each other's postures, form, and positions, as if we are simply sparring, neither of us committing fully. It is clear that he is just as hesitant to harm me as I am him, and we continue to dance around one another, clashing steel against steel. His footwork is better than mine, and I find my feet getting caught underneath me, a feat made worse by the thickening mud. Further up the street, I can hear Vireo fighting the rest of the crew, but I remain focused on Darmour and our own fight.

"You are getting rusty," Darmour says. "Your footwork is off."

"This is not some training fight!" I lash out, but Darmour slaps this away with ease using the outer edge of his sword.

"You're letting your emotions get the better of you. Have you not learnt anything from me?" He steps back, waiting for my next move, his words grating against my spirit.

Does he blame me? Does he think I am not human enough for this to affect me? This whole situation is madness, and frustration builds up in my core, igniting a fire within me.

"Emotions!" I cry out. "You want to talk to me about fucking emotions while we brawl in the street." I attack over and over while Darmour continues to move around me. I take wild swing after swing of my blade, each time catching nothing but air, and with the last blow, I scare myself with the intent that I hold. The realisation that I would kill Darmour if I had to makes me feel nauseous. Have I lost all my humanity?

Then, with a flurry, Darmour has me moving backwards and I fumble, struggling to knock away his strikes. Each time I take a step, my foot catches in the mud, each block taking me longer to recover from. And then, with a crashing blow, Darmour knocks my sword from my grasp.

He raises the sword to my throat as the two of us breathe heavily, staring deeply into each other's eyes. In his, I see the future I had dreamt of for us. Chickens pecking in the dirt outside. A child bouncing on his lap in our cottage. A peaceful life, free from all this. It is a life we both craved more than anything else, and I can see that he still wants this. There is a sadness in his eyes, his honour cutting through the threads of our future.

"Do you yield?" he says with a sigh. He has played into my weaknesses, and I have been foolish enough to let him.

"What do you think?" I say, my hands coiled by my side.

He lowers his blade. "I think," he says, "that you will not kill me."

He is giving me an opening. He is allowing me a window of opportunity, daring me to take it, and I do. I whip up a ball of fire, not one intense enough to kill him but certainly enough to knock him off his feet. In a flash of light, it blasts into his chest and sends him skiing through the mud. I stand rooted to the spot until I hear him groan and his chest heaves with breath.

The skies above are flashing brightly in the now darkened sky. I turn quickly to head through the house and out of the back door.

Esara is standing in the garden, holding someone closely in an embrace. My heart sinks. I am too late. She has already raised him from the dead.

"What have you done!" I cry out.

A woman turns to face me, her blond hair darkened by the rain, causing it to cling to her face. She is an adult now, and it is strange given that the last time I saw their true appearance, they were a child.

"Esara?" I say in disbelief, and then my feelings turn to horror when Ulrik turns his head to face me. I would love nothing more than to see the man that I was falling for one last time, but not like this.

His face has the appearance of someone in between life and death. His skin has returned only partially, with the death and decay that a body succumbs to clearly not reversible. He offers me a polite smile. It is a smile I have not seen from that face for so long.

"Move away, Esara, I can't allow this," I say. "Ulrik, you must understand, this magic, it is tainted. It comes at a cost."

"No!" Esara cries as she steps in between us. "I won't let you take him, not now that I have him back. We can fix him. There is always a way of fixing things, of fixing curses."

"Then you admit that a curse is what this is. You may have brought Ulrik back, Esara, but in doing so, you have cursed him for eternity. He is neither living nor dead." I have never seen her so vulnerable, never seen her fight to defend anyone, but it is what I would come to expect when it is her brother that stands behind her.

"It's okay, Zerina, I understand." Ulrik's voice is pained and crackled, and his breath is wheezy, as if each word is agonising. And then he walks towards me.

I am paralysed in this moment. I can tell by how he carries himself, how he walks, that it is really him. His soul hasn't been corrupted from the resurrection. At least there is that to be grateful for.

"Ulrik, no! I won't let you go again, I won't let her take you from me." Esara sets off past Ulrik, anger and hurt in her eyes. Ready to sever the bond we have formed since we first set sail in an instant to protect her brother.

Ulrik grabs her arm and tries to make her see sense. "Esara, this is not the way. Doesn't magic come with a price?" he says.

At least he listened to me when we spoke about magic.

Esara does not answer, so I answer for her. "It does, and with this kind of spell, the rules are encased in stone that cannot be manipulated."

"What is it? The price?" Ulrik asks with concern.

"To bring life back from the afterlife, you must sacrifice another."

Esara continues to struggle against Ulrik, seemingly oblivious to what I have just said. "Get off me, Ulrik, she wants to send you back to the afterlife!"

Ulrik's face drops. "Whose life?" he asks quietly. "Tell me whose life must be lost so that I can once again walk this world."

Before I can respond, a bright light coming from Ulrik's grave takes my attention. The Resurrection Stone is levitating in the air, spinning quickly on the spot as it seeks to replenish its spent magic.

Esara stops struggling as she turns to face the blinding light that illuminates our surroundings. I can feel the power of its core emanating outwards, looking for the one who called upon its magic.

"No!" Ulrik shouts, his eyes wide with realisation. "Take me back, I did not wish for this! You cannot have her life in exchange for mine!"

"It's a price I am willing to pay," Esara says, standing in between the stone and Ulrik. "I have done things I am not proud of, Ulrik. I just hope you understand. Know that I love you."

"Esara, no!" he cries as she steps towards the pulsating Resurrection Stone.

I know what must happen, yet despite everything we have been through, despite how Esara left things with me, I understand that this is the price she must pay. Tears fall from my face as I watch her move towards the light. Why couldn't she have just listened to me when I tried to warn her?

Green magic spins around the stone as it rotates at an inhuman speed, the surge of power threatening to throw me from my feet.

"Esara!" I cry out at the same time that Ulrik does.

She offers us a smile. "It's okay, I am ready. It is done." And then she turns to face the stone.

A bolt of green magic leaves a stream of mist behind it as it fires from the Resurrection Stone like an arrow. Esara stands with her arms outstretched, ready to accept her fate.

"Captain!" Darmour dives through the air, knocking Esara from the path of the blast. I am unable to see what happens fully as a flash of green blinds me. When the flash is gone, I rush towards them, my heart racing.

"Esara!" Ulrik roars as he races to her side with another rasping breath.

"No, no, no!" Esara yells. "This wasn't meant to happen! Darmour, Darmour!"

When I reach them, Esara is struggling to get up from the ground, and the storm above us has started to settle.

Beside her, Darmour lies on his back, his arms and legs stretched out, his eyes wide open. A green energy charges around his body.

"No!" I scream, sliding onto my knees as I reach him. I lift his head and wipe my hand down his cheek. "I'm here, I am with you, don't go, don't leave me." I keep brushing my hand down his face, each time hoping that he will gasp for breath, that life will ignite in his vacant eyes, that he will tell me that everything is going to be okay one last time. Everything I am, everything I have, I would sacrifice it all for him in an instant. "Please Darmour, I need you." My voice breaks as I plead with him to stay with me. My words are bereft of reason as I shake him, pleading with him to come back to me, not to leave me.

My words mean nothing. He can't hear me. He is gone.

10

MORGANA

"Orjan, is that you?" My throat is dry and my voice croaks as I try to speak. It hurts just to breathe, let alone sit up in bed.

The man sitting at the desk across the room is wearing Orjan's armour and colours, but he looks nothing like the Orjan I have come to know.

When he turns his head to look at me, I gasp, which in turn causes me to wince with pain. His face is not that of a lizard man, but of an olive-skinned, weary lord. One who has sacrificed so much for so long. I can see that his face is wet with tears, and I know in an instant that it is truly him.

"How? How is this so? Am I dreaming?" I have tried so many incantations, brewed so many potions, researched so many grimoires, but I have never been able to find anything to free him from his curse, yet here he sits before me, his curse broken.

Then my mind races and my heart panics as I remember about my sister, about Gillam and the Gondoron Pass. "I need to find Yaelor," I say. I try to push myself up, but I am

83

still too weak, and my arms buckle as I collapse into the bed.

Orjan rushes towards me and takes hold of my hand with a tenderness I have never felt before.

"It is okay, she is here," he says, his cheeks still wet with tears. His voice is choked, but he looks more relieved than anything.

"She is here?" I say, confused by his words, still processing the rugged man who sits by my bedside. His skin is rough against my own, but softer than the scales that were previously bound to him. "How – what has happened? How did we get here?" The room seems to spin as I try to comprehend how I have ended up here. I raise my hand and place it lightly on Orjan's face, my fingers grazing his rough stubble and taking in his strong jawline, and then our eyes meet. He has deep, dark eyes, almost black, and I find myself transfixed, unable to find words as I get lost in them.

As Orjan smiles at me, another tear falls from his face and lands on the bedsheets. He wipes them away with his sleeve before laughing. "I found a way to break the curse, Morgana." He kneels down beside me. "But I would have gladly embraced my curse once again if it meant you would be okay."

A tight knot forms in my throat and I find it difficult to swallow as I continue to examine Orjan's face. His voice is different than I am used to, no longer blighted by the hiss that would often form in his words along with that all-too-familiar growl.

"Is it really you?" I ask, still not believing that this isn't all a dream and that I may wake up at any moment.

"It is," Orjan says with another smile, "truly." He traces

my fingers down to his neckline where I notice that his skin is badly damaged.

"What is this?" I say, a horrible feeling rising in the pits of my stomach. The texture around Orjan's neck feels like bone.

"An amulet. A curse-breaker. Wherever it is from, it has magic inside it that has broken my curse. I am free of it, Morgana, I am truly free." The joy in Orjan's face is a picture I wish I could hold on to for a lifetime. Everything he has had to endure, the selflessness he has shared with this kingdom, always putting them first – if there was ever anyone who deserves any semblance of happiness, it is him. But I know the cost of magic, the true cost of such powers, and I know all too well that all forms of magic come with a price. So the question is, just what has Orjan had to pay?

"Where did you come across this?" I ask, examining the necklace further. It has fused with his skin and become one with his body. It looks painful, and the skin around it is blackened and charred.

Orjan shifts awkwardly and releases my hand. "That is not important right now. What is important is that you rest and recover. You were so near to death when we found you that I feared that you would not survive. Even the healers, despite their hope, thought that your injuries were too severe."

I can see through his tactics. He is just not very good at distraction, which tells me he is hiding something. There is something about this amulet that he does not want me to know.

"Orjan," I say, cutting him off, "how did you come about this amulet? How did you learn of its existence?"

He exhales and shakes his head as if battling his own

thoughts. "It was in Hora, hidden in the ruins deep beneath their temple."

"Hora?" I say, confused.

"I went to see the destruction caused by Rhagor for myself, with Rior."

"Rhagor?" I muse, then I remember that Rhagor had wiped out the farming village. I focus on the amulet, then shift my gaze to Orjan's weary face, slowly piecing everything together.

If Rhagor flexed his power to disintegrate an entire village, he must have wanted something – there must have been a reason for it. Orjan said he found this amulet, which clearly has magic stronger than anything I have come across before.

And I realise that I have seen this amulet before. The bone material used to craft it is unmistakable from my visions.

"What have you done?" I say. "Orjan, truly, what have you done? If this is something that Rhagor desires, he will not stop until he has it." Panic overcomes me as a flush of heat rises up inside me, knocking me sick. I fight a wave of nausea and start padding around the bed.

Orjan reaches for a pan and tosses the water out of it, then passes it me. I spew out burning bile that stings my throat. I retch and retch, over and over as my muscles tense, the pain in my body intensifying the feeling, somehow making it even worse. What has he done? Not only has he put himself in grave danger, but also the people of the kingdom he cares about so deeply.

Orjan's hand meets my back and he rubs it soothingly, his other rough hand wiping away the hair that is matted to my face.

When I finally stop retching, I sit up, my eyes watering and my throat burning as if I have breathed fire.

"Here." Orjan passes me a cup of water and I drink it quickly. It soothes my throat and quenches my thirst, and he fills it up again. This time I take my time to sip it rather than drink it in one like a person of the wild.

"Orjan, we can't stay here," I say, my voice trembling. "If Rhagor knows that you are responsible, if he knows you are holding something so powerful that he desires, I fear what he will do to you in retaliation."

Orjan stands and moves to the large window beside the bed to look out over the kingdom of Eltera. The light from outside lands on him through a gap in the drawn curtains, allowing me to see his full form in detail for the first time.

He closes his eyes as if savouring the warmth of the sun against his skin. "This was never my intention," he says. "I was not thinking clearly when Rior and myself landed at Hora. The destruction was like nothing I have ever witnessed, all those lives taken, all those souls lost as if they were insignificant. History will never tell of their names. In a moment of madness, one self-proclaimed god-king thought it absolutely acceptable to wipe out generation upon generation of families. There are people in this very kingdom who will have lost family members or friends when Hora was wiped from these lands. Nothing is left, Morgana, nothing but smouldering ruins. The only traces of people are the ashen husks that line the streets."

He takes a deep breath. "I was angry, I was hurt. I wanted to let him know that I would not stand by and let him do this. That I would not allow him to extinguish lives like they mean nothing. They mean everything. Each and every one of them had a name. They had families, husbands, wives, parents, and children."

Orjan leans forward and places his hands on the stone that surrounds the window as he looks down at the ground. The pain in his voice is so raw. He is grieving for these people, his people. People who have accepted him, who trusted him to keep them safe and lead them into prosperity. A man who helped free them from the confines of the tyranny that they had to endure for so long.

I sense he has more to say, so I remain silent, watching him.

"When I saw Codrin overseeing labourers digging, I knew that there was a reason for it, that they were looking for something. And in that moment I had to know, I had to find out what it was that they desired that badly that they would destroy a village without any hesitation. I had no clue what this was, but when I found it, there was a pulse of energy that I was drawn to, like I had to wear it, as though I was not complete unless I did. What happened next was agonising, even more so than when I drank the tainted waters of the Fountain of Youth. I passed out from the pain, deep beneath the village, underneath their once sacred temple. When I woke, I was free. The curse had been lifted. It was on our way back to Eltera when I came across a child with terror in her eyes near the Gondoron Pass. Her mother had been taken by slavers. We went to help, and in doing so, we came across the child's mother, Yaelor, a face that I recognised from the Barbaraq incursion. Although last time I saw her she was standing beside Laith in the Forest of Opiya. This was when I came to you to report your sister was in fact alive."

He looks at me scoldingly and I feel a pang of shame. I will never forget the look he gave me when I ordered Lek and my soldiers to advance on the forest, despite Orjan's pleas for me not to. I was driven by the visions that I have had to endure for a lifetime.

It was in that moment that I knew that no matter how hard I tried, no matter how much I had grown to care for him, that we would never be together. The hurt that I see in his eyes now is apparent as it was that day. For that day, Laith was lost, replaced by Rhagor, and that is something that I do not think Orjan will ever be able to forgive me for.

There is still so much for me to understand, and it causes an intense headache. Orjan's curse, Yaelor, Gillam, and myself. What are the chances of all our paths crossing at the same time? There must be a reason for it. Either way, we need to prepare ourselves for what will come next.

"I need to see my sister and niece," I say. "Then we need to prepare for what is to come, Orjan. I know all too well what the consequences of our actions will be."

Orjan studies me in silence for a moment, and I cannot tell what is running through his mind. He has the look of someone trying to catch me in a lie. Then he asks, "Who is the child's father, Morgana?"

"Her daughter, she is the child of the boy. Laith."

Orjan stands quietly and turns to look out at Eltera through the window once more. This time, however, his jawline is clenched and his knuckles whiten when he grips the stone.

"You have to understand, Orjan, I have done what I have needed to. It was a secret I needed to keep, for them."

"I am used to the lies and the deceit, Morgana." There is a coldness to Orjan's words that I do not like.

"Orjan," I say, but he does not turn his head or acknowledge me. Surely he must understand why I have wanted to keep the knowledge of them a secret?

"This is above you or I," I protest. "By technicality,

Gillam is the rightful heir to Rhagor, she shares his bloodline."

"There it is. There is the play that you have been meaning to make. Have you been calculating this the whole time, manipulating everything into place for your own purposes?"

He misunderstands my intentions and what I mean. If Rhagor were to discover that Gillam shares his bloodline, I dread to think what he would do with her. I have kept her hidden to keep her safe, not for me to take power.

"Orjan –"

"Why tell me this now?"

The way he is looking at me hurts me in a way I was not expecting, and I realise that even if I try to explain, he probably will not believe me. "Because we need to prepare for Rhagor," I say instead. "We need to have a plan for when he arrives. Because when he does, we are going to be met with his fury. I will do what I must to ensure that you, Yaelor, and Gillam are safe."

"Well at least if we did have to fight Rhagor, having the most powerful sorceress in Levanthria will have its benefits." There is a bitterness to his words as he speaks.

I am about to tell him more, to open up to him about the spectres that haunt me, that sapped away my power and left me no longer able to wield my magic, but then his demeanour changes and he stands up from the window, his powerful frame suddenly more on edge, more aggressive.

"What is it?" I say, trying to sit up straighter. "Is it him? Is he here already?"

Orjan shakes his head. "It is Codrin," he says, and he turns and heads for the door without another word.

II

ORJAN

Send word to Codrin, somehow the dwarf has escaped from the dungeons in Askela. I would perhaps offer caution with letting her know that the weapon that he crafted was also taken. Someone was on the inside and they aided him, although it is still not know who this was.

Captain Vance Kregain, Initial report of escaped prisoner VIIV,

Seeing that Elven brute trot into my courtyard like he owns the place fills me with enough anger to rip his throat out. I look down at my bare hands, wishing just for this moment that I still had clawed fingers.

I hurtle down the hallway, down the stairs and towards the courtyard. My morning star and shield are hanging in a rack by the door, and I grab them as I rush by.

I have no doubts why he is here. He knows I have taken the amulet, which means that Rhagor knows, too. If not, he'll know when he sees that I am no longer a lizard man.

This is a moment I have been waiting for. I despise Codrin and everything that he stands for, the pain that he enjoys inflicting on others. His is a sickness that needs eradicating from this land once and for all.

Everything seems to move in slow motion as I step out into the courtyard. My morning star is gripped tightly in one hand, and in my other, I hold the shield made from the hardened shell that was torn from my back – a reminder of the cruelty that I vowed would never befall these people again, a reminder of the courage the people of Eltera showed on that day. It is what I stand for, for them, I fight for them, to stir the fires that will help ignite the change that is needed in this world.

The Elteran guards look at me confusingly, as do the people who are in the courtyard. As I would expect; they would not understand why I am greeting Codrin with such aggression. Come to think of it, they are probably wondering why a human is parading around with Orjan's weapons, given that most have not seen me in this form.

Codrin has already dismounted and he stands with about twenty of his own guards. If they are riding with him, he must have confidence in their abilities, and I assume that these are the best he has to offer. Looking at their frames, I can see that he has opted for those with a more powerful build on them.

Codrin's own powerful frame stands smugly in the centre of the courtyard as I approach. He does not have a weapon drawn, and his arms are folded across his chest as he dead-stares me.

He is not intimidated by me, and neither I, him.

"Orjan," he says with a confused tone, "you look different. Still, the Rashouyan colours you wear give you away.

You know why I am here. You have taken something that does not belong to you. The king has given me permission to imprison you until his arrival."

"He is no king," I roar, "and you are no magistrate. You are nothing more than an enforcer."

I do not wait for a reply, neither do I care how many men he has with him as my anger takes over me. I swing my morning star at him, aiming for his head. Codrin simply smiles before hopping backwards, causing me to miss, having foolishly let my anger drive the worst strike. I swing the outside of my shield at him, forcing him to brace himself with his arm. The Elf is like a boulder as I quickly realise that the strength I once possessed is now gone. He grunts disapprovingly before shoving me backwards, and I adopt a defensive stance.

His guards draw their weapons, ready to attack me, but Codrin raises his hand, bloodied from the spikes of my shield. My own soldiers draw their weapons without hesitation. Their allegiance is to Eltera, not to the fake king. Rior moves to stand beside me, both his blades in his hands, his eyes fixed on Codrin. He wants this fight as much as Codrin does.

"Let him have his moment," Codrin tells his guards, beckoning for them to stand down. He reaches for his back and draws his greatsword, the blackened blade shining as if it were made of glass. "Or at least try."

I nod at Rior in silent communication to stand back as well. Then I let out a cry of frustration and attack again. Codrin steps out of the way, and with an almighty swing, his sword comes at me from the side. I raise my shield, bracing myself for the impact, the force of which is incredible as it reverberates through my arm. His greatsword bounces off, and he uses the momentum to swing the blade over his head and come at me from the other side. I quickly turn into this, once again using my shield to take the full force.

The power is enough to send me sprawling through the dirt, a cloud of dust spitting up into the air. Before I have time to think, he is already rushing at me, a pleased grin on his face. He is enjoying every moment of this, his smugness reminding me of Grush. I defeated him in the battle for Eltera just as I will defeat Codrin.

Codrin trails his sword behind him as he runs at me, and when he reaches me, he raises his boot high to stomp on me. I pull my shield in front of me and his boot meets it.

"Tell me, Orjan," he says, pushing all his weight onto it, "how does it feel to know that when all this is done, these people will belong to me?"

I press up against his boot, but his sheer bulk and strength is incredible. Why is it I find myself wishing for the strength I used to have as a lizard man? I am not used to the constraints of my own human body as I desperately try to push him off me, but I find myself pinned by my own shield. Codrin grins at me as he readies himself to bring his sword down on me.

A stone bounces off the side of his head, forcing him to stop.

Infuriated, he looks around, raising a hand to his head before inspecting the blood that now clings to his fingertips.

"Leave him alone!" Gillam's voice echoes around the courtyard. Silence descends on the courtyard as the stone bounces off the ground. Codrin turns his head to look at the stone as it skids to a stop before raising his gaze to the child. It is as though mechanical cogs are turning in his head as his face slowly turns into one of rage.

I see Yaelor almost shudder with what her daughter has done, but I admire Gillam's spirit. She reminds me of Rior when I first met him.

Yaelor grabs hold of Gillam and pulls her behind her, but she is unable to hide the panic in her eyes.

"Kill them all," Codrin sneers as if he was only looking for an excuse to slaughter everyone. His guards cry out in tandem and flood through the courtyard.

"On me!" I hear Rior cry as he rushes forward from beside me, a sword in each hand. Elteran guards follow him without hesitation, weapons bared and ready to fight, this time not to defend Eltera, but to defend me.

The roar thunders in my chest as the blur of blue from Eltera and black and gold of Askela meets on the courtyard to the sound of steel crashing against steel.

While Codrin is distracted, I push him up enough for him to lose balance, which affords me enough time to clamber from the floor. I try to lift my shield once again but it is too weighty and is slowing me down. If I am to win this fight, I am going to have to fight with my head and my speed.

I drop the shield to the ground and grip my morning star with both hands.

Codrin raises his greatsword with one hand and points it at me, his eyes wide. "Your head will look good on a pike at the gates of Askela."

"Yours will be fed to the wolves," I sneer as I wait for him to make his move.

The two of us exchange blows. Codrin is slower than I am, and I'm able to make a few quick attacks, but despite my speed advantage, Codrin manages to parry these.

Behind him, Rior is making his way through a thicket of Codrin's guards, each of them dropping to the ground as he slices through them. Unfortunately our own soldiers fall as the dirt starts to pool with the blood of soldiers on both sides.

There are already too many that have fallen, especially in my name, but I use it to inspire me as I continue to exchange strikes with Codrin.

I can see his frustration building as he is unable to land a blow on me. I dart around him, and as he takes a wild downwards swing at me, I step to the side, then drive my morning star into his upper arm. The spikes tear through his thick flesh, and blood begins to pour out from his wound. I then rake my weapon down his arm to the sound of his scream of pain.

The blade slips from his grip as he turns to face me. I raise my morning star above my head, ready to end him. It is no less than he deserves. I have waited for this moment for so long.

"Enough!" Morgana's voice pierces through the courtyard like a wild arrow.

The battle nearly stops immediately. After all, she is our queen, and as far as I know, Codrin and what is left of his guards will not have known that she was here.

It freezes me to the spot. As much as I want to end Codrin right here, right now, there is a reason she is intervening, and despite my wishes, I cannot be seen to defy the queen in front of everyone. To do so would put her in a difficult position, which would likely end in my execution.

"Do it," Codrin snarls. "End it now!" He starts laughing, blood seeping through his teeth.

"Death would be too much of a kindness!" I say.

Instead, I drive the base of my morning star into the side of Codrin's head, knocking him unconscious.

"Lower your weapons," Morgana demands as she staggers into the courtyard, barely making it down the steps. I fear she may fall at any moment.

Reluctantly, everyone does as she asks. Rior is breathing heavily with swords in hand, soaked in the blood of our enemies. I am impressed by how good of a fighter he has become.

Morgana stumbles slowly across the ground, her skin deathly pale as if she might collapse at any moment. "Orjan, have Codrin and his remaining guards taken to your dungeon. We need to move fast."

I give the command to Rior, who leads our own guards in escorting the remaining Askelans away. It takes three of them to drag Codrin away in his unconscious state.

Yaelor stands with a bloodied axe in her hand. "Gillam!" she calls out, breathing heavily.

"Mama," Gillam says, running out from behind some barrels just beyond the training grounds. She wraps her arms around her mother tightly, and it is warming to see the embrace. It reminds me of what it is that we are actually fighting for.

"Yaelor," I say, disrupting their moment. "Can you fetch the healers to tend to our wounded?"

She nods and heads towards the castle, tossing the axe on the ground, Gillam following closely behind.

"Why did you stop me from killing him?" I ask as Morgana reaches me. Codrin's blood drips off the end of my morning star. I was so close to ending his deplorable life.

"Because enough blood has already been shed on this day," Morgana says, but I know it will be because she has some form of affinity for him. After all, he used to serve her every call prior to Rhagor crowning himself king. I am no fool. "Regardless, we do not have time or the resources to lose soldiers in a fight that can be avoided. If Codrin has already arrived looking for you, then I can assure you that Rhagor is not far behind."

She looks around the courtyard. "We need to make it look like no battle has taken place. That would only arouse his suspicion and draw him to attack sooner."

"I will meet him head-on if I need to," I say, gripping my weapon tightly. "I am not afraid of him."

"Put your pride to one side and think of your people, Orjan. We still do not know why he needs this amulet, and are you forgetting that it is now a part of you?"

I barely have time to think about what she is inferring when she says, "I cannot and will not let him take you or that amulet, for more reasons than you will ever know. Rhagor could be here at any moment. He could already be at the castle gates. He has no clue of my involvement, so you must do something for me, Orjan. You must hide, somewhere deep in the castle, somewhere he won't find you."

"What about Yaelor and Gillam? Do you need them to come with me?"

"No, as soon as Yaelor is back from the healers, I will send them on their way with a horse and supplies. They cannot be here when Rhagor arrives, it is too much of a risk. One that I cannot take. You cannot both be in the same place. As things stand, he has no clue of Gillam's existence or Yaelor's, so they should be able to get by on a horse without drawing his attention."

"I don't like this, Morgana. I am happy to turn myself over to him if it means the safety of these people."

"But that is precisely the problem. He will expect you to

do that, and we still do not know his plan or why he needs that amulet. Let me find this out. Hopefully I can redirect him away."

"I hope you are right," I say. Not just for her sake, but for everyone in this kingdom. How could I have been so foolish? I have endangered everyone.

12

RHAGOR

Pure blood elves are long considered extinct, their bloodline now diluted. That does not mean that they are and I believe that they choose to remain hidden amongst modern society.

Hector Valerin, Elven Bloopdlines Volume II, 27KR

I feel nothing for the sister I have left impaled on the ground in front of the burning Elder Tree. She got what she deserved, only this time I regret not staying with her to watch her life shift out of those blackened eyes, to see her fae skin fade and wither away as the precious tree that granted her eternal life and rebirth burned away in front of her.

My plan is bigger than that, however. This is only one part of it, and I must get my hands on that blasted amulet if I am to finally have the revenge that I have sought for the last two thousand years.

Then doubt creeps into me. Should I have waited? Should I have confirmed that her petulant life had truly faded away before continuing on?

I look over my shoulder to see the shroud of smoke billowing into the clouds above as though a volcano has erupted, but I know it is the Elder Tree. That in itself will cause chaos not only across these lands, but for the gods, too. If they were not taking notice before, they certainly will be now.

I grin to myself; the sight of the smoke in the distance all but cements my dear sister's fate, a move which will leave our darling mother reeling. Seeing her forest, her blessed tree, and her daughter destroyed in one swift movement. She'll need to bear the responsibility for her own grief. After all, it is because of her, because of Opiya, that this had to happen. If she had not imprisoned me for so long, I would not harbour such vengeful thoughts. If she had a shred of dignity, she would realise that this is in fact her fault, that everything that has happened is a consequence of her actions. I cannot wait to see the fear in her eyes when she finally sees what it is that I have planned for her.

All of this destruction, all the chaos that I intend to bring to this world, it is all because of her, and what I have planned for my mother is a fate worse than death itself.

I have no doubt that Codrin will see the fire as my signal. He will already be advancing on Eltera, he may already be there.

Ultimately he's one of the few people that I can trust, which says a lot about this world, given that the man is an Elven brute.

My chest is pounding and my breathing is heavy as I continue my own advancement on Eltera. I can see the towers of the castle ahead of me. It is somewhat inferior to the castle that I have called home for the last eight years, but I am told that after Askela, it is the best remaining castle in these lands.

How pathetic these people are, that despite the resources they have had for so many years, this is all they have managed to achieve. When I am done with these lands, there will be nothing left but smouldering ruins. Hora was just a small example of the power that I have imbued in the sword at my side, and although it is frustrating that my own power is limited, the other gods will soon find out what that feels like. I grow tired of this land and its people. What good am I as a god of chaos and war if there is never war or chaos in my presence?

With a heel, I kick my horse, frustrated that it is not moving as fast as I would desire. How these limitations have grown to irk me. My horse is breathing heavily – it is probably in need of rest – but I do not care. I will not stop until I reach Eltera and I have my hands on that blasted amulet. If Codrin's thoughts are true and it is in fact Orjan who has taken this magical artefact from me, then I will certainly make an example of him in front of all of his people before making an example of them, too.

I don't know what his intentions are, but he could not have known what the amulet was capable of. Given that he is bound by a powerful curse himself, I imagine he will now be aware of what the amulet is. For it is a chaos-bringer in my eyes, imbued with the power that I harnessed two thousand years ago. An artefact that I have managed to keep hidden for all this time, even from my mother who apparently sees everything. Oh, the irony.

If Orjan is the one who now holds this ancient power – my power – then his lizard curse will undoubtedly be broken now, for the magic inside the amulet is like nothing else in this world. It contains the power to break magic as a construct. And given that the self-proclaimed gods of not only Levanthria but across this entire world only exist because of this magic, I for one cannot wait to see it stripped from their very bones. For them to endure what I have had to endure, imprisoned, powerless, human.

The thoughts of my plan bring a smile to my face, and as I look up into the sky, I wonder if she is watching, and if so, why she has not intervened. Then I remember that she is bound by her foolish laws, the ones that I so easily broke. My focus then drifts back to Eltera. As I continue with my approach, I am so close to achieving what I have always wanted, and I will not let anything get in my way, nor let anyone think they can try without facing the full force of my wrath.

When I reach the front of the city gates, I can see some guards who lean through the gaps in the turrets, their bows pointed at me. I must admit, from the outside, Eltera looks as though it is in fine condition, a stark contrast to the rest of Levanthria. It is formed with large, light grey stone which is forged from the Kragoan Mountains if I am not mistaken. Barely any moss or green can be seen clinging to the walls, a trait that I know the greystone is used for.

A large drawbridge is raised, leaving a wide moat between me and them, circling around the far sides of the kingdom as far as I can see. The moat is half-filled with dark water, which I sense has some form of oil-based substance in it to keep their enemies away. But I am no enemy, I am their king.

"Who goes there?" a voice bellows at me. "State your business with Eltera or be on your way."

I find the statement insulting, and I raise my head to stare in the direction of the voice. "Open the gates," I say, my jaw clenched. Whoever called to me like some commoner had best hope I do not cross paths with them. I will not suffer such indignation, such insolence.

"Shit!" I hear a voice say, "it's King Rhagor."

Adjusting my gaze to the gap in the turrets, I bow my head and offer a wry smile, my horse jolting and tutting about as if it is more impatient than I am.

"Lower the bridge!" a woman's voice calls, who I assume is the captain. I still cannot see any faces but am pleased when the bows are lowered from pointing at me.

With a loud clunk, the chains begin to lower, grating against each other as the drawbridge groans from the strain until it is completely flat against the ground in front of me. Perfectly engineered. I admire the craftsmanship that has gone into this. Perhaps I will have something similar put in place around Askela.

At a canter, I head across the bridge, taking my time to cast my judgement over the guards that quickly mobilise to greet me. As I approach, the large iron gates to the kingdom peel back, allowing me to gaze upon the people of Eltera hard at work by the markets. They continue their day, blissfully unaware that I have arrived, but word quickly starts to spread as hushed words and eyes begin to reluctantly fall on me.

I have not been here for so long, they must be wondering why I am in fact here.

A woman stands ahead of me with her arms by her side, her white hair tied back, her helmet tucked under her arms. She is wearing the blue tunic of Eltera over her mail armour, with what looks like a wyvern etched onto the front of it.

She is nervous, her body language shifting as she awkwardly adjusts herself to ensure a proper posture to greet her king, her head raised slightly. She does not make eye contact with me directly aside from quick, intermittent moments that pass by quicker than a blink of an eye.

As I approach, I wait until my horse is near enough on top of her before stopping and waiting for her to raise her head towards me.

"Where is Orjan?" I growl, unable to hide my frustration towards him and this wretched place.

The captain looks to her right at the soldiers lining the sides of the courtyard, then across at the other side to the others.

"Answer me!" I snarl, my voice elevating. "Where is your lord?"

"H–he is in the castle, or so I heard. I have not seen him, he has been in his chambers with the healers since Morgana arrived."

"Morgana." My nostrils flare at the sound of her name. Why is she here? Does she have something to do with all this? Is she the one responsible for Orjan stealing my amulet? She must be. I figured as much.

"Yes, she arrived in a sorry state. Folk have been saying she was attacked by a wyvern. I don't know if that's true, but word is the healers have managed to save her."

Good. If she has survived, I can take great pleasure in being the one to draw the last breath from her with my hands wrapped around her neck. If she is behind all this, I will be sure to make her suffer for as long as her body will allow.

Heeling my horse once more, I rush forward without a care for the captain who is unfortunate enough to still be in my way as I race through the streets. My horse tramples her as I charge towards the castle gates. When I arrive, they are wide open, allowing me to pass through. The courtyard is busy, but I care not about the people around me, only

Morgana and, more importantly, Orjan, her pawn in all this.

"Orjan!" I call out as I drop down from my horse which is still moving. I reach for my sword and draw it in one movement before slamming the blade into the ground. I limit my magic, suppressing the flames but allowing a low grumble to shake the earth round me. It is enough to garner everyone's attention as they stop what they are doing and look over to me, no doubt dumbfounded as to why their king has arrived in such a hostile state. I can see the terror in their eyes, but then I notice one woman in the corner who does not show fear for me – it is for someone else, and she presses her child behind her.

I pace up and down behind my sword impatiently for a few moments before calling out again, "Orjan!"

Then I notice a horse to the side that I recognise as Codrin's, but there are no signs of him or his guards. And that's when I smell it: the scent of iron in the air. Breathing in deeply through my nose confirms this. There has been blood shed here, and by the looks of it, a poor attempt to cover it in the dirt. I breathe in heavily again. It is fresh blood. There has been a fight, and not long ago.

"Do not keep me waiting much longer, not unless you want a repeat of Hora!" My impatience grows, amplifying my frustration. When I am about to shout again, a rather bedraggled Morgana staggers out from the doorway to the castle. She is wearing a black dress that fits her nicely. She tries to walk as elegantly as possible, but I can see from her heavy limp that she is injured and in a lot of pain. Her face is bruised with a stitched cut above one eye, and her left shoulder appears sunken.

Unlike everyone else here, she meets my eyes with a

sternness that tells me she is not intimidated by my presence.

"I am so glad you have arrived, my dear," she says, clearly trying to keep up the facade of our marriage. She has had her uses, but she is long past that point now. If only I knew what exactly it is that she has been hiding from me.

"Where is Codrin?" I ask.

"Incapacitated," she says confidently. "He is in the dungeons, accused of treason." She continues her staggered walk towards me.

"Treason?" I growl. "How so?"

"He tried to raid this castle. As a lord of Askela, he is not allowed to encroach on another lord's lands." She stops a few steps away from me, resting her hands in front of her. I do not know whether it is confidence or arrogance that she carries, but either way, it is a fine line and a very dangerous one to draw in the ground between us.

You could cut the tension in the air with a knife as I try and figure out what her play is here. I have demanded Orjan, yet she is the one to greet me. She is delaying me, all but securing my thoughts that she has had something to do with him stealing from me. The question is, why? Does she intend to use the magic of the amulet against me? To steal my power so she can take my throne? After all, power is all that she has ever desired.

"I have no time for your games, Morgana." I stand behind my sword, resting my hands on the crossguard. Its power pulsates into my hands, letting me know that it is ready to be wielded whenever I so wish it.

There is a flicker of panic in Morgana's eyes, which she tries to mask. It is only present for the briefest of moments but long enough for me to notice.

"You care about him, don't you?" I smile teasingly

before it turns into a wide grin. "Ooh, what a twisted tale we weave."

Morgana's shoulders drop as she rather pathetically says, "I have no idea what you are talking about. You are my king, and my husband."

I must admit, she puts on a good theatrical show for everyone in our presence, but I truly know her. I have seen and shared the power she has so desperately built throughout her life. To think her capable of harbouring such feelings for another is, quite frankly, nauseating.

"Now now, there is no need to pretend, Morgana. If I am honest, you do not have much more time in this world. The darkest parts of the afterlife are reserved for cowards and traitors." I stare deeply into those emerald eyes of hers. "Trust me, I know the god who created it." I exhale deeply, growing frustrated with her tactics. "Guards, fetch me Codrin at once."

They mobilise quickly and do as I say; they know all too well what I am capable of, how easily I could destroy them all.

"Either get out of my way or tell me where Orjan is. He has something that I want and I do not like waiting."

"He has already gone," Morgana says defiantly, her arms moving to her side as if she is ready to wield her magic against me. My gloved hands groan as I squeeze the crossguard of my sword, a low rumble trembling in the ground ever so slightly.

"Then you leave me no choice," I say as I ready myself to obliterate everyone in my vicinity.

"If you do, you will never see that amulet again," Morgana spits.

I grin. "So you do have it." Now the question is, how do I obtain it? I cannot risk reducing Eltera to rubble just yet. If

I'm right, the amulet will have bonded itself to Orjan, and I cannot risk destroying it by eviscerating everything like I did in Hora. That would risk destroying the amulet.

I feel a smile tug at the corner of my mouth as I think about how I will get the amulet back. No, it will have to be a lot more intimate than that, as I will need to extract the amulet from him myself.

13

YAELOR

The castle is in disarray as everyone around us is doing what Morgana has instructed. Having reached the healers and instructed them to Morgana's wishes, I head back towards the courtyard. If Rhagor is on his way, we must leave. We have already outstayed our welcome and something bigger than us is at play.

One thing is clear: Morgana is not by Rhagor's side as I had thought. Whatever happened in the courtyard tells me that tensions have been rising for some time. She may be my blood, but our father would be ashamed of the things she has done, how she has turned out.

"Mama, did you see my throw?" Gillam beams proudly as we hurry back towards the courtyard. I have been sure to grab a satchel and some basic supplies to last us at least a day, but we do not have time to wait around.

"I did." I want to praise her for her accuracy, I want to tell her how brave she was to stand up to the man who helped kill her namesake. I want to reassure her that given the chance, I would have driven an axe into his face, but that is not the life that I want for her. She has already seen more violence recently to last her a lifetime, and that is enough. All I want is for her to be safe and able to live her life, as far removed from the life that I had to live as possible.

Yet despite my wishes, despite never training her how to fight, despite always steering her away from conflict, she somehow always seems drawn to it like a moth to a flame. "I need you to stay away from fights from now on, Gillam."

"But Mama —"

"No," I cut her off. "Do you understand? Unless your life is in danger, you run. Do you understand?" Being her mother has been the hardest thing I have ever done but it has forced me to see the world through different eyes.

Gillam pulls her hand away from me and stops following. When I turn, her shoulders are sunken and she has withdrawn into herself.

I kneel in front of her and place my hands on her shoulders, and she reluctantly raises her eyes to meet mine. In them I see her father, I see Laith. I am so proud of this child, despite how difficult she can be at times, and I know that Laith would be too. That, given the opportunity, he would have been a great father to her. I'll never know what kind of life we could have led together, but I do know that Gillam shows the spirit and fight of both of us combined.

"What is it?" Gillam says.

"You have his eyes," I tell her, something I have never said before. "There are times when I look into them and it reminds me of your father."

"When we get away from here, can you tell me stories about him?" Gillam asks. "I promise not to start any more fights."

She raises her hand out towards me, bending her

thumb and first two fingers, only leaving her last two outstretched. It is something she has always done with me when making a promise, and I do the same, interlocking my fingers around them, like links in a chain. I place my hand against the back of her head and pull her face forward, pressing my forehead against hers. Tears sting in my eyes. "I am so proud of you, Gillam. I am so proud to be your mother. Just know that everything I say, everything I do, it is to keep you safe. I hope you understand that."

"I understand," she says, wrapping her arms tightly around my neck and squeezing me tight. I do the same, and we embrace for a moment before I tell her, "Come, we need to leave before more soldiers arrive." I do not want to go into the full details of why she cannot be around Rhagor.

"Ferelda?"

It is a name that I have not heard for so long, it makes me not want to look over my shoulder, to face my sister. She is the only one who knows me by that name.

"I think you have the wrong person," Gillam says over my shoulder, "that's not my mama's name."

I look over my shoulder to see Morgana standing underneath the archway in the corridor. She is leaning into the wall as if it props her upright. Her red hair is loose and matted, her face bruised, her eyes bloodshot. I turn to see her and am overcome with a swell of emotion that I can see she shares.

"How silly of me," Morgana says softly and offers Gillam a smile. I can tell by the way she looks at her that she knows she is mine, and there is a softness to her that contrasts starkly against the stories that are spoken of her.

"Are you the queen?" Gillam asks, tilting her head. "You don't look very well." She stands at my side, holding on to my hand.

Morgana laughs, but I can see the tears that she is suppressing. She clears her throat and says, "Well, I wish I had aides at my side that were as honest as you are."

"My name's Gillam," she says proudly. "My mum says it means strength, but Gruya at home told me once that it means scarlet, like the colour of your hair."

One thing I cannot forgive or forget is that Gillam, the warrior who she is named after, had her life taken by two of Morgana's thugs in Askela. Regardless of whatever redemption she seeks, I am not sure I can afford the price.

Morgana gathers herself and switches her attention to me. The last two times our paths crossed, we were in battle in this very kingdom. It is strange, the paths that fate weaves. Whatever ordeal she has been through, it looks to have been far worse than the path we have walked. Part of me is grateful for that, for she deserves what comes to her for the things she has done. But she is still my sister.

"Come, I have readied a horse and supplies for you to leave at haste. It is not safe for you here," Morgana says before turning for us to follow her.

Does she know? Does she know Gillam's parentage?

I follow her outside, and when we reach the courtyard, you would not think there had been a fight at all. People are still rushing around, but I am amazed at the speed and fluidity with which they move.

"Over here," Morgana says, leading us to a dark brown horse that already has a saddle along with bags and a satchel.

"I made a point of attaching a sword just in case you need it," Morgana says. "There are enough supplies to last you for at most a few days."

"Thank you," I say.

Before I have a chance to say anything else, Gillam

wraps her arms around Morgana and hugs her. Taken aback, Morgana first winces, but then lowers her arms to hug her back. She looks uncomfortable, like she has not seen such affection before, but I can see in her face how tender the moment is for her, and I know in an instant that she knows everything about Gillam.

"I can't forgive you for things you have done," I say.

"And I would not expect that forgiveness. All I need in this moment is the knowledge that the two of you are safe. When all this is done, I will spend a lifetime making up for it all. For now, you both need to leave. Gillam is more important to Levanthria than she could ever realise."

For some reason I believe what she says. She squeezes Gillam one last time, then turns to leave, heading back into the castle. There is a softness to her that is foreign to me, her usual cold exterior warming like a rising sun. I spend a few moments tending to the horse, checking through everything and making sure that everything is secure.

"Are you ready?" I ask Gillam who looks on after her auntie, unaware that Morgana is her family.

Gillam smiles and nods, and I reach under her arms to pick her up and place her on the horse.

Then there is movement at the gates, and I freeze to the spot when I see who is sitting atop a strong, black horse.

It is Laith.

He's older now, with his face hidden behind a beard, but it is him. The sight of him causes me to hitch my breath. I was not prepared for this moment, and I find myself frozen at the sight of him, longing to just run over and hug him, to let him meet his daughter.

I quickly remind myself that it is not him as he hops down from his horse and slams his blade into the ground.

The earth rumbles under my feet. I have heard so much about Rhagor, about the sword that he possesses.

My worst fear is realised as I come face-to-face with him after all this time. I have failed. Gillam is dangerously close to him.

"Orjan!" he bellows. It is Laith's voice I hear but there is a rasped anger in it that is not truly his, and it forces me to remember that the true Laith is gone.

He is pacing around now, and it is clear that Rhagor is furious. "Orjan!" he roars again to the deathly silence of the courtyard. Everyone is on edge with him being here, his power causing the ground to continue to shake ever so slightly.

I panic, my heart racing as I have no idea what to do. To make a run for it now would only garner his attention. Attention that I do not want to fall on us.

"Is that the king?" Gillam asks through hushed breath.

I place my hand in front of her and push her behind me. "He is no king," I say.

Then to my right, Morgana exits the castle once more. She is struggling to walk now, and her legs look ready to buckle underneath her. Despite her best efforts to hide her injuries, it is clear to see how much pain she is in.

She starts speaking to Rhagor, telling him that Orjan is not here, but I know that she is lying. He is somewhere within the castle walls, and she is protecting him for some reason. It is clear there is so much more to this than I first thought, but I care not. I simply need an opportunity to make my escape with Gillam, however that presents itself.

Morgana manages to keep her cool as she continues to distract Rhagor. He is talking about an amulet, and Mogana acts surprised, but I imagine she is hiding the truth about this, too.

"Where is he, Morgana?" Rhagor demands, and I can tell that his patience is waning. "He is here. I know he is, you know he is. Now hand him over or I will level this entire kingdom."

"And run the risk of destroying your precious amulet? It would take you an age to dig through all the rubble," Morgana replies, the confidence and aggression in her voice commanding and manipulative. "And that is if he was here," she adds with the faintest hint of sarcasm. "Think of all the time you will have wasted when I have already told you that he is not here."

I am rooted to the spot, powerless as all this unfolds in front of us both.

"I have no time for your games, Morgana," Rhagor snarls, his face contorting with anger as he raises his voice. It is a dangerous game that she plays. "Perhaps you just need some encouragement. Remember when you fled Askela in the dead of night, you left your little tracking spell in the dungeons? Do you take me for a fool? And given it was my blood that you used, that only leaves the question, who were you tracking?" Rhagor scans the courtyard and my heart plummets when his eyes set on me.

Morgana steps into his path, trying to distract him with her words, but he pushes her to the side when she refuses to move.

He starts walking straight towards us.

"Are they my own eyes staring back at me?" Rhagor says, stopping to inspect Gillam who is peering at him from behind me. "Morgana, you have been busy, you treacherous whore. Hand the child to me," he demands.

I keep Gillam behind me, my hand trembling. "She is not yours to take," I say, a quiver in my voice.

"Is that so?" he says darkly. When I refuse to move, he

strikes me. The anger in his features is something I am not used to seeing on Laith's face.

"No!" I say as I snap my head back and throw a punch at him. His lip explodes in front of everyone watching, and this serves to only enrage him more. "You cannot have her!" I scream as I strike again, but he blocks my punch and slams a fist into my stomach, knocking the wind from me. Before I can react, he grabs my hair and yanks my face towards his.

I can feel his breath against my skin.

"I will not hurt her," he says through gritted teeth. "But if you try and strike me again, I will break her scrawny little neck in front of you right here!"

"Please, don't take her!" I beg. She is all I have left in this world. Despite the urge to fight him, I believe what he is saying. He is cold and cruel enough to kill her in front of me.

"Then you best hope Orjan does the right thing and return to me what he has taken." Rhagor slams me to the ground as Gillam rushes to my side. I still struggle to see Laith's face, the warmth of his smile, the light in his eyes, now replaced with a cold-laced darkness that is not him.

"Leave my mama alone!" Gillam screams.

Rhagor is quick to her, however, and grabs hold of her, wrapping his arm around her from behind and pinning his forearm under her chin.

"You have two days," he says. "I will be waiting at Askela. Find him, make him return what he took, and I will spare this pathetic child." He carries Gillam with one arm and plucks his sword from the ground with the other, then climbs onto his horse.

I am dazed as I try to get to my feet as fast as I can. "Gillam!" I cry out after her.

"Mama!" she says as she starts to cry. My heart splinters into pieces.

"Two days!" he growls. Then he spins on his horse and leaves.

As I scream after them, my voice grows hoarse with rage and anguish.

My daughter is gone.

14

ZERINA

Do not fool yourself into believing the world ends beyond the territories of Levanthria. There is a vast world out there and I want to explore as much of it as possible.

Darmour Larka, Diary entry, KR unknown

"I am so sorry, Zerina, I never meant for any of this."

It is strange seeing Esara stand before me in her true form. It is the first time I have heard her apologise for anything. There is no hiding, however, that this is the same person who left me trapped on our ship, locked away, the person responsible for the death of Darmour.

I look at her, finding myself devoid of any emotion, for I fear the fury it will ignite if I allow my emotions to get the better of me. Instead I don't acknowledge her as a half-dead, half-alive Ulrik pulls her away to allow me to process what has happened.

There is so much to process, so much to comprehend about what happened last night and the consequences that will live with all of us forever. Standing at the foot of the jarjoba tree where Ulrik was buried, I instead stand at the grave of Darmour. A man whose bravery and kindness was unparalleled. My heart has not ached like this since my sisters were taken from me at the witch trials. The day that shaped my life, who I am now.

My clothes are sodden from the rain last night and I am covered in dirt from filling Darmour's grave. This is not where I would have chosen to rest him. Darmour deserves to be laid to rest at sea, like a man who has dedicated his life to the ocean should be.

I can only hope that one day I can return and take his body to lay it to rest properly. Perhaps then I will be able to find peace and calm from the storm that now stirs within me.

Vireo spent the night helping me tend to Darmour's grave, something he didn't have to do but something he insisted on. When we were done, he didn't say a word. He seemed to know there was nothing he could say, so he simply turned around and left, waiting for me inside.

I find myself now simply staring at the raised bed of soil and the pile of rocks I have collected and stacked – the only marker that shows he is here, laid to rest.

"Zerina?" The voice is one that I should be happy to hear but I am not. Cranky and pain-filled, it is not the voice of the man I once knew.

Looking over my shoulder, I see him standing there, but not as I now know him. Esara has been hidden behind his anger-filled eyes for so long that it feels foreign to see the hurt and kindness in the ones looking at me now.

His face is gaunt and pale. Some of the colour has returned in places, but other parts are simply too decayed, too beyond the magic of the Resurrection Stone. One of his cheeks is simply a hole, with sinew and skin desperately trying to patch it back together.

It's the face of a monster.

But behind it is the heart and soul of a man I once cared for, one who would be dismayed to hear the things his little sister has done in his absence, in his name.

"I am truly sorry, he was a good man, an even better pirate." Ulrik removes his tricorn hat and places it against his chest as he stands next to me to pay his respects.

Silence fills the void between us and, despite my anger and my grief, somehow it is a comfortable silence as we simply process everything that has happened.

"People keep telling me that," I say after a while, my voice shallow and broken. My chest hurts from the tears that I have shed, my throat burns from my roars of anguish. I am bereft, I am empty and broken. "Yet no one truly knew him, not like I did." The longer I stare into his grave, the more I yearn to be given one more day with him, one more chance to tell him how much I cared for him, to tell him how he held my heart like no other man ever has, and that I held his. I would have forgiven him over time for siding with his captain. I understood the conflict within him, from being oath-bound.

"We were to be married one day," I say quietly. "We didn't know when, but we were going to marry and leave this life, step away from it all. To try and find some semblance of happiness in this place. Now I know that was all just a dream."

"What was it that stopped you?" Ulrik asked. He is sincere in his question, and I have to remind myself that this is not the same Ulrik I have spent the last eight years protecting as they morphed into a pirate with a heart darker than the cracked, blackened land of a volcano.

I look at him again, his soft features and expression such a contrast to what I am used to, even despite his monstrous appearance. "A foolish promise we both made to a dying man," I tell him. "One that somehow stands next to me while I mourn."

"I am so sorry, Zerina," Ulrik says with sincerity. "I wish there was something I could do, something that I could say to atone for everything that has happened while I have been gone. There is so much that I do not know, so much that I do not understand. I would gladly walk into the ocean to bring him back. I never wanted this, I don't want this. The price we have paid, the price you are paying, is simply not worth it." There is a different kind of pain in his voice, a visceral, emotional pain that replaces the laboured gasps between the words that he forms.

"You will live," I say, a sharpness in my voice that I know Ulrik is not used to hearing escape my lips. "You will walk this world and you will honour his name. Otherwise, what was the point? His death would mean nothing." My throat stings as bile rises. "You walk this world now because he cannot. I need you to know that. I need you to understand that how you feel, that pity you may be feeling for yourself, it pales in comparison to the anger that I am feeling. You will honour him, Ulrik. You will."

I am not seeking his blessing. He is alive now from a situation that was completely out of his control, I understand that. It doesn't deter me from speaking with such venom as I stare into his deep, darkened eyes. "You will spend this lifetime walking in his shadows, Ulrik Thatch."

"All I ever wanted was for Esara –" he stops himself short when he sees that flicker of hatred in my eyes. If only he knew the monster she had become, the vile, selfish sibling that is a far cry from the sweet, innocent child he rescued from the witch trials.

"If you only knew the things she has done, the things she has proven herself capable of, Ulrik. All in your name."

Ulrik looks down at the ground and I can see the shame oozing out of his pores which he wears like a heavy wax coat, one that will weigh him down. I know him, I know how he thinks. He will carry the burden of Darmour's death on his shoulders, and he will do the same for Esara's actions.

"My sister will atone for the things that she has done. I cannot begin to imagine what you have been through. Just this moment, seeing her walking around, glamoured to my appearance, the hatred in her eyes . . ." His voice cracks. "To know there is a further eight years that I need to catch up with and make amends for . . . Well, that alone is going to take me a lifetime." He looks back at his ramshackle family home, decrepit and falling apart. I can see the crew moving around inside. They are likely more confused than anyone else as to what they should do now.

They had no clue that their captain, the most feared pirate of the seas, was in fact Esara. They have never seen her before. In fact, I have spent longer knowing her as Ulrik as I did Esara. This whole situation is simply a mess.

"She is my sister, however, and as her older brother, I have to take responsibility for all this, for everything she has done, because she has done it in my name."

"Then you are a fool," I say coldly. "Do not make the mistake of walking the same path that I did. I tried to mentor her, I tried to help her, but she only got worse. Everything I have done, everything that ultimately led us to this moment, is because of that blasted vow I made to you when you were dying." I turn to face Darmour's grave once again and I am unable to suppress my broken heart anymore. My legs buckle and I drop to my knees, my hands planting in the cold mud. I start sobbing uncontrollably. Each breath hurts, each second that I cry feels as though my heart is shattering like a mirror that has been smashed to the ground.

"I am so sorry, Darmour," I say, my voice broken. "This is all my fault. If only I had told her, if only I had stopped her, then you would still be here." I reach into my pocket and retrieve one of the rings he had on him. It is a silver band that he had promised he would give to me the day that we married. I sit up and look at the ring, rolling it through my fingers, and then I place it over my third finger on my left hand. "We may not have said our vows to one another, but we had given our hearts, that I can be sure of. I will carry this ring in your honour. I will not give my heart to another, because it will always belong to you. Our souls, our lives are intertwined in this life and the next."

Ulrik remains quiet until I stand and turn to speak to him. "I need you to know that I do not hate you," I tell him. "That is an emotion I reserve for Esara. She will bear the consequences of that hate one day, for the things she has done. She has wronged too many people. That said, she has been like a sibling to me all these years, and as much as I despise her right now, I could not draw a blade on her. I do not hold you responsible for everything that has happened. After all, I need to take my share of blame for that, and I will."

"I understand," Ulrik says. He reaches out and hugs me. I close my eyes and, despite the urge to fight him, to push him away, it takes me back to when we were on the Isle of Voraz, when I was simply a witch who did not understand the extent of my powers, when we went swimming in the ocean and I could simply forget everything that was going on in the world.

The stench of death still clings to Ulrik, however, and I pull away from him.

"But I can't do this, I can't be around you. There is so much that has passed, so many tainted memories that I now associate with your face." I then look at the house and see the back of Esara's head sat at a table. She isn't moving, and is likely lost in her own thoughts.

"And the things that I want to do to Esara, to make her pay for what she has done, means that I cannot be around her, either. I fear for what I will do if she is in my presence for too long. I will, however, leave you with something that I hope will aid you in whatever path of redemption you choose to walk. Do you still carry your mother's trinket?" I ask.

Ulrik reaches into his jacket pocket and gives me a soft, reassuring smile before pulling the rose quartz pendant from his pocket. The silver chain sits nimbly between his finger and thumb.

"Put it on," I say. "Esara!" I call, hostility in my voice as I demand she come here.

It doesn't take long for her to come to the door. I see a sorrow in her eyes, but also an excitement because I am finally ready to speak to her, as if she thinks I will absolve her.

Instead, I stretch out my arm towards her and root her to the spot with my magic, suspending her arms in the air as if she were on a torture rack. She cries out in pain, and I would be lying if I said I did not savour the moment. There is so much I could do to her in this position.

"Zerina, don't!" Ulrik begs as he steps towards me, but I quickly raise my other arm, freezing him to the spot with my magic as well. His eyes grow wide with fear and shock, and I know this is a type of magic he is not accustomed to seeing me use.

The pain of the magic channelling through my arms is excruciating, but I savour it, I acknowledge it, and I use my grief as an outlet as I start to syphon Esara's power into the trinket around Ulrik's neck.

Esara gasps for air as her magical essence escapes from her mouth and drifts towards Ulrik like a thick fog being guided by the wind. As it pours into the amulet, I see the undead face of Ulrik slowly change into the one I remember from my memories: beardless, with features softer than when Esara took his form.

With a snap of my wrist, I break the connection, and the two of them drop to the floor, gasping for air.

"What have you done?" Ulrik says, his voice returned to normal, his words no longer riddled with agonising pain.

"It is both a gift and a curse," I say. "The two of you are now tethered. Esara's essence is now inside that pendant, and as long as you wear it, it will hide your undead appearance." I walk over and kneel beside Esara, whose head is lowered in shame as she gasps to catch her breath. I grab her chin, forcing her to look into my eyes. Hers are large and green. I still see the wildness in them that I am used to from her magic. After all, no glamour in the word could hide the madness that has seeped into her thoughts and soul.

"And you —" I pause as I speak through gritted teeth — "you will no longer be able to take the form of another." If she was so desperate to save her brother, willing to sacrifice anything and anyone to get him back, then she can be tethered to him for the rest of his life. I will leave it to her to figure out this curse, but perhaps being bound to another might teach her to not only think about her own wants and needs.

She stares back at me. I can see she wants to respond, that she does not appreciate me grabbing her face like this, but I want her to know, and I know that she does, that I am far more powerful than her, and now that her glamour magic is gone, she only has her skill with a blade to account for.

"This will be the last time you see me. I cannot travel with either of you. You best hope that our paths do not ever cross again, Esara, for I can never forgive you for what you have done."

I walk past her and make my way to the front of the house where Vireo is already sitting on his horse, ready to leave.

I have a promise to uphold to Vireo, and I'll be damned if I break another oath.

As if reading my mind, Vireo says, "Zerina, you don't have to do this. You are not oath-bound to me. After all, I was not able to help as I wished I could have."

"That is kind of you to say, Vireo. I want to help though. I am from these lands, and I want to help protect them. It is what my sisters would have done. If not by oath, then I will lend aid to your quest simply because it is the right thing to do."

Vireo grins, the relief on his face clear to see. "I have no doubt you will prove more than helpful in the fight that is to come."

"Where is it we ride to?" I ask. "Back to the forest you spoke of?"

He shakes his head. "Eltera," he says. "There is someone there whom I hope will join forces with us. His soldiers will help swell our own, and from what I have heard, he is less than favourable of the king. Even if that's only slightly better of his opinion of me."

"Dare I ask?"

"I will tell you all about it on the ride over. Please understand that the person I am now and the person I was are completely different. I can only hope that Orjan will see that." There is remorse in his voice, a shift in his body language that says he is not perhaps proud of some of the decisions he has made in his life.

"Did you say Orjan?" I ask, surprised.

"Do you know of him?"

"Our paths have crossed," I reply. "In truth, it would be good to see him, although when we parted ways, he was not in the best of places."

"Then perhaps having you by my side will help with winning him over."

"I wouldn't count on that," I sigh. "It would seem we have much to catch up with on our journey."

I look at the house behind me one final time.

Esara is still sitting in the mud, staring at me wordlessly as if in shock.

Then I take Vireo's hand and climb onto the horse behind him.

15

VIREO

We ride north from Osar to Eltera. I have not seen Orjan since the day he confronted Laith in the Forest of Opiya, but from what I am told, he is a good man and an honourable one. Out of all the kingdoms in Levanthria, Eltera is the one that's progressed and seems to be improving in what is now proving to be a diminished landscape.

Zerina has forewarned me that the last time she was here was during the witch trials that I have heard so much about. So many lives were lost that day, including her sisters'. All for the crime of being women who could channel magic.

It shames me how I used to enable the systems that were put in place by King Athos Almerion, something that I will spend a lifetime repenting for.

We ride in silence for two days as I respect Zerina's need to grieve for Darmour, a man who it would seem shared similar values to myself.

He died a good man, protecting his captain. Despite the

things Ulrik – Esara – had done, he stayed true to his role, an admirable trait indeed.

Our horses tire, but we manage to maintain a steady pace. Now that I have the most powerful witch in Levanthria by my side, my plan is to try and get Orjan to agree to join us in battle against Rhagor. Gossip amongst Esara's crew members told me that he does not favour King Rhagor, and his forces would definitely be beneficial to our cause.

I can only hope that he sees sense and understands the need to remove Rhagor from the throne. Only then can Levanthria truly begin to recover and be allowed to breathe once more.

Orjan and I will need to put our history to one side. I hope he can see beyond what I used to be and understand that I only want to fight for what is right.

Behind us, Zerina's former shipmates follow, but they keep their distance, as if worried Zerina might enact revenge on them at any moment for their complicity in leaving her imprisoned in the cell on *Esara's Revenge*. It is only a handful of men, but it's better than nothing. They chose to remain with Zerina when it was clear that Esara and Ulrik would now be forging their own paths.

I just pray that Zerina does not allow her grief to consume her, though I can empathise with how she is feeling. After all, I still wear the cloak of the woman I lost, who died by my own hand. Something I will never truly forgive myself for. For now, all I can do is lead the way to Eltera, and be grateful that Zerina has agreed to follow me.

When we reach the gates of Eltera, I am surprised to see

that the drawbridge is already down, yet there are no guards manning the gates.

"Something isn't right," I say, slowing my horse. "Where are the guards?"

"Keep your wits about you," Zerina calls back to the others. "I can't imagine them being too welcoming to a witch and a group of pirates," she says back to me.

"I will do my best to ensure that Orjan sees reason," I reply – brave words given that Orjan's pride has often got in the way, even if he believes what he is doing to be true. This whole situation is a massive risk, but one we have to take. Although our numbers in the forest are growing, we cannot hope to fight back against Rhagor and Askela without reinforcements.

"Come, let's head inside."

The crew follows us as we traverse the streets of Eltera, heading up to the castle. The streets seem solemn, with the people of the kingdom holding low heads in a subdued manner. Some try to go about their days, but others seem somewhat disinterested in tending to the markets that we pass.

As far as I understood, Eltera was a vibrant kingdom. The streets look usable and the houses are well maintained, so why is everyone so subdued? What is it that has happened here?

Again, when we reach the castle courtyard, the gates are open, and I hop down from my horse. Guards are in full armour, readying their horses and their weapons as if going into battle at this very moment.

"Vireo?" a woman's voice calls out, one that I recognise yet was not expecting to hear.

I turn to see a battered and bruised Yaelor. She is also readying a horse, but she stands apart from the guards. Her eyes are sunken, and her face is blotched as if she has been crying.

"What has happened?" I ask at once. "Why are you here?" My words become more frantic with worry as I look around for Gillam, unable to recognise her in the sea of silver- and blue-armoured guards.

I rush towards Yaelor, momentarily forgetting about Zerina and the crew. "Where is Gillam, Yaelor? Where is the child?" I place my hands on her shoulders, fearing the worst. She stands before me with a numb vacancy in her eyes.

"He has her, Vireo." There is a distance in her eyes that I do not like. I can see she has strapped an axe to her horse, but she is not wearing any armour other than her leathers. She is not prepared for a fight, let alone fit enough to fight by herself.

A mixture of emotions swell in my stomach. Relief that Gillam is not dead, tinged with the fear of who it is that has her.

Yaelor pauses, as if too shocked to speak. I shake her shoulders lightly to try and snap her back into the moment. "Who has her Yaelor? Who has Gillam?"

"Rhagor," she says in desperation, and the fear that grips me intensifies. This is exactly what we have sought to avoid her entire life.

"Does he know?" I ask.

Yaelor shrugs her shoulders. "He has taken her as a bargaining tool. For some reason he wants Orjan. I do not fully understand why, but I think he has something Rhagor wants."

"And he knows Orjan well enough that if he uses a child as a bargaining chip, he will have to act. Where is he?" Zerina asks.

"Orjan, you can't go, this is madness," a woman's voice echoes across the courtyard, more irate than concerned.

"I can't stand by and let an innocent be taken by him!"

I recognise Orjan's Rashouyan accent.

"This is what he wants!" the woman's voice continues. "He wants you to respond like this. You're falling into his trap!"

When I raise my head, I can't prepare myself for the anger that consumes me when I see Morgana. How is Orjan still aligning himself with this monster, after everything that she has done? Morgana looks in even worse condition than Yaelor. Her bare arms are covered in gashes and her face is swollen and bloodied.

Then I notice Orjan – but I am surprised to find that he is no longer bound by the scales of a dragon, but back in his human form. His skin has aged and his hair is greying, but there is no mistaking that it is him. He rushes out into the courtyard, Morgana trailing slowly behind him. She is clearly injured as she struggles to walk, her focus solely on him.

"If it is what he wants, then he can have it. He has taken a child! I cannot have that on my conscience," Orjan protests, waving his arms angrily as the two of them continue to argue.

"Trust me, I do not want any harm to come to this child. But if he wants that amulet, if it is so important that he doesn't want to risk its destruction, then I dread to think what he has planned." Morgana places an arm tenderly on his shoulder, but Orjan shrugs it away, pain etched in his face.

Orjan heads through the courtyard towards the horses. Needing to stop him, I step out from Yaelor and call his name.

"Orjan!"

He stops in his tracks, eyes locking on me with the realisation that I have stepped foot into the kingdom that he presides over. Morgana has a look of shock on her face. This is not what she would have been expecting.

"There is much that we need to catch up on," I call, raising my hands and taking a slow step towards him, all the while choosing to bite down on the bile and the vitriol that I harbour for Morgana. "Just know that I am here to ask for your help." I continue my walk across the courtyard towards him. He has drawn his hand to the hilt of his weapon. "I have no intention to fight, Orjan. It seems that we both want the same thing."

"You should listen to him," Zerina says.

Orjan looks surprised to see her.

"It is good to see you, old friend, and even better to see you returned to your former self," she adds.

"What are your intentions, Orjan?" Morgana snaps. "What is it you want?" She looks panicked at seeing me, as though she has seen a ghost. She looks ready to summon the guards on me which causes me to question why she has not used her magic.

"There is a lot at play, just know that I want the same thing as you: the child returned and an end to Rhagor," I say.

Orjan walks towards me, stretching out his arm. "Consider me your ally for now, Vireo. I will spare you what time I can afford. Zerina, are you joining us?"

Zerina nods, smiling.

"That's all I ask," I say. "Just know if it is a choice between you and the child, then you will lose every time."

"I would expect nothing else." Orjan smiles before walking back inside, beckoning me to follow him. "To the war room," he demands. He looks at a young knight who has his hands rested on a hilt at either side of his waist. "Rior, you will join us too."

The young knight nods and allows me to follow. I usher Yaelor and Zerina to follow me in, and Morgana trails behind, unable to move as quickly as the rest of us.

For a moment, Yaelor hesitates, glancing at the horse she has prepared.

I give her a stern look. "We need a plan if we are to get Gillam back safely. We cannot let our hearts lead us into this battle. We need to think with our heads. Please, do not do anything stupid, like heading off on your own."

"She is my daughter, Vireo. I would shatter mountains to get her back."

"Let us shatter them together, then."

We follow Orjan down a large corridor lined with blue banners of the kingdom. The castle looks vibrant and well kept, and the stone surrounding us is in pristine condition.

When we reach a set of large wooden doors, the top of which are oval shaped, Orjan pushes the doors open and marches inside. I follow him into the chamber, the proposed war room. It is bare save for a single banner of Eltera and a large round table that sits in the centre.

Orjan pulls a chair out and takes a seat at the table, and the young knight sits by his side. I can't help but think that Orjan must have taken a new squire, for there seems to be a strong bond between the two of them.

I choose to sit opposite him, pulling a chair out first for Yaelor, who reluctantly takes a seat. I place my hands on the large table and admire the simplicity in its design. Next, Morgana staggers through the door and chooses to take a seat between where I sit and Orjan. Her breathing is heavy and laboured, and she winces with pain as she sits down.

Zerina follows in behind, sitting on the other side of Yaelor. She gives a casual look around the room as Orjan looks at her nervously.

"She is here as my guest," I say, responding in a more formal way that I haven't used since I hosted at my manor in Askela.

"I've told the crew to wait in the courtyard. I figured there would not be enough room for all of us," Zerina says as she leans back in her chair.

There is a tense, charged atmosphere in the air which is understandable given everything that has passed between us over our intertwining histories.

Things are not exactly favourable between myself and Orjan, and the way the young knight beside him glares at me tells me that he does not trust me. His hands are placed beneath the table and I would be forgiven for thinking that he was holding a blade tightly.

Then there is Morgana. Although I despise the woman, I can't help but feel as though she is lost. Her body appears broken, and she has a nervous air about her as she shifts about uncomfortably at the table.

"I don't have time for this," Yaelor says through gritted teeth. "I shouldn't have followed you here, Vireo."

I lean in to Yaelor and tell her quietly, "You know as well as I that if you go charging in to confront Rhagor, you're as good as dead. To do so would do nothing but burden your daughter with being an orphan."

She leans back in her chair and sighs. Her body language is pent-up and erratic, but I do not blame her; I would be the same if it were my child.

"Shall we get started?" I say, resting my elbows on the hard wood.

Orjan gives Morgana a disapproving look, and in this

moment my eyes are drawn to an item that seems painfully attached to his neck, just above his collarbone. His skin is charred and black on the edges, and it doesn't take me long to deduce that this has something to do with his lifted curse.

"If you would be so kind as to tell me what you know, then I will be honest with what I know," I continue when no one else speaks. "But know that at this table, we are all equal. I do not take kindly to harboured secrets. If we are sharing information to come up with a plan, then I need to know everything."

16

ORJAN

We sit and argue around the table as we try and come up with some kind of battle plan. I can't help but feel it is all a pointless endeavour. I cannot see how we can stop this wretched king.

"I will turn myself in, it is as simple as that," I say, cutting everyone off. "I can't allow a child to bear the consequences of my actions. Or this kingdom."

"But what is he planning to do with that amulet, Orjan? Surely I am not the only one to see sense. We need to find a way to save Gillam that doesn't allow Rhagor to get what he wants," Morgana says, "and I think I know how."

The room quietens as Morgana speaks.

"Oh really, and how is that?" Vireo does not manage to mask his hatred for Morgana, but he does manage to fight back the vitriol to allow her to speak.

"Because I know something about Rhagor that he is desperate for no one else to know," she says. "I know that he is bound to a mortal's body, which means he bleeds like the rest of us. If we can get close enough to him, then we can kill him. All of this will be over."

"You make it sound so easy," Vireo says. "If that is the case, why haven't you killed him already?"

"Because believe it or not, Rhagor does not trust anyone, let alone me. I left the castle the night that I found out he could bleed, and I have no doubt he would have killed me in my sleep had I stayed any longer."

"I only sit at this table because I need an audience with Orjan. The things you have done to this kingdom, they are unforgivable," Vireo says, struggling to keep control of his temper. I see a flicker in his eyes and a frayed edge to his voice that reminds me of the Vireo I once knew, not the one that people tell me legends about.

"This is my table, and I choose who sits at it," I raise my voice and I am surprised to see both Morgana and Vireo stop their quarrelling for a moment to let me interject. "We will all have opportunity to speak." I look at Morgana and tip my head for her to continue what she was saying. Vireo sits back and folds his arms, but respects what I have said.

Morgana's eyes are on Vireo, though she can't quite make eye contact with him. Is that shame I see her wearing? Is she truly penitent for all the wrongs she has committed?

And yet I know that she has done good, too. She helped me liberate Eltera from the Wyverns. If not for her, I fear to imagine where the people of Eltera would be now. Granted, I know she has done questionable things in her past, she has told me about them, but she has assured me that she strives to do better, to be a good queen. And for some reason I can't help but believe her, even if she did lie to me about breaking my curse. Yet I still sit here at this table with my curse broken, free from the suffering of being a lizard man. And Morgana is sitting by my side.

"There is too much that has passed between us for me

to truly make amends, but I can assure you that I want Rhagor's reign to end as much as everyone." Morgana steadies her gaze onto Yaelor as if her words are meant for her alone, but Yaelor could not look more frustrated. I do not blame her; she must be desperate to leave and find her child. "I am trying to do the right thing, especially when it comes to my niece and my sister."

"How long have you known about Gillam?" Yaelor's voice is surprisingly calm, though I can hear the tinge of her Barbaraq accent on the tip of her tongue.

"Since she was at around her first birth year, when you turned up in Osar," Morgana says. There is a softness to Morgana's voice that I am not used to seeing her share with others.

"You have known all this time?" Vireo asks, appearing confused.

"And you never once sent word?" Yaelor adds. "Much has passed in our lifetimes, Morgana, but we are bound by blood."

"If I had sent word to you, it would have raised Rhagor's suspicions. I have done everything I can for so long to ensure that he remained ignorant of Gillam's existence. It would be catastrophic if he knew who she really was."

There is tension in the air. I can feel an almost static charge between everyone as though magic is being drawn on.

"I'm sorry, who is the child?" Rior asks, and I realise he is the only one present who does not know.

"She is the daughter of Rhagor," Morgana says.

"That monster has nothing to do with her!" Yaelor corrects, a flash of anger in her voice, and I don't blame her for her response. "She is Laith's child. Yes, Rhagor may have control of his body, but that does not make him her father."

"That's why the child is so important to you. Not only is she your niece, but you want to use her for power. Is that it?" Rior is straightforward with his interpretation of the situation and I see him drawing the same conclusions I usually would have. It seems that some of my bitterness towards Morgana over the past few years has rubbed off on him.

And yet, he voices the same concern that I myself have. "Is Rior right?" I ask. There is so much to pick apart from this whole situation, we need to be clear on what everyone's motives are. "You plan to leverage Gillam's status as heir for your own benefit?"

Morgana's eyes lower again and her shoulders drop. "Is that what you truly think of me, Orjan?" she says. "After all this time? I would forgive Vireo and the others for thinking this but –" she pauses, and when she meets my eyes, I see sadness there. "Well, I thought you of all people would have known me better than that."

"What do you want me to think, Morgana? I am still only now at this very table learning all the threads of silk that you have woven like a spider. How can I trust you fully if you are not fully honest with me?" I reply.

"Because Gillam is of my blood. She is family. Yaelor and Gillam are all that matter to me. I would give all of this up. My title, the kingdom. I would be rid of it all in a heartbeat if it secured their futures." There is a steeliness in her voice that I recognise, and I can't help but feel that she is being truthful in what she says.

"By the laws of the land, Gillam is the blood heir to Rhagor," Vireo says. "If we can defeat him, then Gillam would rightfully be in line for the throne. She would be queen of Levanthria." There is a tense pause as everyone at the table seems to ponder his words.

Vireo glances at Yaelor, who nods, before he continues, "We simply wanted to wait until she was at the right age to rule. We always intended to gather the forces that we needed to defeat Rhagor."

"He is too powerful," I say. "How can we hope to defeat him? He is more dangerous than anyone else in this world, and his forces in Askela are larger than any other land's in the region. And if I do not turn myself in, he will not just kill Gillam – he will level Eltera to the ground."

"He has weaknesses though," Morgana says. "As I said, he bleeds like the rest of us, something he has wanted to keep secret all this time. If he bleeds, it means –"

"That he can die?" I finish Morgana's sentence. If what she says is true, then all we'd need to do is get close enough, and we could end all of this. We could be free from his reign once and for all.

"So we take to him on an open battlefield, and we kill him," Zerina says boldly. Rior nods his head in agreement while a worried look passes between Yaelor and Vireo.

Morgana shakes her head. "Yes, he can bleed, and that means he can be killed. But there is still the matter of the sword. I believe that in order to truly kill him, we must get to his sword."

"No!" Yaelor protests. "Laith is still in there, I know it!" She slams a hand on the table.

"I met the boy once," Zerina says, flicking her long black hair from over her shoulder. "He was honourable and courageous. He travelled with Jordell."

"You knew of them?" I ask.

"A long time ago," she says. "But long after you and I parted ways, Orjan. If all this is true and there is an opportunity, I think we have to take it. We have to kill him."

"No!" Yaelor protests again. She leans forward like she is poised to dive over the table and pummel Zerina's face.

"There has to be another way," Vireo says as he looks at Zerina and then at Morgana. "You two are the most powerful sorceresses in Levanthria, if not the world. You must have some knowledge on Rhagor's power. Is there a way of us breaking the possession, of saving Laith?"

"I don't have my power anymore," Morgana confesses what she told me in my bedchamber just a short time ago. "The gods seem to have deemed me not worthy. I am bereft of magic. I have nothing."

The room falls silent. Her power would have been a valuable asset against Rhagor, and it weakens us greatly not having it.

"Power or not, that wasn't my question," Vireo fires back, showing no concern or remorse for Morgana's plight. There is certainly no love lost between them. I thought my relationship with Vireo was strained enough, but if his and Morgana's relationship was tethered by a rope, it would be severed entirely.

"What I do know – or what I believe at the very least – is that Rhagor's power is intrinsically tied to that sword," Morgana says. "If we could just get the sword from him, that could be enough to free Laith."

I turn to Zerina, knowing that she acquired special knowledge of magic after our ill-fated excursion to the Fountain of Youth all those years ago. "Is this true?" I ask her.

"I cannot be certain," she says. "My knowledge falls upon all magic of this world, gifted to me by the Fountain of Youth, but I do not have the foresight to understand the inner workings of a sword created by the gods themselves.

In theory, it could work, but unless we can get in a position to remove the sword, we will not know."

"So we just need to get close enough," Vireo says with a hint of sarcasm. "As if it is going to be that easy to just walk up to him and take it."

"Well, there is a window of opportunity," I say. "Rhagor has the child, and he wants me in a trade. If I can get close enough to him, I can try and remove the blade from his possession. Only then will we know if this theory is correct."

"Don't be so foolish, Orjan," Morgana scolds me, her voice elevated as she pushes herself up from the table. "There is too much at risk. Gillam, you, that blasted amulet that is bound to your neck."

I understand and appreciate her concern, but I do not really see any other option. "Rhagor will offer the child in exchange for me," I say firmly. "If we can make that happen, you can leave with her, and her safety is all but guaranteed. I can try and remove the sword from his possession, and if I can, we could end all of this."

"And what if you fail, Orjan?" Morgana's voice chokes. "He will kill you, and then he will have the amulet. He'll be free to put into motion whatever his plan is."

"I do not believe Rhagor will kill me," I say. "He wants this amulet, and it is attached to me. He wasn't willing to kill me before, and I do not believe he will kill me now. He can't risk destroying the artefact."

"Or we can just try and kill him," Rior says from my side. I nearly forgot that he was in the room. I know him well enough and I have trained him all of these years to know that he has become a master tactician, waiting to hear all the information before offering an opinion.

"No one asked you to speak, boy," Vireo says dismissively, and I suspect it is because Rior is my squire that he speaks this way.

"Do not speak to him this way, Vireo. Rior has proven himself more times than I care to count over the years. His bravery is far beyond his age, as is his knowledge of battle." I nod to Rior to allow him to speak.

"There are two options, and both of them involve Orjan," Rior says. "Either way, he is going to do what he feels is right, and I know more than anyone that when his mind is made, you will not change it."

I do not know whether Rior is calling me out with his words, but he proves that he knows me well.

"So we escort Orjan to Askela, right up to Rhagor," Rior continues. "Orjan has something that Rhagor desires above all else. I am amazed he did not level this city to get that amulet. If I had to bet coin on it, I think that is because if he had done to Eltera what he did to Hora, then it would have taken him an age to find this amulet. That tells me he is getting desperate, which means he is more likely to drop his guard. And when he does, that will give us a perfect opportunity to end his life."

"We can't kill him," Yaelor repeats, and this time Vireo has to stretch his arm across her to keep her seated.

"I understand your desire to keep Laith alive, truly, I do," Rior says. "It is an impossible situation. I do not know him, and therefore I can think more logically and detach myself from the situation. In the grand scheme of things, you are asking us to prioritise one life over the rest of Levanthria. I simply can't do that."

Rior talks sense, and I can't help but feel proud of his conclusion, despite my own care for Laith. After all, Laith was once my squire, long before I met Rior. "The boy speaks the truth," I say. "But if I can get close enough to remove the sword, I will. Failing that, I will do what I have to, to create an opportunity to strike. And when I do, well . . . We cannot miss."

"It isn't just as simple as that, Orjan," Vireo says. "We need a plan for what happens afterwards. We have numbers. We can mount an attack on Askela. I can try and get word to the people through the tunnels, tell them to make their escape."

"That will take too long," Morgana protests, "and it will all but alert Rhagor to what our intentions are. We need our numbers to be low, at least at first."

"Morgana is right," I say. "We need him to not see us mobilise. Vireo, you have my soldiers. They are well trained and disciplined, and they will follow under our banners into any battle. There is a lot of discourse amongst our people after what Rhagor did to Hora. I know them enough that they will fight for our cause. I fear though that my soldiers will not be enough."

"Combined with the numbers we have been growing in the forest, it is better than what we had. Can I count on all of you to fight?" Vireo asks.

"You have my hatchets," Yaelor says at once, standing from the table. "I would fight any god to get my daughter back."

Zerina rises and leans onto the table. "I will do what I can with my magic," she says, a ruthless determination in her eyes.

Rior stands proudly next to me and places his hand on my shoulder. "And you have my blades."

"And my morning star," I add, rising to my feet.

Last is Morgana. She looks hesitant at first, but slowly, she stands. "I do not have much that I can offer now that my magic is gone," she says, "but I give you my word that I will do what it takes to make sure my niece is brought back safely. Even if I do not agree with the method."

"Right," I say, "we need to mobilise the troops in a way that will not draw too much attention from Rhagor. I would suggest mobilising from the north. I will travel to Askela with Morgana and Yaelor to get the child back."

"And I will try and get word to the forest in time for our forces to ready themselves to join the fight," Vireo says. "I can only hope that they are ready for what is to come. You are a brave man, Orjan." Vireo walks around the table and offers his hand to me. I grab hold of his forearm and we shake firmly in agreement.

"Then it is settled. We go to war."

17

ESARA

In the depths of the Forest of Opiya grows the Lumina Bloom, a flower that only blossoms in complete darkness. Its petals are said to glow with captured moonlight and are highly prized by alchemists.

Ivy Mentara, Flora of Levanthria, 201KR

My brother is here, he is really here. So why is it I still feel a void of emptiness inside me? What is wrong with me that I can cause so much chaos and destruction to everyone's lives, despite only ever wanting to do a good thing? To bring my deceased brother back from the afterlife. It is all that I have strived for. I have searched this world over for treasures long lost by man to get to this point, faced monsters that mankind only ever told about in stories. I have done truly unthinkable things. Taken lives, stolen, abandoned people, sacrificed others. All so that I could deal with the grief I was burdened with when his life was taken.

I have carried his identity as my own for so long that my

own body now feels like a shell, empty and devoid of any happiness or emotion.

Ulrik is right here, sitting opposite me at this very table, his expression one of frustration, concern, and sorrow. He looks solemn, like he is in deep thought. His shoulders are sunken and his spirit seem truly broken. Thanks to Zerina, he is no longer of undead appearance; he looks just as I remember him before he passed. Before that day in Treventine.

He taps his finger repetitively on the rotten table. The damp has got to the wood so much so that I am surprised it does not crumble from the pressure. He is lost in his thoughts as I am mine. He has not spoken a word to me since Zerina cursed me, since she took my magic and buried it deep in the pendant that is tied around his neck.

It is strange being in this home, to have spent so much time here as a child. There are so many memories tied to the very walls of our old family home, where I had the best childhood that my mother could give me. I was cared for, I was clean, I had clothes and food. We did not struggle. Ulrik saw to that when he was away in the King's Navy that money was sent back to us. Along with our orchard, it meant that we could live a good life when I was young.

Up until King Athos Almerion decided he wanted people capable of magic in his ranks. The day that they took us will remain with me for the rest of my life, like a carving etched into stone. The splintered door, reminding me of the sheer force and brutality they showed when they removed us and took us to Eltera to be tried as witches. Where they executed my mother. She put up a fight. It was the first time I saw her use her magic, and it gave me the courage to use mine, but what use was a glamour? It couldn't do anything other than change the appearance of things. The magic within me contained no such destructive properties. If it did, perhaps she would still be here.

It is why when Ulrik died that I knew I needed to bring him back, that I needed to be with him again. It is why I have done all the things that I have done.

So why is it that I feel no remorse? What is wrong with me?

Darmour is dead. My first mate, a man who gave his life to protect mine, despite everything that I have done. We had been through so much together, I had seen the world with him. He taught me so much, he had become more like a father figure than anything else. Yet I feel nothing but a blackened void. I don't feel a need to cry, a need to grieve for him. I feel empty and devoid of any emotion.

Even with Ulrik here, there is no flutter of excitement in my stomach, there is no giddiness about me. He is right here, just a few feet away from me, neither dead or alive. Instead, he's trapped in a cursed state. This is not how it was meant to be.

The air around us is riddled with damp, the mouldy smell clinging to everything in the kitchen where we sit. There is nothing left in the room other than the broken table and rickety chairs where we sit, most likely ransacked by the locals once we were taken.

My thoughts then wander to who it actually was who reported us to the King's Guards all those years ago. Who accused us of harbouring magic. A little spark ignites within me at the thought of exacting my revenge on them.

Getting lost in my thoughts, I see Ulrik's lips parting as he speaks, but I have been oblivious to the words that he is speaking.

"Esara!" he says, his voice elevated, almost shouting to me. We are alone, the crew having chosen to leave with

Zerina. I do not blame them. I would have done the same if I were in their position.

I don't know what to answer back to my brother. It has been so long that I have heard him speak, it sounds different than it was when I was using it. The fact that he is using my actual name is going to take some getting used to. After all, I have been known as Ulrik for the best part of a decade.

This whole situation is going to take a whole lot of getting used to.

"Darmour was a good man," Ulrik says.

"He was," I say. My voice is soft and young. After all, I am a young woman. That doesn't make it feel any less strange for me to hear. I pause when I speak, raising my hand to my throat in surprise.

Ulrik studies me as if reading a book. Then he leans forward and says, "So, you have been walking around as me, all this time?"

I nod. I can't actually tell him why I did it. I don't actually know myself. It was all I could think to do. At least when I was glamoured as him, I could see him, I could still talk to him.

"You must think that madness has taken me," I say.

"Has it?"

"Probably," I say with a wry smile.

"It isn't funny, Esara," he scolds, his voice tinged with frustration.

But I find that I do not appreciate his tone. I am not the child that I once was. I am a grown woman, the most feared pirate Levanthria has ever known. I would kill crew members for talking to me in such a way.

And yet, somehow I find myself shuffling in my seat as though I am a child again. All I ever wanted was Ulrik's approval. Everything I have done my entire life as long as I have known it has been for him, in his honour, in his name.

"A good man is gone so that I can be here. Do you not understand the severity of that? What makes my life more valuable than his?"

"You don't need to be so high and mighty," I bite back. "I know the severity of the situation. I sailed the world with Darmour, he has saved my skin on more than one occasion. Still . . ." But I stop myself.

Ulrik scowls at me from deep within his eyes, a disapproving look that is all too familiar to me. "Still?" he asks. "Is there anything else you want to add about Darmour's death?"

Why must he prod and poke me? What does he expect me to say other than the truth? "It's isn't like I asked him to push me out of the way of the Resurrection Stone. I was quite willingly giving myself to it. His death is on him and him alone, not me." I would have gladly embraced death. That was my plan, and Darmour got in the way of that.

I know what I say is cold. I know what I say is heartless. But it is all I know, and it is an honest truth. It was Darmour who rushed into the situation and took the force of the magic from the Resurrection Stone. If he hadn't, he would still be here, and I would be gone. Either way, my brother would be alive which is ultimately what I wanted throughout this whole thing.

"Is this what has become of you, sister?" he says, and I can't help but note his disappointed, condescending tone. "Is this what my death did to you? What it has turned you into?"

"Turned me into?" I stand from my chair, knocking it over, and it takes every ounce of my restraint to stop myself from tipping the table over. "I am not some monster. If you want a monster, I will leave you to have a catch-up with Orjan!" I spit, bile rising in my throat. "I am not going to apologise for speaking the truth. It isn't my fault if others do not like me being honest with how I think and act."

Ulrik remains seated. He doesn't flinch, and he isn't intimidated by my actions. He simply leans back in his chair and sighs loudly. "Perhaps this is all my fault," he says. "If I hadn't taken you with us . . . You were just a child. The things you were exposed to at that age, you were too young. You shouldn't have witnessed them."

I snap, grabbing hold of the table and flipping it after all. "Is that what you think? That I am broken?" Anger surges through me. I have waited for this moment for so long. I have dreamt about it so many times, rehearsed the conversations we would have in the mirror while glamoured in his form. In none of those moments had I imagined the disappointed eyes that he casts upon me right now, that he would be so ungrateful for everything I have done for him.

"Calm down, Esara," he says, raising his hands aloft. "I do not wish to fight you."

"You can get fucked! If I want to fight you, I will fight you." I lower my hand to the hilt of my blade, but stop myself. What am I doing? Why am I reacting and behaving like this?

"Is this why you brought me back?" Ulrik remains calm, but I can see his own anger rising like a tide, swelling within him, as though he is restraining himself. "So you could fight me?"

"It is you who looks down at me with judgemental eyes," I spit, the venom in my voice only becoming more poisonous.

"I didn't ask for this!" he says, clenching his fingers into a tight fist.

"And you think I did?" I roar. "This wasn't the world I wanted to grow up in! I took my first life when I was ten. I watched my brother who I adored die, right in front of me. I did the best with the hand that I was dealt, and I am not going to apologise or show remorse for anything that I have done in this life. Whether you approve or not, I am the person I am today because of everything that passed before me."

I want to lash out, but he is my brother. I haven't brought him back just so I can kill him today, so I let out a growl born of anger and pent-up frustration, and then make for the door.

"Esara!" Ulrik calls after me, but I ignore him, kicking the front door as hard as I can on my way out. What remains of it splinters from its hinges as I storm down the garden.

"Esara!" Ulrik calls after me again. "ESARA!" This time there is a pained gasp in his voice, like when he was first raised from the dead.

I turn and see him leaning against the broken doorway. His appearance is now as decayed as our family home. I don't understand. Why does he look undead again?

I walk back towards him slowly. As I do, his appearance slowly changes into his normal self. I stop in my tracks and take a few steps back once more. Lo and behold, his skin rots away as his glamour disappears again.

"What has that bitch done?" I curse as I walk back towards the house and push past Ulrik.

"It seems that whether you like it or not, you are tethered to me. Zerina did say it was a curse," Ulrik says, examining his hand as if it does not belong to him.

"So what, you are now stuck with me for the rest of my life?" I say, picking the chair up and sitting back down. I cross my legs and fold my arms like a petulant child.

"I guess you are," Ulrik says. "I have no clue how Zerina's magic works or how she did it, but your magic is clearly in this pendant. And as long as you are with me, this glamour seems to work, but if you leave, it's gone."

"Why are you explaining this to me like I am some form of imbecile?" I sigh as I look at the back of my nails. I did just see his glamour vanish with my own eyes.

"If I leave you, people will see you for what you really are, and if that happens, they won't ask any questions. It looks like you are stuck with me."

Ulrik takes a seat in the chair opposite and we both sit in silence in the centre of the broken room.

18

RHAGOR

"Get off me! Let me go!" The child squirms in front of me, desperately trying to wriggle free from my grasp. It is pointless. She is not strong enough to shrug me off.

"Listen, you half-witted fuck! If you carry on, I will snap your neck like a twig and your mother will know nothing but the grief of knowing that I buried you in a shallow grave for the wild birds to feast on your corpse," I snarl, slapping the back of her head. It is in her best interest to listen to me. "You are lucky, I do not usually take prisoners, and I certainly do not usually barter with them. But you are a means to an end."

The child stops squirming but frustratingly it doesn't stop her from talking.

"My mama is going to find you and when she does, you are going to pray to the gods for forgiveness."

I can't help but laugh at her words. The little shit has got fight, I'll give her that. If only she knew that I was a god.

"My dear child," I say with a pompous sneer, "did you

not know? Even the gods fear me." There is a growl in my voice as we make our way towards Askela.

I have no doubt they will be forming some semblance of a plan. In fact, I expect it. They can do whatever they want, as long as I get Orjan and that amulet. When it is finished, I will be able to make my mother and all those other gods pay for what they forced me to endure. For everything they put me through.

"Why would they fear you?" the child says with a sincere tone, and I can't help but muster a laugh. "You're not that scary."

"You are a spritely one, aren't you? Still, keep quiet, or I will end you," I say coldly. "The sooner Orjan gives himself to me, the better."

The child does as I ask, and we continue our journey back to Askela in silence.

I can feel a hole boring through my chest as I pace up and down on my horse on the plains between Askela and the Forest of Opiya. A fog-like mist settles eerily on the ground. Behind me, my forces stand in wait. I am expecting an uprising, and I am not foolish enough to think that a battle will not be had on this day. If anything, it excites me.

The child sits on the front of my horse, fidgeting. It was not so long ago that Morgana was tending to the laceration on my face. Now she knows too much, and is likely the master tactician behind an attempted coup of my throne. So much has passed in such a short time.

The sun has set, and we are fast approaching the deadline I gave to the Elterans. Orjan would be a fool not to show up. Even though he knows what is at stake, there is no way in this world that he would allow me to destroy his kingdom or bring harm to this child.

"What if they don't come?" the child says.

I stop the horse in its tracks. "You will not want to know the things I will do," I say.

She doesn't even flinch, nor does she recoil in horror as so many others do. I can't decide if its bravery, naivety, or stupidity that drives her.

"My child, have you not heard the stories about me?" I ask, actually welcoming the distraction. "Perhaps I need to indulge you a little."

The bells ring, followed by the sound of a battle horn, and I laugh out loud.

Orjan is so predictable.

Excitement courses through me. I am so close. They may have soldiers, they may even mount an attack on me, but they would not risk it here, not when I have the child.

I slap the child around the head, and then I grab hold of her chin from behind and force her to look ahead.

"Ouch!" she says, trying in vain to pull herself free.

Ahead, a long line of soldiers has emerged over the dip in the landscape, ready for battle. I see flags and banners raised high into the sky as they march on me. Could they actually be foolish enough to think they can defeat me in battle?

The sounds of battle drums as they march echoes in the air, and it invigorates me. It has been so long since I had a good fight. Perhaps I will play with them for a bit, and then I'll kill them all. Foolish little bastards. I am impressed at the numbers they've amassed, but it is clear they are only the forces from Eltera, and my own forces far exceed theirs by at least three to one.

A group of riders march at the front of the army, and as

they draw closer, I see what I am waiting for: Orjan, sitting at the very front. It is clear it is him from his armour.

"Come with me, it's time to take you to see your mother."

"My mama is a warrior, I have seen her fighting," the child says with a sense of pride.

"Wait here," I say to Codrin, ignoring the child's words as I move forward slowly with my horse. "Wait for my word."

He simply nods, growling.

Even from this distance, I can see the necklace that is bound to Orjan's neck, the curse-breaker. And my chest flutters with anticipation. I am so close to achieving what I set out to do.

Orjan does not travel alone. Morgana rides on one side of him, and the woman who I assume is the child's mother on the other.

"Mama," the child says, swinging from my grip. I hop down from my horse and then grab the child, forcing her to stand in front of me.

"So glad you accepted my invitation, Orjan. You have fewer scales than the last time I saw you," I sneer. The wretched fool has caused me no end of inconvenience. I purposely look beyond them as the approaching army comes to a stop a distance away. "I see you brought reinforcements."

"I have done as you asked, Rhagor," Orjan says. "Let the child go."

"Hello, wife." I wave to Morgana, who dead-stares me. She does not show an ounce of fear in her cold eyes. I then look at the woman on the other side of Orjan, who looks ready to murder me. There is no hint of nervousness in her, either. "You must be Mama." I raise the child up from the floor and she cries out in pain as she hangs limply from my grip.

"We have taken care of your messenger, by the way," I goad, "not that those forest people will be any help to you. Still, a promise is a promise." I point at Orjan. "You for the child."

Once I have the amulet, I could destroy all of them in one blast with my sword, but what would be the fun in that? I relish the prospect of battle. It is what makes me feel alive, it is how I live up to my name as a god of war.

As Orjan climbs down from his horse, I see something in Morgana that I haven't seen before. Fear. She cares for this man. This situation could not be any more delightful.

"It's okay," Orjan says, meeting Morgana's eyes. "As long as the child is safe, that's all that matters." He starts to make his way slowly towards me.

"Orjan!" Morgana calls. She hops from her horse and stands before him. I have never seen her looking so stressed, so desperate. She looks up at him and without saying a word, leans forward and kisses him.

I am in shock. I didn't think she was capable of such emotion. The two share an embrace before he steps back from her and places his hands on her shoulders. "I have made my peace," he tells her.

I clap slowly and sarcastically as Orjan turns and starts walking towards me once more. Only then do I release the child. "Off you go. Walk slowly or I will slaughter every last one of you," I growl threateningly, all the while my heart rate quickening. I am so close to achieving everything I have desired for so long.

As Orjan and the child pass one another, he rests his hand lightly on her shoulder and nods at her. How admirable. Even in this moment, he is trying to reassure her.

Time seems to stand still as he approaches. When he reaches me, he stands proud and defiantly, like a soldier awaiting inspection. The child reaches its mother and after a warm embrace, the woman sits the child on her horse, gives Morgana a subtle nod, and then rides away, back towards the rest of their pathetic army.

"Do what you must," Orjan says without any hint of fear in his voice. "All I ask is you wait for them to leave."

"Why would I do that?" I lunge for him, but Orjan is wise to my move and pushes his weight into me, hooking his arm around mine. He then spins so that he is behind me, using what strength he has to trap my arms behind my back.

"Now!" he cries, holding me firm.

Rage fills every part of me as I struggle against him, bound by the weaknesses of this mortal's body. Orjan struggles to hold me as I flex my muscles and push the strength of this body to its limits.

Morgana pulls a bow from nowhere, firing an arrow towards us. I don't have time to react as it buries into my shoulder.

"Attack!" I scream, and the thunderous steps of my forces advance without hesitation, causing the ground to rumble.

Searing pain burns into my shoulder where it is buried deep within my flesh. Morgana clearly told them about my mortality. She will pay for her treason.

I continue to wrestle with Orjan who desperately holds on to me. I throw my head back and feel it connect to his face. With a grunt, his grip loosens enough for me to create a small bit of distance between the two of us.

Snarling, I grab hold of the arrow and rip it from my shoulder, barely acknowledging the pain. It is anger that fuels me now, and the gods know that I do love a fight. Orjan swings a punch at me and the two of us exchange blows.

Granted, the man can fight, but he is no match for me. I have no clue what goes on around us as all my focus and attention falls on Orjan. He will bear the price of my punishment, and I will set an example to strike fear into the hearts of anyone else foolish enough to cross paths with me, let alone fight me.

Orjan goes to punch me again, but despite being limited to a mortal body, I still have more strength than a normal human, and I catch his hand. This time, he lunges over me, grabbing hold of the hilt of my sword which he starts to pull free from my scabbard.

I instinctively wrap my hand around his wrist and strain against his surprising strength as he tries to steal my sword. But as Orjan nearly wrenches it free, I grip him even tighter until I hear his bones crack. When he swings with his other arm, I grab hold of it, and with a flick of strength, I snap his wrist. He grimaces and cries out in pain, with no option but to loosen his grip. It is my turn to catch him by surprise, and I step into his space and swing behind him, wrapping my arm around his neck. Ahead of us, Morgana stands in defiance, despite the pain on her face.

"I want you to see this!" I spit as Morgana's eyes widen in fear, and I savour the moment.

I stamp down into the back of Orjan's leg, and the crunch of his bones is most satisfying. He lets out an even louder scream of pain that satisfies me to my core.

"No!" Morgana screams, her voice cracking.

But I am not the god of remorse, I am the god of war, and I bring chaos to the battlefield.

"Look into her eyes," I whisper into Orjan's ear, "and know that you will only ever see her again in the afterlife." I punch him in the side of the head to daze him, then kick him in the back of the knee. I let go of him, grabbing hold of the back of his head to keep him upright, and strike him again, one more time.

Then I lean around him and grip hold of the amulet – my amulet – and dig my fingers into his flesh.

Orjan cries out in agonising pain as I use all my strength to pry the amulet from him slowly and painfully. He continues to scream out until, with one last tug, I feel the amulet rip free from his body. Suddenly it feels light in my hand as Orjan's body goes limp. I push him forward face-first into the ground and stare at the blood-covered amulet as I hold it aloft in the air. The widest smile erupts in my face, as Morgana's shrill scream fills the space between us.

Orjan's body, convulses in the dirt, and his blood pools around him until eventually, after one last twitch, he ceases to move.

"Kill them!" I roar, reaching for the sword strapped to my back. "Kill them all!"

Morgana is gripped by anger as her face contorts with a rage only grief can cause, and I reach for my sword. They should have left when they had the chance.

Morgana looks frozen for a moment before she reaches to her side and raises her own sword. She lets out her own battle cry as her forces advance to join her.

I savour every minute of the battle that is about to start.

19

YAELOR

The Sunken Library holds millennia of knowledge, there is no way of accessing the tomes that remain submerged, swallowed by the ocean.

Archivist Coral Vorel, Treasures of the Deep, 88 KR

I have her, and that is all that matters. I will never forget the bravery that Orjan showed in sacrificing himself for her, and I will make sure that Gillam knows his name for the rest of her life. He gave his life so that she could have hers.

The question is now what that freedom will look like, especially if we do not defeat Rhagor on this day. I can only hope that the gods show us favour. It is in their favour to do so.

We gallop on the horse to the side of the battlefield, the earth churning up under the horse's hooves. A rumble in the ground tells me there are horses in pursuit of us.

"I'm scared, Mama," Gillam says.

While holding the reins of the horse, I squeeze her with my arms as tightly as I can. Taking in her smell, the innocence of a child, tainted by being in the centre of a battle that she has no control over.

All that matters now is getting her to safety, as far away from this as I can get her.

So far what Vireo had planned is working, and I am grateful for all that he has done for us. He has played his part in ensuring that both of us still draw breath.

"You will be okay," I reassure Gillam as best I can, but we need to get away as fast as possible. Get as much distance as we can before changing course to the forest, for it is there where we will be safe.

Get to the fae. Vireo's message had been clear. Get Gillam, get to the forest, alert the people there of the battle. Then, get Gillam to the fae. He was certain they would protect us.

I hope he is right, for I do not trust them after they did not come to our aid last time.

A group of Elteran knights head towards us at speed. I count at least twelve of them as they charge forward, and behind them, I can see Vireo's green cloak as he keeps the row of archers steady, waiting for me to get to safety.

As the knights draw closer, I recognise one of them as Rior. He looks stressed, angered, and as though he has made his peace with the fight he is charging headlong into.

They slow down as they reach me and two of the knights change their course to ride alongside me.

"Fiora and Noran will stay with you and make sure you get to safety," Rior yells me. His horse bucks as he raises one of his swords into the air. "For Orjan!" he roars in a battle cry, pain etched into his voice.

"We are here to help," one of the knights says, pulling up on my right as he draws level with us. "If Orjan gave his life for the child, we will make sure you make it there." His face is obscured by the thick plate armour that he carries. I appreciate their help and support.

As we approach the front line, I hear Vireo's calls in the distance, and the sky is littered with streams of arrows that fly over us. Pushing Gillam forward, I lean over the top of her, just in case a stray arrow were to land upon us.

We just need to get past the front line now, then we can turn towards the forest with a smaller chance of Askelan soldiers following us.

We continue forward at speed until we race past the front line. I give Vireo a nod of thanks as we approach, and then he quickly disappears out of eyesight and is replaced by a sea of soldiers. So many people have laid down their lives for this cause. Not necessarily just for Gillam, but for what we all stand for.

They go into battle knowing that the scales are weighed heavily against them, that there is a vast chance none of them will see the sun break its dawn, and that fills me with pride and honour, yet saddens me to my core.

Although I was raised as a Barbaraq, these are my people. They all hail from the same land where I was born. I appreciate each and every one of them as I try and catch as many faces as I can. I want to remember them, in as much detail as I can. That will be the final honour, for if we are victorious in battle, they will go down in the legends and stories that will be told of this day. For they fight for the freedom of not just Eltera, but for everyone in Levanthria.

Some faces carry the burden of battle, their eyes heavy with fear and apprehension. They tend to be in the central ranks, surrounded and led by the soldiers that are more experienced, their faces stern and focused, ready for the word.

As we make our way through them, I hear Vireo give the

command, and they all start to press forward. I feel like a fish swimming up river as I push through the ranks, slowing my pace so as not to hurt anyone as they march.

My horse is slowing, panting, and getting harder to control as she struggles with the sway of bodies around us. I try my best to steady her nerves as we continue forward.

"Where are we going?" Gillam asks, a quiver in her voice. The pain that is etched into her words tears me apart. She should not bear witness to this. She should be free, playing in a field somewhere, swimming in the river or ocean.

But at least she is alive.

"Somewhere safe," I tell her. "We are heading to the forest we originally set out for. There, you will be safe from these people, from Rhagor." It pains me to lie to her. How can I tell her she will truly be safe when I do not know if this is the case? When I reach the forest, I need to ask them to join the battle as fast as possible. The only chance we have in all of this is if they join our ranks.

Voices start yelling at us as we approach the back of our army's formation, just drawing to a point where we can make a last-ditch attempt to the forest. At first I ignore them, thinking they are all chiming in with the battle cries as our forces advance on the Askelan troops.

When a rock hits my shoulder, I realise the angry words are aimed at me.

Fiora and Noran are quickly by either side of me, drawing on their swords.

"What is the meaning of this!" Noran demands, his face still hidden by his armour.

There is a group of five or six infantry men, all with expressions of anger and frustration. More worryingly, their weapons are directed at Gillam and me.

"You caused all of this," a slender woman says. She is holding a pike which she points at me aggressively. "My husband is already ahead of us in this fight, probably already dead. All so we could save the child of a whore." The venom in her voice shocks me.

"This is neither the time or place for a quarrel," Noran warns, pointing his sword at the woman. "Fall back in rank and join the battle."

"Why should we?" she sneers. "We're fighting a cause for Orjan, to save this child. Tell me, how many lives will fall today, all to save this runt?"

"That's enough," I demand. "Say what you like to me, call me what names you see fit, but keep my daughter off your venomous tongue."

We do not have time for this. The longer we are here, the more danger Gillam is in, and the more we are at risk of being overthrown by the Askelan soldiers.

"Wonder how many lives we will save if we hand you over to Rhagor?" she says, her tone telling me this is not an idle threat.

"Better still, if we give him your corpses, he won't give a shit if either of you are alive or dead." A deeper voice sounds out from a large, brooding man. He is thickset and balding, his skin blackened with grime.

"That is enough," Noran demands, blocking the path between them and us.

It grants me a reprieve from the eyes that burn into my flesh.

"We fight on this day against Rhagor and his tyranny. Do you think if Rhagor knew how important the child was, he would have let her go?"

He has already said more than he should. I imagine Rior has shared the information within his and Orjan's trusted ranks, but as far as I was aware, the rest of the kingdom had no clue as to Gillam's heritage.

"Then I think we should find out," the woman says, thrusting her spear towards the knight. Even though Noran is clasping his sword, it is clear that he is not expecting the strike, and I hear the sound of his flesh tearing as her pike pierces his armour.

He grunts, slamming down his sword towards her, but she pulls out the pike and rushes forward a second time.

"Heresy," he says with a grimace as, for a second time, his armour and flesh is pierced. The woman clearly knows where the weakened points to strike in his armour are.

Fiora darts past me and tries to use her horse to get the small group under control. We are behind the rest of the back line now, meaning we are isolated and alone.

"Noran!" a feminine voice calls out from underneath Fiora's helmet. She swings her sword down multiple times, catching one soldier across the face who screams and drops to the ground, clasping his face as he whimpers. If it hasn't killed him, it wouldn't surprise me if she has removed his nose.

The rest of the group rush at her, and her horse bucks from the assault before the woman leading them drives her pike into the horse's chest.

"Go!" Fiora demands as she drops to the ground with a crack. Her armour does not help as the group are upon her at once. The leading woman's attention is now on Noran, who, despite his injury, chooses to drop from his horse, gripping his sword.

I want to run, I need to keep Gillam safe, but I can't leave Rior's knights like this.

"See those trees?" I whisper to Gillam. "You take the

reins, and you run as fast as you can. Find the camp, tell them what is happening here. They will keep you safe!"

"Mama!" she says, but I drop from the horse, grabbing the two hatchets that are strapped to my side. "Go!" I snap, not looking at her. "I will follow you, I promise."

I charge forward, not waiting for them to make the next move, I channel all the brutal training that I was put through as a child with the Barbaraqs – harsh days where combat training would happen from the second the sun rose until it set, sometimes fighting through the night. We trained in all kinds of weather conditions, not just to toughen my skin or to hone my skills with a blade, but to strengthen something beyond that, something deeper that breeds a resilience that the Barbaraqs are known for, unmatched in these lands.

I charge towards Fiora who is on her back. She is being hacked and slashed at by our attackers, but as far as I can see, there is no blood, at least for her; her armour is doing its job, for now. A man has his sword in the air, grabbing the hilt with both hands as he seeks to drive it through her armour. I slam my hatchet with my left arm into the blade, knocking him off balance before using my right arm to bed my blade into the bridge of flesh between his neck and collar bone. I pull my left arm back, then slam my hatchet into the side of his head with a crunch. There is no escaping death for him this time. With little resistance, I pull my hatchets free from both of them as they drop to the ground, leaving only the large grime-covered man and the female leader who continues to fight Noran.

"We don't need to do this," I say, panting, my face covered in blood. Despite the violence, despite the fight and bloodshed, I feel calm and collected. "Lay down your weapon and I will be on my way."

He doesn't listen. He rushes me, bringing his sword towards me from the side. I run to meet him, which he doesn't expect somehow. I have two hatchets; I have no intention of forming a defensive formation.

His arm is too close for me to drive my hatchet through his wrist, but I manage to brace myself against his blow. His strength is powerful as his inner arm crashes into me, knocking me sideways. I manage to regain my composure, but he is quickly upon me once again, seemingly adopting a more offensive approach. Just how I like it.

It has been so long since my hatchets tasted the blood from battle – true battle – and I could be forgiven for feeling a little rusty after all these years. But after the first few exchanges, I can't help but feel confident.

The two of us continue to swing our weapons, and metal clangs against metal as each of us tries to best the other. Behind the man I am fighting, I can see that the pike-wielding woman has the upper hand against Noran, which then draws my attention to the female knight. Fiora is back on her feet and fast approaching, ready to aid me.

"Help your friend," I tell her, my eyes remaining fixed on my opponent.

He grimaces and snarls like a wild animal as he starts circling me, ready to strike at any moment. Refusing to wait, I run towards him. His frame is large and clunky, and he may be stronger than me, but I am far faster. I jump into the air and raise a knee, and at the same time, I bring my hatchet down on his arm holding his blade and it makes a clean cut, severing hand from arm around halfway down his forearm. His scream turns into more of a yelp as my knee crashes into his chest, knocking him backwards. He stumbles for a few steps, then brings his now stumped arm up for closer inspection, gaping as blood squirts out at the end. The colour drains from him until he is ghostly pale. He looks at me and tries to say something, but he is only able to string together a stammer.

I take a step forward and slam my hatchet into the centre of his head with a satisfying thud. His eyes turn white as they roll back, and he falls backwards, taking my hatchet with him.

As his body convulses on the ground, I step forward, lean down, and claim back what is mine, grasping the hilt of the blood-soaked hatched and prying it free. Blood sprays up on me and I can feel the bloodlust kicking in. The temptation to just dive headfirst into the battle is taking over me. It surprises me that even after all this time, the culture of the people that raised me, the expectations of battle, the excitement that it draws from me, have simply remained dormant all this time, suppressed under a rocky crust waiting to explode onto the battlefield.

I spin to try and find Rior's two knights. Both of them lie on the ground motionless, the wounds from the fight getting the better of them. This is why I don't wear armour. It is okay on horseback, but on the ground, it is more a hindrance than a help. I look for the group's leader, but by the time I see her, it is too late.

A pain rips through my skin as her pike drives into my lower side. The pain is intense and feels like a white-hot poker has been pressed into my skin.

"You bitch," the woman snarls as she grips the pike tightly in her palms. I drop my hatchets and take hold of the wooden shaft, holding it firm and trying to stop the woman from pushing it any deeper.

The two of us grunt and groan as a battle of wills starts, my odds of survival diminishing with every passing moment as the pain intensifies.

"Mama!"

At first I feel I am imagining her voice, but then I see Gillam arriving on the horse. She charges into the woman's side, knocking her over. The woman lets go of the pike and I seize my opportunity to rip it from my flesh before turning it on her.

She tries to speak as she lies on the ground, but I give no further opportunity. "You shouldn't have left me able to breathe!" I say coldly as I drive the pike into her chest, feeling her bones snap and crunch under the force as I spear her to the ground.

Let the corpses of these soldiers serve as a warning to any who seek to harm my daughter.

I spit blood on her, realising my face is busted before clasping my hand to my waist. There is more blood than I would like, and as Gillam rounds the horse and comes back towards me, it is not fear I see in her eyes, but a resilience, the same resilience that was drummed into my very being when I was a child. But she wasn't raised this way. I gave her a good life, a good upbringing.

She rides towards me, but she does not slow as she approaches. Maintaining her speed, she lowers her arm to help me up, seeming to understand the urgency of the situation.

Pride fills my heart.

I grab hold of her outstretched hand and pull myself onto the back of the horse. I am weakened and my body hurts, but my determination remains the same as we make our way towards the forest.

We cannot fail. We have come too far. I can only hope that we are not too late.

20

MORGANA

I feel numb. Orjan is gone, the amulet ripped from him as if he was nothing. I suppose to Rhagor, he was nothing, but to me, he was everything. Why did I never tell him? Why did I never disclose my true feelings for him, feelings that I never thought I was capable of?

I should have told him that I loved him.

I try to scream but no noise leaves my mouth as the world around me falls into slow motion. Yaelor has set off at speed with the child, and I can see the forces ahead of me charging on my position.

Orjan is gone, and there is nothing I can do about it. I should run, I should turn and flee. I have no magic, I have nothing. If the child is free from the battle, if Gillam is safe, then that is all I want.

Rhagor stands ahead of me, his arms folded as he stares at me tauntingly, a wry smile pursing his lips. If I had my magic, I would show him a fury that he truly deserves, but I don't. I can no longer feel its essence coursing through me, no longer feel the charged connection flicker over the surface of my skin.

I cannot do much, but I will give Yaelor and Gillam as much time as I can. I step forward with my sword, waiting for Rhagor's forces to reach me, certain that my death will greet me sooner rather than later. At least this way, it is on my own terms. Perhaps in the afterlife, I can be reunited with Orjan where I will truly be able to tell him how I feel.

Within the gaps between the soldiers that charge towards us, I see a strange flash of light, one that is too similar to that of the spectres that stripped me of my power, that taunted me and attacked me. Just what I need. They are clearly here to taunt me even more, like a dragon poking at its desperate prey, knowing they are helpless.

They will not break me. I may be a master of magic, but I am also well-versed with a blade. As the first horse reaches me, I duck the blade that swings down at me and rake my sword down the horse's side while continuing to move forward.

"Rhagor!" I shout. Noise surrounds me as if I am in a landslide.

Everything stops though, as though suspended in time. I turn to look at the horse I have just slain and find it frozen in the midst of collapsing to the ground. The battlefield has stopped too, as if frozen in ice.

Have I stepped into insanity? I look at the ground, wondering if I will see my body on the floor, wondering if I have already greeted death. I have so many questions it makes me nauseous, but what I do notice is the spectral glow just a short distance away, growing brighter, growing stronger.

And moving closer.

The light continues to grow brighter until I can barely contain it in my sight, as if the power of it forces me to look away. My heart flutters as a strange sensation comes over me. This is like the spectres, but something different.

A humanoid shape comes into view. Taller than a mortal man, they must be standing at around nine feet tall. Their features are hidden behind the light that emanates from them. Their energy radiates from them, but it does not bring me warmth. Instead, I am shrouded in a cold shadow that wraps around me, its gnarled fingers raking against my skin. A feeling of dread, desperation, and helplessness washes over me. Uncertainty, fear – there are so many negative emotions that I feel in their presence, it is truly overwhelming.

"Who are you?" I ask. And what do they want? I have never heard of magic able to freeze time.

A voice echoes around me as if it is in my mind, though I know the figure in front of me speaks the words.

"Apologies," says the voice. "It affects humans differently whenever we choose to communicate with them."

Its voice shakes me. It feels like they are inside me, haunting me. A stab of pain in my head causes my eyes to water. Are they casting the kind of magic I used to when controlling someone's thoughts? Is this their way of retribution, torturing me for the things I have done in the past?

And yet this voice is different – less threatening – than the spectres that haunted me, that stripped me of my magic, but the essence that I feel coursing in the air around me is similar, it is somehow linked.

"You are right," the voice says. I have not spoken any questions, and given the voice is inside my head, I can only imagine it can hear my thoughts somehow. Its voice is strange, ethereal, powerful yet calming.

"Do not let my language lure you into thinking that I

can not bring you harm, Morgana. You have done many an act of evil in your life. That is something you can never repent for, despite how tortured your soul is. You are tainted by darkness, touched by the evil that you have brought to your world."

I don't reply. He is not wrong with what he says.

"You do, however, contain the rare gift of necromancy. Even if you have tipped the scales of natural balance in your endless pursuit of increasing your power and mastering your magic. Our situation is dire, and Rhagor must be stopped. This is why I am here."

"What do you mean?"

"Rhagor plans on using the amulet he is now in possession of to force the gods to walk this earth, to live as he has had to, so he can destroy them one at a time. I am forbidden from intervening, and despite already choosing a path for you, in this moment, I need your help."

"How? I have no power. If not for you making time stand still, I would likely already be dead."

"And why do you think I am here? If you die, then all hope will fade with it. You still have your part to play in what will happen in this battle. I am here to make sure the battle goes in the favour of those who seek to end Rhagor's reign, preferably before he drags us all to this world. And no, you can't kill him in this state. I am present in your mind, time is moving at its usual rate. It just seems slower for you."

"So you are a god?"

"Yes," the voice says. "It was I who stripped you of your powers. You misused them, you caused so much harm. But in this moment, I can return them to you, to help in this fight. But it will come with a price. You see, I control the afterlife, and through your intervention, the magic that bridges between worlds has been heavily distorted. You need to fix that."

"How?" In truth, I will do anything to get my magic back, to be able to stop Rhagor and bring his reign to an end. Not for me. I don't want the crown that weighs heavy on my head. I will ensure the one true heir takes the throne. When she is ready to.

"This is why I am willing to give you a chance. I can see in some ways the way you think has changed, but that does not bring forgiveness for all that you have done. Tell me, Morgana, are you willing to spend a lifetime, if not an eternity, repaying a debt that you owe to the spirits trapped between this world and the afterlife?"

I stand tall and bold, the power of the god radiating through me. "If it will help these people today, then do what you wish. I am willing to do whatever it takes to repent for those that I have wronged."

"Do you vow?" the voice asks. "It will be unbreakable. You will be bound to the laws of the afterlife, helping guide lost souls to their rightful place. You will become the harbinger of death."

The words are daunting, the title even more so, but in this moment, I am desperate and will do whatever it takes.

"I vow to do your bidding," I say, my voice stern. "I will help the souls that are lost as you ask."

"Very well, but understand this: if you stray from the path – if you deviate just a little – your soul will spend eternity being ravaged by demons. You will spend the rest of your existence in excruciating pain as your soul is flayed over and over."

If that is what awaits me, I can only be grateful that this god offers me a kindness in my moment of need. I bow my head. "I will serve you as you wish, just let me help." With my power, I can give Gillam and Yaelor the time they need. I may even be able to best Rhagor.

"Know that the power that I grant you cannot be reversed. It will not just be the power of a necromancer you will possess. It will be beyond that. You will be the conduit between the living and the dead. Do what you must to stop Rhagor. Then you will serve as the harbinger for the rest of your existence," the spectre says.

What he offers is a high price, but one I am willing to pay to protect those I care about most.

And avenge Orjan.

With this, the spectre raises his hand in front of him and opens up his hand, revealing his palm. Spectral light forms above it, dancing around in a swirling motion until its colour turns from white to a darkened green. It's the colour of my necromancy magic, but it looks darker, with flashes of red cracking within it. I can feel its essence as the stream of magic drifts towards me like fog setting at the base of a mountain. It creeps towards my feet until it wraps around my ankles and starts to climb. As its power begins to absorb into my body, I feel energised, invigorated, and my spirits lift. A crack in my rib forces me to wince with a shot of pain as my broken bones snap into place, correcting themselves. This magic is something beyond what I am used to, beyond what I was capable of, and it feels tremendous. Closing my eyes, I embrace the essence as it seeps into me, its power circling around me, blowing my hair around as if I am in a storm.

When I snap my eyes open, I am in the midst of battle, my eyes fixing straight onto Rhagor. He is still staring back, only his smug look seems to evaporate, contorting with anger and confusion. I have no clue what he sees, but I can tell he knows something is different about me.

I am on my own. There are more soldiers passing me, our own Elteran forces not yet level with me.

A soldier moves towards me, roaring loudly as he tries to strike me with his blade. That is his last mistake. I raise my hand and twist it, and his neck snaps as if an invisible force grips him. A bone protrudes from his neck, and he doesn't utter another noise as he crumples to the ground.

Channelling my magic, green energy surrounds me as I use my power against the next wave of soldiers that approach, around six or seven. They all stop in place as I absorb their lifeforces. Their bodies disintegrate before me until they are nothing more than piles of ash. I feel as though I could run forever, an unlimited lifeforce for me to draw on. As powerful as my magic was before, this is something different. And I quickly start moving through the battlefield, each step I take drawing me closer to Rhagor who, for the moment, I cannot see.

I dance in and out of the soldiers, ending every one of their lives who is foolish enough to try and kill me. Each wave of my hands sends out a crack and flicker of greenish red magic that continues to shroud me like a darkened cloud. I have become exactly what the spectral entity told me I would be: a harbinger of death.

I am moving to step forward when the essence of my magic connects with something, and I am frozen to the spot, unable to physically move no matter how hard I try.

I look around me, wondering what it is. Has a mage cast me in some sort of binding spell, or is this something to do with Rhagor? It is something different, it feels linked to my magic, but what is it? I focus on my newfound powers, channelling the notes of magic as if they are a song that I must learn the melody to.

When I look down at my feet, I see what is binding me

in place. Spectral hands clasp on to my ankles, climbing from the bodies of those who I have slain.

"RELEASE US!" the voices rattle as one, like the spirits who attacked me at the Gondoron Pass. "PLEASE," they rasp. The faces are gaunt, their souls glowing as they are still tethered to this land.

"I don't know how," I say, panicking. "I will try, but you must help me. Only then will I grant you reprieve to the afterlife."

"If that is what it takes." The voice speaks as though in pain, desperate to please me in order to ease their suffering.

Is this what the spectre meant about the harbinger? Can I now control the dead and the damned?

It is hard to fathom, but I can feel the fallen soldiers' essences as though they are mine, and as I think about them standing, the power around me surges and the spectres stand tall.

"What the fuck is that!" a soldier cries out, fear etched into his very being.

The horror on his face tells me that he sees what I see, and the others around him do too. I will the spirit in front of me to do my bidding, and he takes up his sword and charges at the Askelan soldier, striking him down before he has a chance to retaliate, frozen in his terror.

Spectres around me start rising from the fallen, standing tall before taking up arms as I will them to stand against the Askelan forces.

Flashes of blue and green surround me as the spectral soldiers start fighting against their former comrades, and I am mesmerised by the way they flicker around me, drifting forward. Their weapons meet the steel of those that fight back, and I find that when they are slain, they vanish in a cloud into the air around them like a whisper on the wind.

I have no clue where the fallen spectres go, but it breathes new confidence into the soldiers they are facing when they realise they can be bested.

It has, however, created the edge that I needed, and I continue my pursuit of Rhagor, looking for Orjan who lies strewn on the ground beside him.

"RHAGOR!" I call out, frantically searching for him, using my magic on anyone who comes too close to me.

Then ahead of me I see him. Orjan's body is still crumpled lifeless on the earth. Rhagor is grasping the amulet in his hand, his sword in the other. I know I need to stop him, stop whatever madness he is about to inflict on this world. It must be bad enough for a god to intervene and grant me these powers, to gift me such an ability to raise the dead. The power is simply unheard of.

"RHAGOR!" I cry out again, consumed by rage and anger for what he has done, for killing Orjan.

He snaps his head up and his arrogance pours out of him as he simply smiles at me, enraging me further. As he draws one hand to the hilt of his blade, I realise he is trying to connect the amulet to the sword, and I fire a blast of energy at him with a scream. The powerful force follows the sound of my voice as if I am a banshee, flooring any soldiers that are in between us and forcing Rhagor back.

It stops him from what he was doing, and his arrogance turns to unbridled rage as he turns his sword and points it to me. I do not fear him.

I charge down on him, ready to drag him to the afterlife with me if I have to.

21

JORDELL

My mind is all over the place as I walk through the dense forest towards Vireo's camp. It has been so long since I have been here, I wonder if people will remember me. I can only hope that Vireo is here so I can tell him of what Zariah has told me – that she has foreseen the great battle as I have, but she has not seen how it will end, or who will come out victorious.

We cannot allow her brother to be the victor. It would be catastrophic for the world, although I don't know what his final plans look like. He seeks to bring the gods tumbling down to this world, to live as mortals as he does so that he can kill each and every one of them.

If the gods are all on the planes of Levanthria and beyond, who will watch over the rest of the world?

Then darkened thoughts enter my mind as I wonder if this would be a bad thing. The gods have played with our lives for too long, as if we mean nothing. One thing is for sure, they own more magic and power beyond the comprehension of anyone in this world.

It takes me longer to travel than I would like at this

stage, but I move as fast as I can. Elara skips through the fallen leaves as she follows me, the odd chirp escaping her beak every now and again as she pounces on an unfortunate critter to feed on.

It has been nearly two days since I left Zariah, so I know I am drawing close to Vireo's camp. As much as my legs ache and my body tires, I cannot afford to rest. The news I bring is too urgent. Vireo told me he wanted to gather soldiers from across Levanthria, but I fear we do not have time; we must mount an attack as soon as we can.

It is a relief when I finally hear the hustle and bustle of people talking ahead of me and I recognise the large trees that tell me the lagoon is not far from where I stand.

As I make my way out of the trees, I breathe a sigh of relief and stop for a moment, allowing my breath to catch up with me. A horde of worried eyes fall on me, and a young woman I do not recognise reaches for her sword. She's clad in leather armour decorated with leaves for camouflage, and her untidy hair is short and blond. She clutches the hilt of her sword, ready to draw it on me. I don't blame her. After all, she does not know what my intentions are and I have travelled into their camp from the direction of the fae kingdom. Behind her, other men and women turn to face me, each of them ready to draw their weapons on me, and not just swords and axes; I also hear the pulling of bowstrings, and I look up to see people leaning out of turrets made of wood, their bows pointed straight at me from afar.

The camp has come such a long way since I was last here, to a point where it could hardly be called a camp any longer. This is a village now, and there are seemingly more people here than ever before. If not for the urgent situation, it would be beyond impressive. Walkways, houses, and huts have been built not only on the ground but also in the tree-tops. These are nowhere as ramshackle as they once were, but are finely crafted homes, built from the resources of the forest and resourcefulness of Vireo and the other people that now call this place home.

Elara scurries in front of me, letting out a warning growl. The girl blocking my path looks confused as she studies the wild creature.

"She is a growlite," I say. "She means you no harm, she just feels threatened."

Elara's scales almost rise into the air like glass, spiked and threatening. She bares her teeth from her beak as she widens her wings to make herself look as big as possible.

I feel humbled by how ready she is to protect me at any opportunity, all because I offered her kindness back in Zakron.

The girl studies me, her hand unmoving from the hilt of her blade.

"I assure you that I am an ally," I tell her.

"How do we know that?"

Again I do not blame her. I look like a wild man, appearing with a growlite beside me.

"Kalia, that will do, lower your weapons." A large man with a thick grey beard runs over to her and places his hand on the woman's shoulder. He then turns and raises his hands into the air to signal the bowmen who are primed to bring down a hail of arrows if they need to. Thankfully, they lower their weapons.

"Jordell," he says and offers me a smile, stretching his arms out wide, "you came."

I appreciate his jovial spirits to see me, but it is not a sentiment that I can return. The weight of the situation threatens to crush my very being.

"Killian," I say in return. I am glad he and Vireo have made it back safely since their attempt to recruit me to their cause.

I step forward as Killian embraces me. His strength is much greater than mine, and as he squeezes me tightly, I worry that my bones may crack.

"I am so glad that you have seen sense. Vireo was worried about you when I left, but I knew you would come, I never doubted it." Killian's beaming smile forces its way through his matted, unkempt beard. Why is it every time that I see him he is even more wild than the last?

"Vireo," I say, panicked and with haste. "I must speak with Vireo. There is so much we need to do. The situation is grave indeed."

"Slow down," Killian says, placing his hands on my shoulders. "Vireo is not here. I have not seen him since we parted ways not long after reaching the southern shores near Loch Bragoa. I came back here to make sure we were ready for when he returned. We are waiting for word from him."

He looks to the treetops above him, and I know it's the thick smoke that still plumes into the sky that concerns him.

"Our attention has been drawn to that said fire. We have never seen anything like it," he says. "We were just about to send a party in to explore." He looks over his shoulder at his daughter who is busy readying the other members of her party for what I assume is for the excursion.

"There is no time, Killian," I say. My body is weak and I am in need of food and drink, but I need to tell him everything that I know. "Rhagor, he has destroyed the Elder Tree.

It is all part of his plan. We need to ready ourselves to fight against him."

"The Elder Tree," Killian repeats slowly, confused by my ramblings. "What about the forest? What about the fae?"

"Queen Zariah was near death when I found her. She is the one who has told me of Rhagor's plan. There is too much to go through right now, but just know that she is ready to lend you her aid."

"You mean like she did last time?" he scoffs, visibly disgusted at the mere mention of her name.

"I understand your frustrations, Killian. I harbour the same ill feeling over what has passed between us, but she cannot let Rhagor succeed in his plan any more than you or I can. The fate of the world depends on it. Now, I need you to be ready to fight, to advance on Askela if needs be. I cannot stop, however. I need to get to Osar, to Yaelor and to the child. They are not safe. Not long after you left, I was visited by Codrin and his guards. I thought they had come for me and the staff, but I believe my being there was happenstance. They were looking for something else. I barely escaped. And in that moment I knew that I needed to get to her."

"Do not wait on my part," Killian says. "Do you need some of my men to go with you? I will send a messenger to Queen Zariah. It doesn't feel right mobilising without word from Vireo though."

"I have just been with her. She is aware of what is transpiring, although a messenger may alert her that we are closer to battle than we first thought," I affirm. I step past Killian and examine the camp one last time. "I do not know if I will see you again, old friend. The battle that is about to take place is much bigger than you or I." As I make to leave, my legs buckle from underneath me and I nearly collapse. Killian catches me before I can hit the ground.

"I know time is of the essence, Jordell, but you need to rest before you go anywhere. If only for a short time. You need to eat and drink, then be on your way."

Killian is right. As much as I need to move, I am close to exhaustion, and despite being able to replenish my health with my staff, that doesn't allow me to neglect my body through malnutrition.

Killian helps me to a bench in the centre of the camp and brings me bread and water. As I eat, the two of us discuss all the finer details of everything that has passed since our paths last crossed.

Others come and join us at the table: a short Dwarven man, an older, stronger looking man, and a young woman with dark braided hair. All look like they bear the scars of many a battle.

"I would like to introduce you to a few people," Killian says. "Jordell, this is Morvin." He first points to the Dwarven man, whose beard comes down to just above his waist. It is charred in places, and there is a musty smell that clings to him. He wears a hat with some blackened, wide-rimmed goggles fixed atop it. He is covered in dirt and grime, but he has a wide and joyous, slightly manic grin on his face.

"Pleasure is all mine," he says with a thick Kragoan accent. He offers a hand which I accept. His skin is calloused and rough.

"Morvin has been with our camp for just over a year. Spent years captive in the dungeons before managing to escape. The things he has had to endure in that time would send a shiver down most people's spines. But Morvin is made of stronger stuff. We found him on the plains, near death, and brought him back here. It turns out, he was part of the party that killed King Athos."

There is a hint of madness in Morvin's eyes that I can forgive him for, following the ordeal he would have faced while captive in the dungeons.

"You were involved in the assassination?" I say, continuing to examine him. "You don't by chance know of the witch Zerina? And Ulrik?"

"I do. Ulrik was the one who pulled the trigger that day. I have heard tales of what Zerina did that day to protect the soldiers at the King's Keep. Both are honourable, if not a little bit terrifying."

"Morvin here is the master of powder," Killian interrupts. "Not only that, he is responsible for helping maintain and improve things here at our camp. He is somewhat of an inventor."

"It's the least I can do after everything that your people did for me," the Dwarf says coyly, seemingly not liking being thanked for his work. "I am but a humble Dwarf who has served his people. When my time comes, I can be happy with what I have done and embrace my wife and son in the afterlife."

Killian's attention then turns from Morvin to the large, powerfully built man who wears a serious expression. He wears a red cloak, which looks more blood-stained than dyed. His scarred face gives an aura of power about him. Out of the cuff of his sleeves, I can see heavily tattooed arms.

"This is Gregor," Killian says. He seems somewhat awestruck, and I can understand why. There is only one Gregor I know of that meets this description. After all, I have written about him in my scriptures when I was at the

Great Temple, when I was just a young apprentice to the apothecary. A lifetime ago.

"The Gregor?" I say, feeling a little awestruck myself. I can't help but find myself staring at him, drawn to his serious face and the intense presence that he has brought to the table without uttering a word.

Gregor simply nods. "You can't believe everything that spreads on the wind," he says, his voice deep and gravelled like he is need of a good cough.

"So the stories of the popobawa, the night stalkers, the Krampus, they are not all true?"

He pauses for a moment, seemingly frustrated. "Okay, maybe you can believe those ones, but I am but a man. Searching for a way to be free of this world."

"How is it you come to be here?" I ask, confused as to why after all the years of wandering the world, he has chosen this moment to be here.

"Your friend Vireo, he helped me, and in return I said I would lend him aid. He helped me to free Leandra here from a curse that she had been bound to for longer than you could possibly imagine. He is a good man, a good leader. I agree with you all that Rhagor must be stopped before it is too late. I know the gods more than all of you combined. I have even met a few of them in my time. I can assure you that most will not agree with what Rhagor does to interfere with this world. It is about time he is stopped."

As I process what Gregor says, I cannot fathom how Vireo managed to find him, let alone get him to help us. The man continues to astound me every day with everything that he achieves. Perhaps we can do this, perhaps Vireo was right after all.

To Gregor's right stands who I assume is Leandra. She is wearing clothes that are from the southern clans of Loch

Bragoa who were wiped out hundreds of years ago. Again I know because I have studied their scriptures. Her hair is plaited, tight to her head, and she seems young, but at the same time gives an air of experience. Her physique is similar to that of Yaelor, which begs me to wonder if Leandra's clan is somehow linked to the Barbaraqs. Perhaps that is something I should research when all of this is said and done.

"Greetings," she says, as I realise I have perhaps been looking for longer than I should without being rude. Her accent is thick, and her posture is confident and powerful, telling me that we have yet another strong member within our ranks, which will only serve to strengthen us further.

"As Gregor said, Vireo helped free me from a curse that I was tricked into. My clan is now consecrated thanks to Gregor. I will help in any way that I can."

I have seen so much in this lifetime, but I find myself dumbfounded that the legendary monster hunter Gregor Yerald is in our ranks. Not only this, but the Beast of Bragoa, freed from her curse, apparently aided by Vireo. I am not a fool, I have written scriptures on Gregor to know her true name. It is the armour of her lost clan that gives her away, the large fur-lined braces and boots not used for centuries.

I try to form words to offer them all my thanks, but I simply stutter. Even I believed Gregor to be nothing more than a legend, a tale told to try and keep children behaving. To have him stood here in our presence is not something that I expected, but I am sure it will give our fighters a much-needed boost with their morale.

Looking at the greatsword that is strapped to Gregor's back, I wonder if it is as powerful as the stories say. I wonder if in fact that sword would be able to take on Rhagor in some capacity.

"Are you okay?" Morvin asks, breaking the silence with his thick accent. When he talks, I am sure I see an ember drift from his beard, and his eyes are wide and ravaged with a mania that only a long time spent being tortured in a dungeon can bring.

Finding it easier to talk to Morvin, given I didn't know too much about him, I say "Yes, sorry, just a little overwhelmed with the situation and the kindness of strangers."

"Kindness breeds kindness in return," the Dwarf says with a smile.

My mood lifts. The words that Morvin speaks, they are the simple message that I passed onto Vireo when we first found ourselves exiled in the forest. The fact that the very thing I discussed with him is the bedrock of this community fills me with pride. If only the circumstances were better. If only we were not about to go to war.

There is a commotion at the far side of the camp. Killian springs to his feet and rushes past me towards a horse that is fast approaching. There are gasps from people as a crowd starts to form.

Gregor, Leandra, and Morvin are all quick to ready themselves for a fight, drawing on their weapons.

My eyes widen at the magnificent contraption that Morvin holds heavy in his hands: a large, cylindrical item made from some form of metal. I heard faint stories on the whispers of the wind before I left for Zakron, but I never expected to see the contraption in my lifetime. It looks heavier than I could lift, but thanks to Morvin's Dwarven constitution, he carries it with little effort.

"What's going on?" Killian demands, his voice booming over the hushed words of the crowd. It brings a silence amongst the people that tells me he commands a high respect from them in Vireo's absence.

Rushing forward, I push through the bodies of people that block my vision, knocking them to the sides as I surge forward to see what the commotion is.

Then I see her. A face that I never thought I would see again, yet one I set off on this journey to find.

"Yaelor?" I mutter, louder than I expect. It is enough to gather her attention as her tired, battle-worn face looks down at me. She is covered in all manner of cuts and bruises, and she is holding her side where blood seeps through her fingers. She offers a smile, but it is clear that she has little to no energy left in her. She slides to the side, collapsing off her horse, but Killian charges forward to catch her, leaving me to see who it is that sits behind her.

It is the child.

22

VIREO

The Order of the Twilight Veil guards the secret of shadow-walking – a form of magic that allows one to step between shadows as if they were doorways. Only those with Umbral blood can master this art.

Shade Master Darkweave, Secrets of Shadow, 178 KR

As much as I did not see eye to eye with Orjan, he did not deserve for his life to end in such a brutal manner. He was a brave man, and I will remember him exactly as the courageous warrior that he was.

"Hold," I demand, leading the archers.

Rior, however, does not hold; his rage over Orjan's death is getting the better of him. I understand his grief, but he is meant to be a master tactician. We are far outnumbered and we cannot afford to be so ill-disciplined.

"Rior, no!" I call after him, but it is to no avail. He raises his sword in the air and cries out loudly, his voice breaking as he surges forward. Some of the other riders follow, setting off at speed.

"Fuck!" I say, cursing under my breath. "HOLD!"

It will take a miracle for us to survive this.

Yaelor is galloping towards us, and I can see that she has Gillam with her, with Rhagor's soldiers in pursuit. Morgana surprises me by staying where she is, staring down the forces head-on. She will not survive with such carelessness.

I have seen many battlefields in my time, more than I care to remember, long before my days of living as a pampered lord when I was King Athos Almerion's debt collector. That feels like a lifetime ago.

Despite those many battles, never has there been more at stake than right now in this moment. I can only hope that word reaches our forces in the forest; we will not survive against an army of this size. Above all else, we must ensure that the child escapes. She is key to everything.

"HOLD," I repeat. We don't have long as I watch Rior and the other mounted knights charge towards the Askelans.

Yaelor rides frantically towards us, her horse churning up the ground beneath her while Gillam clings to the horse's neck. When I know she is close enough to us, I give the command.

"FIRE!"

I wave my sword towards the battlefield and a sea of flaming arrows pepper the skies.

"Shields!" I roar as a hail of arrows comes back in return. I raise my shield above my head and prepare myself for the torrent of arrows coming our way.

Yaelor raises a shield above her head to cover her and Gillam as arrows start to decorate the floor around her and us.

Screams of pain ring out as some of our archers are

skewered to the floor by arrows. My shield thuds as arrows make contact, one piercing my shield just above my arm.

"FIRE!" I repeat, and the archers step forward, stretching back their longbows and quickly returning another volley.

When Yaelor reaches us, I know it is simply about creating as much time as possible for them to make their escape.

"On me!" I surge forward, my horse quick off the mark, my chest hammering against my ribs as I ready myself for the impending battle. I cover the ground quickly as Rior and the knights pass Morgana, clashing with a sea of soldiers that meet them on the battlefield. They are quickly drowned and I can no longer see them. Behind me, our own troops roar their battle cries as the men and women of the kingdom who were willing to take up arms against the self-proclaimed god-king brace themselves to fight. I admire the bravery and courage that each and every one of them shows on this day. They make me proud to fight under the banner of Eltera.

When I reach the battle, the sheer volume of people fighting is intense. Our armies collide, and bodies slam against each other as my horse tramples the first few Askelan soldiers that we reach.

I bring my sword down on a lanky Askelan soldier. He cries out in pain as my blade slices down his face and neck, and his blood sprays across the ground in front of him. I have little time before another soldier rushes at me, and I knock his blade away before quickly ending him. I continue to push my way through the sea of soldiers, hacking and slashing at anyone wearing Askelan colours. However much it pains me to fight soldiers that I once saw as allies, they chose to side with Rhagor, which means today, they are our enemies.

Ahead, a flash of blue catches my attention and I see that Rior is on the ground, dancing in and out of the soldiers. He wields two short swords, which grants him the agility he needs as he quickly plunges his blades into more soldiers than I can count.

"Protect the queen!" I hear him cry as I realise he and the other knights are attempting to form a protective circle around Morgana. I am surprised at the bravery, courage, and leadership that he displays at such a young age, no longer a squire, but a knight – and one that I am sure Orjan would be proud of.

I continue to surge forward until we have reached their pike men, and my horse bucks up in the air. Unfortunately my horse's chest is pierced with one of their weapons, and it lets out a whimpering noise before falling on its side. It sends me crashing into the ground with force, and suddenly I find myself suffocated by the throng of battling soldiers around me as I lie on the ground.

With a roar, a female soldier pulls the pike out from my horse and runs at me with it, but three of our soldiers tackle her from the side, lifting her into the air before slamming her down. The three of them stab at her one after the other until she no longer moves.

The ringing in my ears from the fall almost mutes the noise around me as I survey the ferocity of the fight. It takes me right back to my earlier battles, where I felt safer with Lek and Gillam at my side, when my youth made me feel invincible.

Neither of them are by my side today, nor is my youth. And even though I fight with thousands of brave men and women, I have never felt more alone on a battlefield.

A hand grabs me from behind, then more, and I am pulled to my feet. I do not know their names, but I see they do not wear fear in their faces, and it invigorates me. I lean down and grab hold of my sword, then raise it into the air, urging our soldiers forward.

Somehow, I need to get close to Rhagor. I need to get that sword.

"Forward!" I call.

A wall of five Askelan soldiers stands in front of me, a mixture of builds, both men and women. The battlefield does not discriminate, and each of them is as deadly as they wish to be.

And they all have eyes on me.

"It's him, it's Vireo," says the largest of them. He is a middle-aged man that I would put around my age, and his scarred face tells me he has survived plenty of fights and battles.

"Rhagor will bring us plenty of riches if we bring him Vireo's head to place on a pike to parade at the gates of Askela!"

"A little bit presumptuous," I say, giving them a courtesy bow and adopting a defensive stance. They do not intimidate me. Although I am far outnumbered, I have faced worse odds before. Close calls became the stories I laughed about over drinks with Gillam and Lek. I wonder who I will share the stories with after this battle.

I wonder if there will be any stories to tell.

I step slowly to my side, both hands clasping the hilt of my sword as the Askelan soldiers start to move towards me.

One of them rushes forward, swinging from the side. I step into them, driving my sword through their chest before using their body as a shield against a second soldier who tries to stab me with their blade. With a crunch, their sword drives into the back of the man in my arms. His eyes widen as blood pools in his mouth. He coughs it into my face as the life in his eyes fade. I drop the man to the ground, and as the soldier draws his sword out of his comrade's back, I quickly draw my sword across his chest, then spin and slam my blade into the stomach of the third approaching soldier. The force and momentum is like I am an axeman, hacking down a tree, and although I do not have the strength to cleave a man clean in half, my blade does nearly pass all the way through.

The next soldier swings his blade down at me, and I need to move faster than I can with my blade, so I let go of it before driving my elbow into the soldier's face, causing his head to snap back. I pummel my fist into his face over and over until he falls back, leaving me and the largest of the group. He sneers at me as he lowers the front of his helmet, leaving only his cold, murderous eyes boring into me with hatred.

He slams his sword into his shield and roars out an intimidating battle cry. "Come on!" he says. "Pick up a weapon, I know I can beat you!"

I grab the sword of the soldier I have just pummelled, tossing it up so the hilt points upwards. I snatch it and slice it down on the soldier on the ground, bringing an end to his pain-filled groans with a crunch.

The last soldier runs at me shield first, and I bring my sword around as it slams into his shield with a metallic clang. Metal shields are a rare commodity on the battlefield, and I happen to pick a fight with one of the soldiers that has one. My blow barely affects the solder as he pushes outwards with brute strength. I stumble backwards, nearly tripping over the bodies behind me. I manage to regain my footing just in time as the soldier brings his sword around at my chest height. I just manage to bring my blade up to block the attack, but he quickly rams me again with his shield, forcing me to use my free arm to brace myself from the blow before he is quickly at me once again with his sword.

He continues this a few times over, each blow with the shield becoming harder to block. My arms grow tired and filled with pain from the blows. When he slams his shield into me for a fifth time, it is enough to cause me to drop my guard, and when our swords meet again, the force almost causes me to drop my weapon.

"Do you yield?" I say with a flicker of arrogance that only serves to enrage the soldier even more.

This time, I am not going to wait for him to clatter me with his shield again. I surge into his space, grabbing hold of his shield-bearing arm from behind, then drive the pommel of my sword into his face. The metal crunches his teeth, and as his head snaps back, I bring my sword down on his arm, detaching his shield in the process. He screams out in shock as thick, crimson blood pulsates out of the stump above his elbow. His eyes widen as I swing my sword around one final time, detaching his head from his shoulders. Blood squirts into the air as the metal helmet clangs to the floor. The body falls to its knees before dropping to the ground, convulsing.

I pant, catching my breath. The weight of the battle is already wearing on me. After all, battles do not usually last long. As soon as one force gets the upper hand, it can quickly out-flank its enemies. That is what we are trying to avoid.

I look back at our forces. The battle is fierce, and

although we stand firm, I know that beyond this initial fight, there are so many more Askelan soldiers to contend with. Where is Killian with reinforcements? Surely our messenger must have reached them by now – unless they were intercepted and the message never found them.

"I hope you are looking down on me on this day, Gillam." I look up to the skies and wonder if Gillam is up there, tankard in hand, pissing herself at me struggling against five soldiers. After all, I am not as young as I once was. "Perhaps save a tankard for me, old friend."

There are more soldiers in black and gold than our force's colours. As I continue to watch our soldiers put up a brave fight, I spot Codrin tearing through Elteran warriors with ease. The sight of him fills me with an anger that removes all battle sense from me.

He stands with an axe in both of his hands, hacking through anyone that gets in his way. I swear I see him even take down one of the Askelan soldiers just so he can get a better position as he brings his axe down on the head of an Elteran, near cleaving him in half.

"Codrin!" I roar, garnering his attention. His head snaps in my direction, his chest heaving as he grunts like a feral beast. He is battle-ready and enraged as I point my sword towards him.

He smiles, then charges at me at phenomenal speed, barging through anyone who gets in his way like a battering ram. Soldiers bounce off him as if he is a boulder rolling down a hill, unstoppable and unmovable.

"VIREO!" he roars, his gravelled voice echoing around us. He is clad in black leather armour, his chest bare with a studded strap across it connecting to a spiked metal shoulder pauldron. He has a white scar that runs down his right cheek, which almost looks silver against his dark

Elven skin. His face is contorted with anger and rage as he continues to barrel towards me. One soldier gets too close, and Codrin swings his greataxe to one side, slamming it into the man's stomach. Blood splashes across Codrin's body and face, but he only has eyes for me. His hatred for me, however, pales in comparison to how I feel about him.

23

ULRIK

I should not be of this world. My decomposed body has been reanimated, yet my brain remains my own. My own appearance is hideous, it repulses me. But the repulsion I feel within the very core of my being pales in comparison to the repulsion that I would face if others were to see my true appearance.

When I look upon my sister, all I see is the tormented monster that she has become. A monster that I created.

It is all my fault. We travelled the seas, I put her in situations that she was too young to face at such a young age. It corrupted her. I should have seen the signs, noticed the warnings when we set sail to Treventine.

When I closed my eyes to sleep last night, I was not greeted by dreams, but plagued by nightmares. At the heart of them, all I could see was her – her warped features encompassing my own aged face, filled with a beard that I never knew I carried. The way she carries herself, that confidence, that look in her eyes, that is what differentiates her from me. I spent the night tossing and turning, unable to fully rest. I could not enjoy the comfort of a good night's sleep when Darmour, a good man, lies in my own grave in the garden of our childhood home.

Now, Esara and I ready our horses for departure in uncomfortable silence. I suppose I should be feeling gratitude for everything she has done for me in my name. She has somehow found a way to resurrect me from the dead, but at what cost? I fear the fractures this has put on her soul, how it has splintered what remained of her sanity, all in the goal of bringing me back from a grave I did not want raising from.

Now I am here, returned to these tainted lands, tethered to my sister like an animal bound by a chain. I couldn't leave her side even if I wanted to. We have already found that if I were to walk these lands in my undead form, I would not make it outside this village before I would be captured and killed. Perhaps that would be a kindness. The very reprieve I so desire.

Shame overcomes me at the thought of giving my life away in such a frivolous manner. A good man died just a few days prior, so that I could live. To give in to my thoughts, to allow my life to drift away and be reunited with the soil underfoot, would bring great dishonour to Darmour's name.

It is in his name that I will now ride, his name that I will live my life.

As I mount my horse, my thoughts return to Zerina, to when she bound me to my sister with the curse that allows her glamour magic to course through me. The magic is somehow intrinsically linked to Esara, but tethered to me like I have been bound by rope.

I can see the blackness that was in Zerina's eyes when she cast the spell. There was sorrow there when she looked at me, but that is not what I saw when she looked at Esara.

All I saw then was hatred, something that I do not think can ever be fixed.

Esara has remained tight-lipped since our argument. In fact, we have barely spoken a word to one another. Even now as we ready our horses, I am not entirely certain where it is that we ride to.

Gulls fly over head, and the bright blue sky shows few clouds, allowing the sun to press down on my skin. The warmth is a sensation that I never thought would be possible, something I would never feel again, and I savour the moment. I hold my breath for longer than I should before exhaling deeply. Despite the turmoil that I hold in my chest, despite the questions that I still have about everything that has happened in my absence, I feel a calmness that I do not have the right to claim.

"You shouldn't look up at the sun for too long," Esara says. There is a playful tone to her voice, and when I look at her, her eyes twinkle with mischief, as if she has forgotten about our argument, as if she feels no weight or burden of guilt for everything that has passed.

I remain silent and stony-faced. I have no clue what to say to her. She is far older than I remember her, and it feels like it is a stranger that stands opposite me as she finalises her horse.

"That's what you used to say when we sailed," she says. "That's what Mum used to say." She pauses for a moment. "Before she was taken. Before we both were. Things were simpler then."

I say nothing at first as Esara mounts her horse. It is strange seeing her as an adult.

"You will have to forgive my silence, sister. All this is still so strange to me." In truth, I feel awkward. I do not know how to speak to her. It is as though a stranger sits opposite me, no longer the sweet, innocent child that I once knew.

Esara smiles, and again there is a cheekiness to her expression that is not befitting the situation.

"I must ask though, where is it we ride?"

"I thought we would head north," she says.

"What's north?"

"I have travelled the world, dear brother. I have seen things that you would only imagine in your nightmares. I have read scriptures of treasures that grant all manner of powers to its bearers."

"Is that it, then? You have resurrected me so we can continue to go off galivanting in search of lost treasure? Esara, our days as pirates are done." There is a sternness in my voice that, judging by her flaring nostrils, she does not appreciate.

"Don't make the mistake of speaking to me like a child," she says, but her tone is playful, almost whimsical. I was expecting the brimstone reaction I was greeted with the other night, but the way she is acting is best described as peculiar at best. "Besides, do you want to be tethered to me for the rest of your life? That is presuming that you can die. I never got that far with translating the scriptures around the Resurrection Stone." She looks as if she is deep in thought for a minute, then shrugs her shoulders and says, "Oh well."

"What do you mean?" I ask.

Esara sighs dramatically before trotting forward on her horse. I follow, not wanting to allow the gap between us to grow too great. After all, I do not want to greet the rest of the village in my undead form.

"Well, we can't head south, can we?" She speaks to me as though I am an idiot. "On account of not having a crew. Besides, raiders have probably taken the ship after all this time. We need to head north. If there is magic that can resurrect someone from death, there must be something that can dispel magic." She looks over her shoulder at me, her long, curling blond hair dropping down her shoulders. "That way you can be free of me." She faces forward again and I swear I hear her say, "be free from your burden."

As we carry on through the village, I feel a wave of apprehension. After all, Esara has masqueraded in my form for so long, become a feared pirate. I wonder if people will recognise my face, even if it no longer carries the beard I am known for. A reputation that I do not deserve nor want.

"Is that you?" a voice says. It is older and weary, but I recognise it. Looking to my right, I follow the voice and see a middle-aged man standing in the doorway of the bakery.

The smell of freshly baked bread is alluring, and a hunger grips me that I have never faced in my life. Suddenly I feel ravenous, and a dull pain erupts in the pits of my stomach.

"Ulrik," the man says, "it is you." His eyes trail to Esara who sits impatiently on her horse. "And Esara, you – you survived the witch trials." There is a nervousness about him that I put down to the situation. It has been so long since he would have last seen either of us.

"I thought you might have returned," he continues, stepping towards us. "We saw a crowd of people at your mother's house. We have left it all these years in case you returned. Of course there had been sightings of you in the past, but no one has touched the house, out of respect, of course." He is trembling as he bows his head, and I wonder if he has heard tales of Ulrik, the fearsome pirate captain.

"Fucking coward," Esara growls out of nowhere,

suddenly becoming more animated, which only confuses me further.

The baker snaps his head up towards her as she rounds on him.

"Why don't you tell him what you did!" she demands, her whole demeanour changing from playful to deadly in an instant. "You have the audacity to come out here and greet us –"

"What are you talking about, Esara?" I ask, feeling confused and alert. We do not want to draw more attention to us than we already have.

"Do you want to tell him, or should I?" she says, pulling up just short in front of the man. He raises his hands to shield himself, cowering in Esara's shadow.

He is more translucent than a spectre, and I think for a moment that he might actually piss himself.

"What is my sister talking about?" I ask, my focus on the baker. His skin is wet with sweat.

"I am sorry," he says nervously. "I have thought about you every single day, both of you."

I feel even more confused at the situation now.

"What are you sorry for?" I ask.

"Why don't you tell my brother dearest, I am sure he would love to know."

"I didn't know what would happen, they promised coin, coin I used to feed my family, to restore the ovens in the bakery."

"Stop talking in riddles and tell me what you did."

"I just wanted to apologise, it has never sat well with me."

My eyes widen and I stare into him, a grimace forming in the corner of my cracked lips. "Last chance," I say.

"It was the baker that sold me and Mother to the

guards, it was because of him that we were taken to Eltera, it was because of him that our mother was taken from us."

"Please, you have to understand!" The baker places his hands in front of him as if he is praying to his gods. "It is not what I thought would happen. They didn't say they were going to put you on trial. When you didn't return, I assumed you had both been executed."

"What my sister says is true then?" I ask, anger rising in my voice as it deepens, that deadly croak returning as my soul is encapsulated by a darkened shadow.

"You are lucky I did not burn your bakery to the ground last time I was here. The only thing that stopped me was your wife and children, they are innocent in all of this." Esara draws on her sword, and it is clear what she intends to do before she brings it down on the man, her face angered and unforgiving.

"Esara no!" I yell. She has done enough. I cannot allow her soul to become any more corrupt than it already has. Bringing my sword up, I block her strike, barely an arm's length away from the man's cowering head.

He whimpers like a babe as I look down on him. The wet patch in his crotch tells me he has pissed himself, and the smell that drifts up confirms it.

"He does not deserve his pathetic life," Esara snaps, baring her teeth. She presses her sword against mine as my muscles strain to keep her in place.

"P–p–please," he stammers. "I – I'm truly sorry. I will spend my lifetime making up for what I did. Just tell me what you want of me."

"Let me end his pathetic existence, Ulrik, he deserves death for what he did."

"No," I say, pushing her blade away with as much force as I can manage. "I can't let you fall any further."

"Thank you," the man says. "Thank you, praise be the gods that look over your good fortune."

"But I didn't say I can't." I spin with my blade and draw it across the man's throat. My hands shake with rage as I breathe heavy, barely able to contain the anger and rage that grows bigger and deeper within me. A hatred that I did not think I was capable of.

The man stumbles back, clasping his hands to his throat. Gargled attempts at speaking fall from his pursed lips as his shocked expression stares back at me. He drops to his knees and collapses face-down in the dirt. Blood pools around his body, and I only wish he could feel the pain of his rotting corpse. He deserved a slow and painful death for what he did, but this will have to suffice.

It is because of him, because of his actions, that our mother is gone, that Esara was forced to flee Levanthria with me. If not for him, Esara could have been safe. She could have lived a normal life, whatever that would have looked like.

"I am impressed, brother. Perhaps all that time in the grave changed you," Esara says.

The screams that come from the doorway tell me that we should make our leave. A larger woman has her hands clasped to either side of her face as she takes in the sight of her husband.

He deserved to die, but the townsfolk do not. That is something I can't guarantee if they choose to engage in combat with us.

"He got what he deserved," I say. And I would do the same over and over again, if it meant I could prevent Esara from losing herself even more. At least this way I can protect her from herself.

Even if my actions corrupt my own soul.

24

ZERINA

The battle unfolds ahead of us, the cries of battle on a scale I have never seen before. So much hatred for each other, and over what? I can't help but feel that there will be so many lives lost on this day that need not be.

I wanted to lead from the front. My magic is destructive, it should be used as a way of diminishing the enemy's front lines, like how I used it in Zarubia all those years ago. However, Vireo requested that I stayed towards the back of the battlefield.

It is hard to keep stationary when I can see so much death unfolding ahead of us. The battlefield is already littered with the bodies of more soldiers than I could ever count. I wonder if each and every one of them will have their own grave, for families to pay their respects. My mind draws back to Darmour, to me at his graveside, and rather than being consumed with grief, I use it to channel my emotions into the battlefield.

"Wait for the setting sun," Vireo had said. Well, I am waiting, and the sun is moving a lot slower than I would have liked. When I turn and look behind me at the sun's position, I can also see the Pendaran Hills far away in the distance. My thoughts immediately return to my sisters, where my life has ended up, my powers, this battle. It is so far from the simple life I used to live.

What I would give to have my sisters beside me, to be able to hold just one more conversation with them, to tell them how much I love them.

"The sneaky bastard." I smile to myself. I have not known Vireo long, but can already see how he works. We travelled together only briefly, but in that time I shared stories with him about the Pendaran Hills, about my home, my sisters, and where I made a makeshift grave for them following the witch trials. It seems like a lifetime ago, but in getting me to wait for the setting sun, Vireo has drawn my attention to my former home, and it only serves to motivate me to do what I must, to draw on my power like never before.

Vireo doesn't want me at the heart of the fight, not initially anyway. He wants me to wait until Rhagor is drawn out onto the battlefield. With Morgana's power gone, there is only me with enough magic to form any sort of threat to him.

I have a few archers and foot soldiers with me, but not many. They stand nervously to either side of me as I continue to survey the battlefield. I can't make anyone out. The soldiers ahead blend into one large body of black, gold, and blue colours. Some banners remain upright as they are buried into the ground, but others have been toppled over.

A war horn catches my attention, but I cannot see which side it sounds from. From what I can see, the black and gold colours of Askela are outnumbering our own forces.

A flash of flame towards the rear of the fight sparks the signal that I need.

"Rhagor!" I say, knowing that Rhagor must have entered the fight, that this is the opportunity that Vireo spoke about.

My heart sinks as the realisation dawns on me.

Orjan must be dead.

"It's time," I say to the men and women beside me. And then I lead our remaining soldiers forward, all too aware that we are now the last line of defence.

I heel my horse and start galloping into the fight, moving faster than those in my ranks. They do not look to me to lead – they know what to do, and they know why I am here: to bring as much destruction as necessary to tip the scales of battle in our favour.

We reach the battle lines quickly, and I start raining down fire on our enemies as I pass them, firing blasts of magic into them as I surge past on horseback. Molten fire melts through their armour, guttural screams of pain leaving the lips of anyone unfortunate enough to be an enemy.

I feel numb to the fight. I feel no empathy for my enemies like I once would have, and at times, it feels as though I am merely a spectator in this body, looking down on myself as I bring down a force of magic that our enemies could not comprehend.

Blasts of force start blowing chunks of earth from the ground around me, showering me in the earth, blood, and limbs of the fallen. I had been wondering where their own spellcasters were, and it seems I have found them. A large blast of energy falls near my horse, and she only just manages to stay upright. Not taking any more chances, I drop down from her side, charging my hands with my latent power, an ancient Elven magic coursing through my veins. A power that once would have crippled me with agonising pain just for using a fraction of it now invigorates me with all the positives of its use, and none of the negatives. All thanks to the Fountain of Youth.

Looking up, I search my surroundings to see where the blasts are coming from. It doesn't take long before I need to dodge another charge of magic that is fired at me. This one is dangerously close, and I can feel the static energy from the storm magic that has been used. It is close enough to sting my skin before it crashes into the chest of a soldier just beside me.

The poor soul lets out a quickened scream of shock and pain as he is hurtled through the air and sent clattering into a group of fighting soldiers, knocking them all over. Ahead of me a mage stands clad in the robes of Askela. I am surprised at how little armour he is wearing as I set my sights on him.

My magic charged, I unfurl a volley of fireballs from my right hand followed by my left, but as they near the mage, they are deflected by an unseen force. Th mage's confidence grows, and he gives me a wry grin, looking to his right where a female mage stands, her hands pushed out in front of her as if she pushes against an invisible wall.

"Barrier magic," I say as I fire another blast of flames at them. It hits the unseen force, confirming my thoughts to be true.

I do not falter, and I continue to surge forward, molten fire dripping from my hands. As I approach, a soldier takes a wild lunge at me from the side, but I slam my hand into his chest before firing a blast of power straight into his heart. It is the last thing he does as he falls to the ground, lifeless, his charred chest smouldering.

The mages don't just fire at me; they are aiming across the entire battlefield, sending volley upon volley of energy into our soldiers' paths. I am grateful that they are not more accurate, otherwise they would have eviscerated our numbers quickly. Instead, plenty of their shots hit the earth, spraying soil and debris everywhere.

As I approach the mages, I use my magic to send out a mild solar flare. It emits from my core with a flash of heat as if I am a sun in the sky. It is enough to divert their attention and draw their focus solely onto me. That should at least afford our troops some breathing space.

There are eight of them in total, standing in diamond formation with the stormcaster at the front.

"Only eight?" I say. "I must admit, I am slightly disappointed."

Another two step out from within the diamond, increasing their numbers to ten, and I can't help but muster a smile.

"That's more like it."

The mage at the front is older, with a thick, greying beard, cracked face, and wrinkled hands. *He doesn't have much magic left in him,* I think to myself as I try to weigh up how best to fight them. So far I know one to be a protector and another to wield the power of storms, but I have no clue what the others are capable of.

It doesn't take long to find out, however, as the two mages on either side of the diamond step forward and stretch their arms out towards me. The ground rumbles slightly, causing me to shake.

"Earth shakers," I say as the two spellcasters, one male, one female, turn their hands over, raising them into the sky. Shards of stone stretch out from the ground like glass diagonally in my direction from either side. I surge forward, darting from left to right as they continue to try and spike me with stones drawn from the ground.

After their fourth attempt, they stop, needing to rest from exerting their powers. All the while I grow closer to their formation. The stormcaster at the front kneels down, revealing the face of the mage at the rear. This one pushes forward and hops over the top of the other, clad in knight's armour, the black and gold of Askela.

"A battle mage," I say. They have adopted the way that the Zarubians fight. I have not seen a battle mage since the battle of King's Keep in the harsh Zarubian desert.

The mage runs at me, but the armour he wears is clunky and it affects his mobility. He lashes his storm magic at me, but I raise my hands, shielding myself from the brunt of his power. When I lower my arms, he has already drawn his greatsword which he is bringing down on me.

The first mistake he made was thinking he could beat me. The second was wearing metal armour against a witch who can control fire hotter than a volcano. My hands are still dripping with molten fire as I clap my hands together on either side of the blade. The panic and surprise in his eyes are clear as my fire melts through his sword. Before he has time to react, I lunge forward and clasp my hands to either side of his helmet next, increasing the intensity of my magic. He squeals like a pig as his skin starts to singe inside. I hear the crackling as he falls back with a thud, convulsing on the ground.

As I step forward, the ground shakes, and another stone column erupts from the ground, crashing into my side and sending me sideways into the ground. I wince, but I have no time to inspect for injuries as the earth shakers summon their magic again. Rolling to the side, I barely dodge the next stone spike that aims to skewer me.

I climb to my feet as fast as I can before unfurling two blasts of fire towards them. The barrier mage isn't able to withstand both, and although they stop the first, the second hits the earth shaker on the left, erupting them into flames. The shock on the barrier mage's face tells me she is not use to combat, not as much as the others. I see the flicker of fear in her eye, so I choose to target her next.

I charge forward, my arms trailing behind me. I only need to move forward a few feet before I am close enough to bring my arm down her chest like it is a sword. I slice her open before firing a blast of fire so hot, so powerful, that it passes through her chest, emitting large flames that swallow up three of the mages behind her.

All of them are engulfed in flames that lick high into the sky, their screams a warning to any others that want to face me.

Three mages remain. One of them looks horrified at the death around them, and I see at once that they are a coward, probably used to fighting from afar, a safe distance from the heart of the fight. He breaks ranks and turns to flee. With a flick of my wrist, I send a blast of fire into the centre of his back, and he falls face-first into the dirt, aflame.

Someone's fist greets my face with a crash; the storm-caster has struck a fierce blow into my cheek, and with a flash of light, I see stars. It has been some time since I received a blow to the face, and I can sense the hatred exuding from the mage as he pulls his hand back, static energy charging in the palm of his hand.

"Fuck!"

He brings his palm towards my face, seemingly wanting my head to explode. I bring my own hand up just in time to catch his in my molten palm, then send back my own charged spell of magic. The forces combine, causing our arms to fire back from one another as we create a small explosion. It sends me rolling across the ground, where the world suddenly falls silent, muffled and disconnected from me. A high-pitched ringing noise pierces the centre of my mind as I stagger to my feet, the world around me hushed and blurred. The battle continues to intensify as muffled metal against metal chimes.

My arms throb as my magic starts to waver, and when I look down, my hands are no longer glowing; they have returned to normal. They are soaked in blood, and given the searing pain in my right arm, I can only assume it is not only the blood of our enemies that I am bathed in. I step forward with a limp, searching for the remaining mages while the world continues to be nothing but dulled noise. It is a strange sensation that disorientates me. When I step forward, the storm mage is writhing around in his own blood. His face is charred, and only a black stump remains of the arm he tried to attack me with. At least my fire magic has cauterised his wounds. Although given his blackened face and burned body, I can only imagine that he would want to greet death as soon as possible.

I oblige him, taking my dagger from its sheath before drawing it across his throat, allowing him to drown in his own blood. I wonder how many lives he has taken, not just on this day, but in his life.

By the time I notice the earth shaker, he is already too close, my ringing ears having disguised his approach. He slices a dagger of his own into my side, and I scream out in pain.

Without hesitation, I swing around and slam my blade into the side of his head. We stare one another down as we hold each other in a bloody embrace.

"You should have aimed for my dead heart!" I say coldly as I twist the blade, and the earth shaker's eyes roll to white before I let go and allow him to drop to the ground.

Blood seeps through the gaps in my fingers where I clasp my hand over my hip.

"Shit!" I press my hand down hard against my skin, and I can hear it crack and sizzle as I use my magic to seal the wound. I cry out from the pain. The sooner I can find a healer, the better. My body aches, part from my wounds, part from my magic use. I reach for my flask and take a drink to replenish my energy and reverse the effects of my magic use.

It works to a degree, but the aching does not stop. My arm and hips throb, and the world around me is muffled as I take in the chaos of the battle.

Our forces are simply outnumbered. We can't hold them off for much longer.

In the distance, I can see Rhagor, recognisable by his gold-emblazoned black armour. He is actually stepping into the battlefield which I find odd. What would trigger him to do such a thing?

Then I see the sword that all have spoken about in front of him. His face is snarling and grimacing as he raises it into the air. In this moment, I know what it is that he seeks to do. Orjan warned me about the power of this sword, and I have heard stories spoken on my travels of the things Rhagor's blade can do.

He seeks to level the battlefield with a blast of magic so powerful, it will destroy both armies. He can't – that can't be his plan. Is he really that callous that he would destroy his own army to see his enemies fall?

I run as fast as my legs will allow me towards him. I have to stop him before he kills everyone.

25

JORDELL

The child is a perfect blend of Laith and Yaelor. Her tired face is soft and speckled with freckles, and her blond hair is plaited, with the side of her head cut short like her mother's. She has a look of panic on her, and I don't blame her. For now, though, my focus needs to be on her mother whom I can see is badly injured.

"Let me see her," I say. Yaelor clings on to her life, her injuries grave. She clasps her hands to her waist to try and stem the bleeding, but I fear she does not have much more left to lose, her lifeforce dangerously low.

"Get away from my mama!" the child says. She jumps down from the horse and throws herself over her mother, displaying every ounce of fight in her that I would expect from Yaelor's child. She buries her head into Yaelor and starts sobbing. "No, you can't leave me, you promised me you would keep me safe."

Yaelor's eyes flutter as she tries to focus on her daughter, but she is struggling to keep them open. She raises a weakened hand to the child's face, her eyes welling up.

"I am proud of you, Gillam. All this time I have thought

it has been my duty to save you, when really, it was you that saved me." She manages a smile. "These people will keep you safe."

"No, Mama, no! You promised me!" Gillam slams her hands down on Yaelor as her mother's eyes roll back into her skull and close. Her shrill scream startles the birds in the trees and draws a silence from the rest of the camp.

"Let me get to her," I say, knocking a couple of people I do not recognise out of my way.

"Get away from her," Gillam says, trying her best to protect her mother from me. She has fight in her, a true warrior spirit for such a young child.

"I want to help. There is still a chance, we have not lost your mother yet." I nod to Killian. "Killian, find out what the child knows," I tell him.

It is not what I want, but Gillam will get in the way, and I need to be left to it if I am to save Yaelor's life.

I cannot imagine a future for Gillam without her mother, not when Yaelor has seemingly sacrificed everything to get her to the forest, to us.

Killian steps forward and picks up a flailing Gillam in his arms.

"No, get away from me, put me down, she can't be gone, she can't!"

"Let the wizard do what he can," Killian urges the child. "If anyone can make sure she is okay, he can, and when he does, your mother is going to need all the hugs you can give her. Okay?"

Gillam continues to resist, but eventually caves, realising that she stands no chance against Killian's strength.

I close my eyes and place my hand over Yaelor's wound. I can feel her lifeforce ebbing away, drifting slowly to the afterlife. As I concentrate, I can feel the rhythmic beating of her heart as I try and draw the connection that I need, one strong enough to tug on the threads of my magic. I have never tried this with someone so close to death, and as I keep searching, the thread is dangerously thin and frayed, threatening to snap at any moment, an action that would see her life beyond repair.

"Don't go, Yaelor," I mutter under my breath as I continue to delve deep into my own magical resources, trying my hardest to connect with her.

"Yes, that's it." It is dangerously thin, but I manage to grasp it, and I start channelling the power of my staff to allow my power to cascade into her, hoping it isn't too late.

My staff vibrates in my hand, and pores of light pull from the forest itself as if the staff draws its energy from the enchanted trees around us. My magical grip on Yaelor's core grows stronger. It feels more like a rope that I grasp rather than a thin piece of string. But despite this, she does not respond to my magic. I press my hand down harder against her skin, my eyes shut tight as I concentrate.

In my mind's eye, I see a blackened void, empty and desolate, as though we have been transported to another place.

It is Yaelor's consciousness. And the fact there is nothing here terrifies me.

"Yaelor," I call out, my words bouncing around like a hollowed echo. "Yaelor!"

I continue to focus on the threads of her life that I am pulling on, drawing on my magic from one side as I search to connect the two, but there is still no response.

"Jordell," Yaelor's voice calls back, but I still cannot see her. "We do not have much time."

"I need you to let me in, Yaelor. I am trying to cleanse

your lifeforce, but I don't know if I can, you are so far gone. Your injuries may be too grave."

"That is okay, old friend. I need you to promise me something," she says. "I need you to take care of Gillam. Please, make sure she is okay."

It breaks me to hear her speak in such away, giving up on the life that she has. Or perhaps it is acceptance, and I am wrong to try and drag her back to me. "I just need a little bit longer, Yaelor," I call out. "I know I can still save you."

"Time is what we do not have, Jordell. Vireo and the others seek to end Rhagor's reign once and for all. You need to help them. Their forces are far outnumbered. The longer you are here saving me, the less time they have. Promise me you will protect Gillam, Jordell. That you will raise her like you did her father."

What she asks of me, it is not something that I am prepared for. All the feelings I have suppressed for Laith push to the forefront of my mind, a cascade of emotions I simply cannot withstand.

With this, she pushes me out with a jolt, and as I open my eyes, Yaelor lets out one last exhale of air, slowly taking her last breath.

"No!" I cry, tears streaming down my face. I can't do this again, I can't raise another child, not after what happened to Laith.

Why has she asked this of me?

"I am sorry, Yaelor." My tears fall onto her clothes as I bow my head in respect.

"You said you would save her!" Gillam screams.

"I am sorry, I truly am," I say, struggling to form words.

Yaelor's lifeless body lies motionless as Gillam pushes her way forward to be with her mother. She sobs uncontrollably, and my heart breaks for her, it truly does. I am bereft of what to say. How do you comfort a child who has lost their mother, who never met their father?

"Ready your forces," I say, my voice hoarse. "Vireo and the others are trying to defeat Rhagor as we speak. We must mobilise at once." I turn back to Gillam as a flurry of motion erupts around me and I can hear Killian's daughter barking orders. "You must stay here in the forest, child."

"Leave me alone," she says, her face hidden under the weight of her grief, her head resting on Yaelor's stomach. "Mama, please, please, Mama, don't go, I need you."

Yaelor's eyes stare blankly into the air. As a mark of respect, I lean forward to close them, exhaling deeply as I struggle to contain my own emotions. She was a great warrior. If we survive this day, people will tell stories of her courage.

As I connect with her, I feel the faintest of pulls.

"It can't be," I say. At once, I channel everything that I have into my staff, and it starts glowing again as magic beyond my control flows into her. Before my eyes, the wound on her waist begins to heal, leaving only a faded scar.

"What's happening?" Gillam asks as more and more of the power from my staff continues to absorb into her skin.

Yaelor's chest rises as she takes one large gasp of air and sits bolt upright. Her eyes are wide, and she pants heavily, but she is alive, she is still here.

"MAMA!" Gillam shrieks with delight as she wraps herself around her and squeezes her so tightly that that I fear she may squeeze the life back out of her.

Yaelor's worried expression softens as she wraps her arms around Gillam. I leave them for this moment as they embrace. She then pads her hands all over Gillam, turning her grime-covered face from left to right as she inspects her for any injuries. Aside from the odd graze, the child looks as though she is okay.

"Jordell," Yaelor says with a smile, although her face looks saddened and worn. "There is so much to tell you, there is so much that has happened."

"And we will have all the time in the world soon," I say. "But for now you need to rest. I have no clue the impacts that bringing you back will have on your body. I dare not think how close you were to the afterlife then."

"And I am grateful, Jordell, truly, I am." And then her eyes widen as if remembering. "The battle has already started. Vireo, he needs your help, Rhagor's forces are too great."

Yaelor kneels in front of Gillam and pulls her close, resting her head against her daughter's. The two of them close their eyes for a brief moment before Yaelor pulls back and looks her daughter deep in the eyes.

"You know what I must do," Yaelor says.

Gillam nods, tears still clinging to her wet cheeks.

"And you know why I must do it?"

She nods again.

"I promise you, I will come back for you."

I can see that Gillam is trying her hardest to be brave. Her breathing is stifled as she tries to suppress her feelings.

"You have been so brave throughout all of this. You have been the bravest child I have ever known. We are nearly there now, just one more battle, and we will be free. Truly free."

"Do you promise?" Gillam asks, a little untrusting.

"Have I been wrong so far?" Yaelor says, her grip tightening on Gillam's arms. "I want you to have this, it will keep you safe." She reaches for one of her hatchets and passes it to Gillam.

The girl's eyes widen with glee. "Really?"

"My hatchets have kept me safe all these years. I want you to have one of them, like two halves of a coin. I pray you will never need to use it, but you will be safe and I will be watching over you if you have it."

The hatchet looks more like a woodcutting axe as Gillam grips it with both hands and waves it around in the air.

Yaelor stands and looks at me. "We can't afford to delay, Jordell. We need to move quickly. I fear we have already lost too much time." She stands battered and bruised, but all the while ready to battle again. "I pray that with your magic, you can help tip the scales in this final battle against Rhagor."

"I would save those prayers," I say. Such things no longer bring me comfort. Long gone are the days of trusting in the gods. "I believe our fates are in our own hands. As long as we are all united, then I can make peace with my maker."

"Will Gillam be safe here?" Yaelor asks.

"Yaelor, this forest, this village, it is your true home," Killian says, moving to stand beside me. "Gillam is as much a part of our people as you are. I can assure you, she will be safe here."

Behind him, his daughter stands, she and the rest of the fighters armed and waiting on the word.

I am surprised at how fast everyone has mobilised, and after a few more hurried preparations and rushed good-byes, a handful of us are perched on horses, ready to ride. Everyone else is on foot, wearing leather armour that has been crafted from resources within the forest. Green and brown leaves of various sizes and shapes are integrated with their armour and tunics, and I am surprised to see that they have even crafted banners to represent themselves: a simple white design around six feet in height with a wolfaire etched into the fabric above a row of embroidered trees. This community has come a long way since the days of it just being Vireo, Gillam, Lek, and myself.

As I search across the faces of the men and women that stand ready to fight, young and old eyes greet me. Some will have hardened battle experience, others less so. I am proud of each and every one of them. They show fight, they show spirit, and despite not knowing what the future holds, each of them are ready to lay down their lives for one another.

"Thank you," I say, unnerved to realise that they are looking to me for leadership. There is a slight restlessness about them, and I feel as though I have no right to command these people. After all, they have not seen me for eight years, since I exiled myself from these lands. My appearance has changed now. I am no longer the strong, thickset man that I was. Age has crept upon me like ivy up an ancient tree.

"Where we head, some of us will not return," I tell them. "But what we fight for is far greater than all of us. It is not just for the people here, but for everyone across Levanthria. Today, we will charge into battle and stare into the belly of the demon. Today, we fight for a new world." I raise my staff in the air and allow it to emit a soft glow of blue magic. It pulsates lightly, and I see a calmness wash over the sea of faces.

Killian raises his sword high into the air. "For Vireo!"

A thunderous crescendo of noise hits me like a wall of water, hammering into my chest. It causes the hairs on my arms to stand. Killian sets off into the clearing, and I follow, with Yaelor, Morvin, and Leandra horsebound beside me. Gregor rides on his sleigh, his large yakulas pulling him with ease, despite not being on their traditional snowy terrain.

The yakulas' horns are impressive in size, the creatures far bigger than the stories gave them credit for. I would not like to be on the wrong side of one of them bearing down on me.

We continue at pace through the trees, slightly ahead of our forces, and when we reach the outer edge of the forest, battle drums sound. The cheers and jeers of battle reign ahead of us, magic tearing the earth apart as though flaming rocks are being launched by a trebuchet.

A rustling in the trees to my right alerts me that a trap has been set for us. Surely Rhagor would know that we are here, that there would be forces within the trees. Have we been naive in our approach already?

I ready myself to fire a blast of energy, but then I realise who it is.

"Zariah?" I say aloud.

She emerges from the trees at speed, her movement and agility far beyond the reaches of a mortal man.

She has a serious look on her face, and she holds a poleaxe in her hands that must be twice the length of my staff, the blade at the end unlike anything I have ever seen. "My brother needs stopping," she says. "I cannot leave my kingdom weakened, but I have brought with me those who are able to take up arms. We will not be as strong outside of the forest, but we can still fight."

My chest swells with gratitude for her presence, for her willingness to put her fear behind her and take up arms outside the boundaries of her realm. Such an act is unheard of from the fae.

Now I can only hope that we are not too late, that we can help turn the tide of this battle.

As we clear the trees, Zariah continues at a sprint, leading the fae into the battle.

"Charge!" I raise my staff as we emerge from the forest. The fae and our own kin roar a fearsome battle cry that would make the gods sit up and listen.

Our horses charge forward as I take in the battle scene ahead. There are bodies everywhere, the battle already well underway. I raise my staff again and send out a blast of magic. If anything, I hope seeing that reinforcements have arrived will spur on the Elterans.

Zariah shouts something in her native tongue that I don't understand, but judging by the response of her own soldiers, it serves to inspire and invigorate them. With a hop and a skip, she suddenly draws level with my horse, her speed underfoot incredible. Then she jumps forward and unfurls two ginormous butterfly-like wings to bring her flight.

Above her, I see Elara keeping up, still refusing to leave my side.

My focus falls on the wall of fire that I see ahead of me, a blazing inferno that is desecrating the battlefield and any soldiers that get in the way of its destructive power.

And then I see Laith. But my heart sinks, because it is not truly him; it is Rhagor, grabbing the hilt of his blade as he drives the spell forward.

He is met with resistance, however. Something is stopping his flames from eviscerating everything in his path. That's when I see a witch clad in the armour of a pirate, standing firm as she uses her own magic to push him back. I know in an instant that it is Zerina. Her sisters, her mother would be so proud of her, and I can't help but think they fight beside her, helping her channel her colossal power.

We continue to move as fast as our horses can carry us. I only hope Zerina is able to stay the magic long enough for us to reach her.

The colours of Elteran and Askelan soldiers heave behind her, penned in by Rhagor's flames. He is too powerful for us.

Rhagor's head turns to us now, and there is a flicker in his power, allowing Zerina to push back against him. He fights back, but he can see us advancing on his position. Surely he could not fire a second blast our way.

He stops the onslaught, one knee dropping to the ground. He is weakened.

"This is it!" Killian cries out. "We have the bastard!"

I fear for what we must do, what I must do, for we will have to strike Laith down if we are to truly bring Rhagor's reign to an end.

Smoke and flames lick up from the scorched battlefield when I see a woman advancing on Rhagor's position, far ahead of the others, enraged, ready to kill.

As I focus on her, Killian says, "Is that –?"

"Morgana?" I say, finishing his sentence and feeling just as confused. Why is Morgana allied with Elteran forces?

She leaps through the air at Rhagor, but something happens, something unexpected.

Rhagor flicks his sword into the air and she catches it as if by instinct, suddenly in possession of the sword. As she lands on the ground, Rhagor's body crumples, as if he was being held up by strings.

Morgana inspects her own form before looking down at the sword. Then, somehow, she slams the sword into the ground and vanishes from the battlefield.

26

VIREO

Codrin charges at me as explosions of magic burst into the battlefield around us. Soldiers soar through the air as the mages wade into the battle, their power far greater than us normal men. I run at Codrin myself, all my anger, all my rage that I feel for him coming down to this very moment.

All that he stands for, all that he has done, the pain that he has inflicted on our people – I hold him with the same regard that I hold for Rhagor. He must face justice for everything that he has done, and I intend to deliver it to him.

Running at him was a bad idea, though. He is far larger than I, and as we crash into each other, I feel a pressure in my shoulder before it pops. His hulking mass is too much for me. He presses me into the ground and starts pummelling me, snarling and grimacing like a wild boar. I shield myself as best I can as he continues to rain down blows on me. I cannot move my left arm though, and I know in an instant that my shoulder is dislocated.

Despite the pain, I have little time to think as Codrin

continues to strike me with the strength of a trebuchet. He is unstoppable, unmovable.

I keep my good arm above my head to shield myself from the blows, but it offers me little protection from his raw power. When he grabs me by the scruff of the neck to pull me towards him, I am grateful for the reprieve from his onslaught.

"I have waited so long for this moment," he sneers. "You have been a constant thorn in my sides for so long."

I smile through blood-soaked teeth, my mouth tasting of iron. This only serves to anger him further, and he draws his hand back, then crashes a fist into the side of my head before slamming me into the ground.

When he tries to stomp on me, I roll out of the way, and although dazed, I manage to climb back to my feet. He will not beat me so easily. I raise my fist, ready for his next strike when a stray blast of storm magic erupts on the ground between us, closer to Codrin than it is me, and I take the opportunity to look for my weapon. As I pick it up, an Askelan soldier approaches, axe in hand high above his head. I drive my blade into his chest until the hilt reaches his flesh before allowing him to fall to the ground.

Codrin, recovered from the blast, rushes me again, this time with a greataxe in his hands. My left arm droops by my side, and I jolt my shoulder with enough force to pop it back into position. The pain stops to a certain extent, but I know it will take me a while to recover.

Provided I make it through this battle.

"You must be tiring in your old age," I goad as Codrin continues his rampage towards me, snarling and slamming his axe into an Elteran soldier as he passes. I can't simply allow him to keep charging into me, I do not have the strength to fight him like this. I need to be more offensive.

I swing my sword at him, forcing him to slow down and use the metal shaft of his axe to block the blow. He tries to ram me again, but I step to the side this time and offer a quick jab to his chest with the hilt of my sword.

It is like punching stone. My blow barely affects him.

Knowing I can't allow him to gain any form of momentum, I start swinging my sword again, quickly, from the left and then the right, then the left again, waiting for an opening to present itself. But Codrin continues to block my strikes, over and over again.

The battlefield becomes even more dangerous as flashes of the elemental magic continue to disintegrate the terrain along with any soldiers unlucky enough to get in the way. Askelan magic begins to dominate the field. In the distance, I see Zerina fighting against a group of mages, her power unlike anything I have seen before. It causes me to swell with confidence. Perhaps we will live through this day. I just need to get past this blundering oaf.

Steel meets steel as each of us continues to try and best the other, yet we seem to be cancelling each other out, my speed against his brute force.

"Is this all you have, Vireo?" he grunts with a grin, enjoying every moment of our fight and the death and destruction around him.

"I'm surprised you could string that sentence together," I goad. I know he has a fragile brain, and if I cannot best him with my blade, I will get into his head.

Codrin's grin widens as he raises his greataxe high into the air before leaning back and hurling it at me, catching me off guard.

I barely have time to dive out of the way as the blade flies past me, slamming into the back of an Askelan soldier who is obliterated by it. With a sickening crunch, the axe pins him to the ground and his blood sprays in the air. I am shocked to see his spirit rise from his body from where I stand.

"What in the fuck!" I curse, looking around to double-check I have not descended into madness. All around me, I see flickers of blues with a greenish hue as other spirits wander the battleground, fighting against the Askelan forces.

"Morgana," I say. It must be her, she is the only one capable of tampering with the dead.

It distracts me enough for Codrin to ready his next move, and like a chain dragging along stone, he lets his spiked whip drop to the ground besides him.

"Shit."

He pulls it back and cracks the whip at me, catching my shoulder. Pain meets me as he tears skin from my already injured arm. He swings it around and whips me again, but this time I raise my arm and step forward, allowing the whip to wrap around my forearm.

I hold it as firm as I can as I try to ignore the searing pain. Codrin's eyes widen with delight as he realises that he has me, and he yanks the whip, pulling me towards him. As he does, I bring my blade down on it, slicing clean through it.

Codrin roars as if it is a limb that I have cut through. As he pants heavily, I ready for his next move.

Now I have a weapon and he does not. For once, I have the upper hand.

He laughs, reaching for a vial strapped to him. I recognise the vial straight away from a mission we undertook long ago, but I thought they were all gone. Codrin must have horded the faerie dust for himself.

"Codrin, don't!" I warn. I know all too well what the

elixir does. I saw it alter Lek the day they stormed the forest. "Shit!" I curse as he downs the concoction. His head starts jerking, and he bangs either side of his head. When he looks at me, all I can see are black eyes, a darkened rage as if Codrin is no longer there. Thick, red veins protrude as if they seek to escape his eyeballs, like molten fire in the cracks of a volcano.

"VIREO!"

I cannot fight him, I have no chance. I throw my sword to the ground and draw on my bow, firing three arrows at him as fast as I can. The first hits his left shoulder, then his right, then his abdomen. He barely flinches as he walks towards me. I fire another arrow at him but he holds his hand forward and lets the arrow bed into it like it is nothing, as though I fire flowers at him. Darkened, thick blood seeps from his hand and down his torso where the other arrows are bedded in, but he merely smiles.

The ground rumbles and I do well not to lose my footing as a quake hits us. Intense heat greets me as a wall of flames moves towards us from above as though the gods are raining down fire. Except I know who is responsible for this power. I have heard the stories of Hora and other places that Rhagor has left in his wake.

I turn and run as Codrin lets out an ear-splitting battle cry. "Coward!" he jeers as I seek to gain as much distance between me and that wall of death. "Fight me!"

As I look over my shoulder, the flames envelop him, and he screams out, his skin disintegrating under the intensity. I don't know whether to be grateful for the divine intervention that meant I didn't have to face the elixir brute, or horrified.

"Fall back!" I shout as I continue to cover ground as fast as I can.

With another rumble, the ground shakes even more. This time I see the form of Zerina stepping towards the flames as she unfurls her own magic.

The stories I have heard about her did not do her justice; her power is truly incredible as she forces Rhagor's destructive flames back with her own magic. The flames wrap around us, but Zerina manages to keep Rhagor's fire back, and instead of running, I turn back.

I just hope that she is able to maintain her power.

27

RHAGOR

Legend speaks of the Moonfire Festival on the island of Voraz, where silver-tongued bards compete to weave the most enchanting tales. The winner is said to receive the blessing of Lunara, goddess of inspiration.

Alderic Smith, Festivals of the Levanthria, 213 KR

I know that power. I know its source, but I have never seen it wielded in such a way. Fallen soldiers raised from the dead, taking up arms against my forces. I am impressed at how Morgana channels their essences so easily. She is unforgiving against my soldiers as she kills them with ease.

How the gods must be desperate if they are bestowing champions with such power, how I cannot wait to see them all again.

First I need to deal with the necromancer. Her magic was powerful enough to force me back, but even with her newfound abilities, she is no match for my power, a power contained within my sword.

"RHAGOR!" she bellows. Behind her, my soldiers

continue to fight against spectres as greenish red magic swirls around her like a thick fog. I swear she could vanish into the smoke-like power if only she knew how to.

"My love," I say, tinged with sarcasm as she approaches and fires another blast of magic at me. I move my shoulder backwards, letting the power pass me. It crashes into the chest of an unfortunate soldier behind me who cries out in pain for a brief moment before falling into eternal silence.

"You will pay for what you have done," she says. "Regardless of what you achieve, regardless of what the gods want me to do. I purely want vengeance."

I look down at Orjan's lifeless corpse beside me.

"You were fond of him, weren't you?" There is a snide undertone to my voice as I seek to goad her. "Such a shame that he took what was mine." I look down at the amulet, then at her. "Well, it seems he took you, too."

Morgana is unable to contain her anger as she sends forward more volleys of magic. I step back again, this time using the power of my blade to deflect the blasts away with ease. She is relentless in her pursuit, however, and continues to push forward, grimacing with pain and anguish as she fires more green energy towards me. I know the power of necromancy and I know all too well its capabilities. I cannot allow her magic to touch my flesh. It is something I am unwilling to risk. As she moves closer, I take a swing of my blade.

Her speed surprises me as she weaves in and out of my strikes, leaving a spectral shadow of her essence behind her. It is a transformation that I would admire under different circumstances, but she is stopping me from enacting my plan, so her actions only serve to infuriate me more.

I kick forward in frustration, connecting with her chest

and knocking her backwards. She grunts but quickly gathers herself, channelling her magic by swirling her arms around her. She stretches out her arms to either side and slowly raises them into the air, her face grimacing with the power she is drawing on. She cannot see what I can, though: that her essence and the spirits she raises from the dead are one and the same, her swirling vortex of power drifting into the bodies around her as they rise from the ground.

She looks at me with only death and vengeance in her eyes, and without her uttering a word, the spirit soldiers charge down on me, weapons raised high.

Well, I might as well have some fun first. Having already seen my soldiers destroy the spectres they face, I step back and wait for them to reach me. The first two I dispatch quickly, drawing my sword against one, then the other. It feels strange when my blade passes through them. I can feel the resistance, but it is different to striking a physical body, like passing my sword through water. It catches me off guard when the first two spirits turn into wisps of green air where I slay them as more spirits run towards me. Their faces are gaunt and contorted, their bodies glowing, shrouded in the same shadows that surround Morgana. I fight them off, my speed far faster than any of theirs. Wisps of green magic flicker around me as I destroy the spectres, but however weak I find them, they are like rats, and they keep swarming on my formation as I continue to destroy them, one by one.

Wave upon wave reaches me until there is a break in them, and for a moment, I think that Morgana has run out of bodies. By the time I realise her plan, I am too late.

When I slice through the last spirit, through the cloud of magic I see her face as she dives through it, blade in hand. With a scream of anger, she drives her dagger into my shoulder.

"FUCK!" I cry out in pain, this blasted mortal body. It will literally be the death of me.

I stagger backwards, grabbing the hilt of the dagger and prying it from my flesh. An eruption of pain burns through my skin. First an arrow, now this. She raises a glowing hand and brings it down towards me, but I am quick to this and grab hold of her wrist, squeezing it tightly.

"You will pay for your insolence," I say through gritted teeth. Her strength is surprising, and I realise that she is no longer a sorceress. She has transcended the boundaries of her necromancy and become something else.

I throw my head forward into hers, knocking her back in a daze.

"Enough of this!" I roar as I raise my blade into the sky.

"You will destroy everyone!" Morgana says, spitting blood onto the ground. She looks over her shoulder at the warring forces and cries out, "Fall back!"

I realise she has no clue what to do or how to stop me as I charge up the power within my blade and it starts to glow.

"It is no less than what you all deserve," I sneer. "I will have my revenge."

Morgana continues to stumble backwards away from me, drawing as much distance as she can. It is fruitless, however. I can easily cover the battlefield with burning rage which will eradicate everything, spirits and all.

When I drive my sword into the ground, the earth shakes violently as if we have been hit by a quake. Morgana turns to run but loses her balance, and I thrive off the hopelessness that I see in her eyes. To think she even thought she was capable of defeating me.

A wall of fire more powerful than I have ever

summoned pushes out around me, the hilt of my sword becoming painful to hold as I channel more power through it than I ever have before. The blast radius is huge as it scorches the ground and soldiers begin to burn and disintegrate into ash. It is only a matter of time before this will be over with and I can drag the gods back to this world.

The soldiers see what is happening and have started to run to escape my blast, but their efforts are futile. They cannot escape this.

Ahead of me, however, someone does not run away from the flames. They move towards them, they embrace them. It is enough to make me pay attention as the fool runs head-on towards my wall of fire.

Then they do something I did not think was possible: as they stop and slam their hands together, a white-hot wall of fire forces itself out from their position.

"How?" I say aloud as the wall of fire crashes into mine. The two negate each other as the furious forces press into one another. Both Askelan and Elteran forces are sitting behind her.

They can see what I tried to do, that I sought to destroy all of them. If my magic fails, they will no longer follow me, despite the threats of what I do. Therefore I cannot let this hindrance stop me. Whoever this mage is, they must know fear, they must know my fury.

My shoulder throbs from my injuries, but I continue to channel the magic within my blade as I try and push pass the barrier flame ahead. It is unmoving, though. The sorceress's power is incredible as I continue to push my magic to breaking point. Cracks form in the ground as it shakes. I seek to obliterate everything, a pained grimace on my face.

"They will not win, they cannot win!" I snarl as, with another surge, I force my flames forward, pushing the sorceress back. My magic is superior and cannot be beaten. My flames grow as my rage does, and it threatens to engulf the barrier as I start to overpower her. My flames begin to form a half-circle, penning all the soldiers in on the other side.

To my left, however, the sound of battle horns garners my attention. A cheer rises into the air along with the battle cries of men and woman as they come running from the trees, advancing on my position from the east.

People on horseback gallop towards me, their weapons raised. Their numbers are not something I should be worried about, but when all my focus is on maintaining my attack, I can't maintain a defence to the east, too.

At the front, leading the charging attack, there sits an older man on a black horse. His hair is long and white, and he holds a staff in the air as he races towards me, the end of it glowing an ice-like blue. I recognise the power within it in an instant, I can feel its essence in the air, suddenly, as if the trees were masking its power before, shrouding it in their shadows.

"How is this possible?" I mutter, for I know at once that this is the staff from the Elder Tree, the last remnants of its power. Smoke continues to plume into the air from the fire that I started, which only serves to inspire these pathetic people into action. They actually think they can defeat me.

But then it hits me: if he is in possession of the staff formed from the Elder Tree, that means the essence of the Elder Tree is still alive, despite everything I have done to destroy it.

That means –

No sooner does everything click into place than I see my sister emerge from the trees, her fae wings spread widely as she glides across the field and draws level with the sorcerer.

"Zariah!" I whisper. I cannot believe she is still alive and that she chooses to side with this pathetic race.

She is like a hydra. Every time I cut her down, she finds a way to come back. I would be lying to myself if I said I was not impressed with her resourcefulness. Is this why she gifted the staff to an outsider? So that she could find ways to fragment her essence? Has she created more than one? I have so many questions that I demand to be answered, but right now, there are a lot more people seeking an end to my reign than I care to indulge.

Zariah is joined by the fae folk as they pour out of their homeland of the forest. It is unheard of, unprecedented for them to leave the protection of their trees. Even I know their magic will leave them. They risk their very existence to side with these animals.

I have no choice. Despite my wishes, I halt my fire blast, letting the flames hiss away.

In desperation, I take hold of the amulet and wrap it around the hilt of my sword, then start channelling the magic energy that now emanates from my hands. This is all I have wanted to do, and I do not have long, as they will be on my position shortly. Morgana, my soldiers, and the Elterans are charging down on me now. Well, those that are brave or stupid enough to challenge me.

I look to the skies and smile, knowing that the gods will be looking down on this moment, hoping that I am defeated. But I haven't been, and I continue to let the magic of my blade pour into the amulet until the two intrinsically combine. With a blinding flash of light, the bone amulet infuses and wraps around the hilt of the sword.

"No more hiding," I say as an almighty blast of invisible power fires out from every direction. I stand at its epicentre, sending out a force of energy unlike anything I have ever summoned. Not destructive, but something far worse.

It is enough to stop the advancing forces in their tracks, and I take my opportunity to focus my magic once more. The temptation to send out another blast of fire is overwhelming, but between my sister, the wizard, and the sorceress, they would likely be able to block this, their combined power impressive on its own. Even if it pains me to say it.

"Rhagor!" Morgana bellows again, this time advancing faster than everyone else.

Her arms are by her side as she charges her power up in her hands before unfurling a blast that I only just manage to block. Then another, and another. Each blast pins me back as I block them. My sword is becoming heavy and my head throbs as my own energy levels suffer because of this blasted injury.

Morgana dives at me, hatred in her eyes, a women possessed by a power beyond comprehension, a power that could match that of my sword.

Then my eyes widen with realisation as she soars through the air towards me. I toss the sword up in the air and she instinctively reaches out towards it, grabbing hold of the hilt of the blade.

I do to her what I did to Laith all those years ago.

In an instant, a nauseating spin takes over me as my soul transfers alongside the sword and I switch hosts. This body has served its purpose. It is broken, futile. With hers, though – with Morgana's powers – I can be something more powerful than the gods themselves.

It only takes a moment before my viewpoint changes and I am holding my sword once again, pushing Morgana to the back of her own consciousness as she becomes a prisoner in her own mind.

I crash into my former body who crumples to the ground.

The connection to the energy I now control is beyond that of what I imagined, and I look down on my new form, embracing the new power that greets me.

But I am inexperienced with this form, and I cannot master this magic in the seconds I have before my enemies will reach me. My sword fully charged with the death from the battlefield, I start channelling its power, I use the latent power within it to summon a portal.

I step into it, away from the battlefield.

With my magic summoned through the amulet, the gods will already be tethered to this world.

Now all I have to do is find them.

28

LAITH

I open my eyes and gasp. The air tastes thin and I pant out loud, coughing and choking as if I am taking breath for the first time. I am free, I am free from him.

The world spins heavily around me as though I'm tumbling down a hill. My body aches, and a searing pain grips my shoulder and my waist.

My body is not in the greatest position, but I no longer feel like a passenger, no longer a prisoner in my own mind.

I raise my arms into the air above me. The sensation is strange; I have seen these limbs moving, I have witnessed everything through my eyes these last eight years, but I have never once been in control of them. Constantly screaming, searching for a way to escape, only to find my words muted, my own personal hellscape unfolding in front of me.

My arms are heavy, weighted by the black armour I am wearing. The pain in my left shoulder is difficult to manage, and I force myself to sit upright.

The smell of the battle greets me first. Charcoaled ground, scorched flesh, and the iron of blood force their way to my senses. It is nauseating, and I continue to breathe in heavily, like panic has come over me. I'm finally in control of my body, but I'm left feeling like I've stepped from one nightmare into another.

As I survey the battlefield, my stomach lurches. So much death, so much destruction, all by my hand. The things I have had to endure trapped inside my own body, the things I've watched Rhagor do to others – it makes me feel as though I am complicit, despite it not being my own actions.

An arrow flies past me, bedding in the ground just by my side. When I look up, I see a green-cloaked man bearing down on me, bow in hand. He has the next arrow ready to fire, to end me. It is an aged, battle-worn face, but it is one that I remember.

"Vireo," I call out, my voice somewhat softer than when Rhagor possessed my body. He doesn't hold back as he fires another arrow in my direction. I close my eyes, embracing my fate. At least I am free from the curse of Rhagor's possession as I greet the afterlife.

The arrow does not reach me though. Some form of barrier seems to deflect it away.

To my left, I can hear horses, churning the earth as they approach. And then I see Jordell with his staff stretched out in front of him.

"Jordell, what are you doing!" Vireo scolds, firing another two arrows in quick succession.

With a wave of his staff, Jordell deflects the arrows once again as I find myself surrounded by my former allies, all wearing the scars from the time that has passed since I truly saw them last. They all look so different, so much older. Jordell's form has completely changed. He now looks somewhat frail, an older man reaching the later years of his life. Vireo carries a faint scar on his face that he didn't used to have, and his chin is covered by thick, dark stubble with flashes of grey. His eyes are darkened and weary.

Then, beside Jordell, I see Yaelor. She has barely changed, save for the blood and bruises that cover her face. My heart skips when I see her. I have yearned for this moment for so long, to be able to speak to her and the others once again. To tell them that it is me sitting here, not Rhagor.

"Stand down, Vireo. Rhagor is gone." Jordell pulls his horse to a stop as the fae fly into the battlefield, tending to the wounded and lending aid. One stands beside Jordell, who I recognise as Zariah.

"Are you mad, Jordell? Let me end him!" There is an anger in Vireo's voice, a hatred that he feels towards Rhagor that is now directed at me.

"Jordell is right," I say, raising my hands while still sitting. "Rhagor is gone, I am free from him."

Vireo keeps an arrow trained on me, untrusting and suspicious. I do not blame him.

Jordell drops from the horse and walks over to me, standing between Vireo and myself, his arms outstretched.

"Vireo, that is enough. I am telling you, this is not Rhagor." He looks over his shoulder at me, seemingly not fully convinced in his words. I give him a coy smile and his expression softens, his eyes welling with tears. He drops his staff at once and turns to face me, dropping to his knees as he plants his hands to either side of me.

I wince as a shooting pain surges down my injured side. My head feels faint; I have lost more blood than I would have liked.

Jordell's ice-white eyes pour into me, as if he is searching for something. I don't say anything, I simply look back. There is so much pain that I see, so much guilt and fear from a man I am used to seeing be so strong.

"It is you," he whispers, his voice almost breaking.

I nod and say, "It is."

Jordell cries out. I can't tell if it is pain, anguish, relief, or something in between. He grabs hold of me and hugs me tightly.

"My boy, it's you, it is really you. My son, Laith, you are back."

Emotion fills me. He called me his boy, his son. I had seen him as a father figure for so long, but I just never took the opportunity to tell him before Rhagor possessed my body. Before everything changed.

My eyes fill with tears as I embrace Jordell back, and the two of us sob into one another.

When he steps away, he reaches beside him for his staff and casts a spell, holding onto my arm. A powerful pressure builds up which forces a grimace from me as an intense light flashes from his staff. Within a moment, the pain in my shoulder and hip fades to nothing more than a manageable throb.

"It is so good to see you again," Jordell says, helping me to my feet. I can't help but notice Vireo still has his bow and arrow trained on my position.

"It is good to see you too," I say, pausing for a moment before saying a word I wish I had spoken when I was much younger, before all of this had passed between us. "Father."

Life lights up in Jordell's eyes, like a spark of magic has ignited within them, and we embrace once more.

"It is so good to see you all again, to be able to speak freely." I turn to face Yaelor who looks confused, and as I take a step forward, my legs tremble. It has been so long since I was in my own conscience, I wonder for a fleeting moment if I would be left as though I was a babe, needing to learn all the basics of my body once again.

"Yaelor," I say. There is so much that I want to say to her, yet I can't. I take another step forward, still wobbling on my feet but determined to get to her. She climbs down from her horse and takes a step towards me.

"She is beautiful," I say. "Our daughter, she is beautiful."

Yaelor charges at me, and for a moment, I do not know if she intends to cleave her hatchet into my skull. I am relieved to find she doesn't. Instead, she wraps her arms around me and pulls me close to her, reminding me just how strong she is. My head falls into the crease of her neck and I breathe her in. I have so much emotion pouring out of me that it threatens to burst through my own barriers. I have so many thoughts and feelings that I need to share.

"She is safe," Yaelor says. Her body is stiffened against me. To see her displaying so much warmth tells me that being a mother has changed her. I have longed for this moment for so long, even though I only learnt recently that I was a father. It changed everything, gave me the motivation to continue, the determination to break free from Rhagor's grasp.

"I'm sorry, truly, I am," I say. "I should have been there, I should have been able to raise her with you." There are so many what-ifs circling around my head that it threatens to send me into a spin. I look around us at the friends and allies that we have, each with their own stories of strength and valour, continuing to fight against a force so much more powerful than them, but no less determined than if it were a mortal man.

Beyond Vireo, a young knight wearing a blue tunic over his armour is standing over a body. When I recognise the yellow colours, my stomach lurches as I am reminded of what happened to Orjan.

"Orjan!" I say, pushing past Jordell and Vireo.

As I approach, the young knight looks at me with anger and disgust, his hands shaking as he grips his blades tightly, ready to strike me down.

I drop down to Orjan. He is covered in a pool of blood, his neck and throat having been brutally torn open. His eyes are open and wide as if searching beyond the skies. I brush my fingers over his face, closing his eyes, hoping that somehow he is at peace.

"This is all my fault," I say, my tears dropping onto his blood-soaked face.

"Remind me why I shouldn't take your head from where I stand," the young knight says. I feel the cold steel wet with blood against the bottom of my chin. I can feel his hatred, his anger, burning into me. I do not blame him. He won't understand everything that has happened.

"I assure you, I am an ally," I say as I cradle Orjan's dead body. "He will be laid to rest, in honour."

"Lower your weapon, Rior," Yaelor demands, stepping forward in my defence. "Our fight is against Rhagor. Laith is free of his curse, just as Orjan was."

I can see Rior's inner turmoil as his jaw tenses while he decides whether he will end my life.

"I suggest you listen to my friend." Vireo's voice comes from behind me, and when I glance over, his arrow is now pointed at Rior. "I assure you we will avenge him, but first, we need to lay him and the others that have fallen on this day to rest."

Rior stands firm for a moment before lowering his blades to his side. He drops to his knees, releasing his weapons to the ground. Then he clasps his hands to his face and begins to sob uncontrollably.

We have lost so many on this day. Orjan has given the ultimate sacrifice. He gave himself to Rhagor, knowing what he would do, knowing that he would likely end his life. And he did it all for my daughter. Did he know her value? Did he know that she was my kin? I have so many questions I would want to ask him, so much that I would want to explore. But I will never have that chance, never be able to make amends for our quarrel in the forest when he was still cursed with the appearance of a lizard man.

Despite the brutal way in which his life was ended, he looks as though he is at peace. I grab hold of his hands and place them on his chest, then stand up and pay my respects to him. My throat burns as if it's on fire, and my eyes sting. He did not deserve this, he deserved so much more. I can only hope that in death he has found the redemption he so desperately searched for.

The Askelan forces surrender as soon as they see our numbers swell. Their king left them all to die, even those who fought for him.

I place my hand on Rior's shoulder, who continues to grieve aloud. "We will avenge him," I say, and then I turn to face the others.

"Please tell me you have a plan." I first look at Jordell before switching my attention to Vireo. He has always tread a fine line between confidence and arrogance, a flicker to his former life as a tax collector for King Athos Almerion.

It is as though he is a completely different person now. He looks over the battlefield and the weight of everything that has happened seems to catch up with him. He looks ashen-faced, and lost, as if he searches for words but cannot find them.

"I don't know," he says, "I didn't think much beyond the battle. Even if I had, this scenario is not one that we could have planned for. I had no clue that Rhagor could switch his host through the sword."

"Neither did I," I say. "But we still need a plan, we need to know where he has gone." I pause. "We need to stop him."

"I am afraid we are already too late," Zariah says, her arms clasped around her stomach as if she is cradling herself.

"What do you mean?" Vireo asks.

"Did you not feel the surge of power before Rhagor vanished? He managed to unleash the power, he has done what he set out to do."

"He has bound the gods to this world," I say, although I do not know what that fully means aside from giving Rhagor a chance to exact his revenge on them. "Where do you think he has gone?" I ask.

"To the very person who set him on this vengeful path," Zariah says. "He has gone to find our mother."

29

ZERINA

We sit at a large bench-like table in the centre of camp, either side filled with strong warriors, some with magic, some without. I can feel their collective power and I am impressed by the forces that Vireo has managed to pull together. I am, however, not surprised.

I sit towards the bottom end of one of the benches. It feels odd to sit with so many strangers, but I feel like we are close given the battle we have already fought together.

I only recognise Jordell, Vireo, and Rior, the three of them sitting opposite me. Rior's mood is solemn as he grieves for Orjan's loss. I can relate to how he feels; I only found another way to cope with that grief.

It has helped me understand that in battle, there are no winners, not truly. We have all sacrificed so much, yet here we are, still breathing. I take a moment to remember the lives of those we lost in the battle against Rhagor.

"What do we do? We can't allow Rhagor to simply walk around exacting his own form of retribution," Vireo says. He is frustrated, and I do not blame him. Following Orjan's burial ceremony he wanted to ride to Askela, to find Rhagor and end this right now, but we cannot be sure that he is even there.

"I agree," Laith says, sitting across from Vireo. Then he addresses everyone at the table. "I know more than anyone how Rhagor works. The longer we leave him while he has control over Morgana, the more powerful he will become as he learns to control her power."

"That is why we need to move quickly. The sooner, the better," Zariah says. She sits taller than everyone else, and is possibly the most beautiful creature I have ever seen. She has slender features and a soft, pale blue skin, and her wings are tucked in behind her back. "This is why I summoned everyone here. I know where Rhagor will be. It is there where we will have our final battle."

"How?" Vireo asks with a stern voice. He is growing impatient, and I have never seen him like this.

"Because Rhagor is my kin, he is my twin. I know him more than anyone else in this world, save for our mother."

"A mother that he hates," Jordell says.

"Exactly. It is her he will seek out first."

"And how exactly do you know where he will be?" Jordell asks, more diplomatic in his approach than Vireo.

"He is in Zakron," Zariah says, a steely conviction in her voice. "Thousands of years ago, long before Zakron became a crumbling ruin blighted by curses and dark magic, it was the capital, a flourishing kingdom, before greed besieged its gates like a plague. It is here where the first shrines to our mother were formed, and it is here where her power reigned supreme, before she created this forest. If Rhagor is seeking revenge against her, he will look for her there."

"Zakron is at least a week's sail across the southern borders. That itself would take us a week to get to him,"

Vireo says, fetching his fingers to the bridge of his nose as if he is in the grips of a headache.

"Not exactly," Jordell says. "When Zariah needed me, when the Elder Tree burned under Rhagor's flames, my staff somehow unlocked a magic that I did not know it possessed. It opened a portal to the forest. I was on the shores just west of Osar. When I stepped through it, I was here in the time it would take me to step from one room to another in a tavern. Yet I had travelled a much larger distance."

Vireo shakes his head in disbelief. I saw Rhagor vanish in the thick of the battle, but even I wasn't aware this power existed even though I possess infinite knowledge, or so I thought. Perhaps the knowledge of the Elves does have its limitations after all. My magic is only sustainable given the waters from the fountain that I use, to negate its effects on my body. After the battle though, I have used the last that I had, with no more reserves for me to draw on, at least until I return to Treventine.

"This is correct," Zariah says. "We must use your staff to open a gateway to Zakron. It is here where you will confront Rhagor. You must end his miserable existence so that the world can once again breathe new life." She pauses, allowing her words to sink in. "You will be limited in who you can take, Jordell. Not everyone at this table will be able to pass through. As powerful as your staff is, it does have its limitations."

Without hesitation, Vireo stands first. "I will go," he says, his hands clenched into fists against the table.

I stand. "As will I," I say. My magic is more destructive than anyone's at the table. It would be foolish for me not to go, even without the means to replenish myself.

Laith stands next. "I have words I wish to share with Rhagor before we end his reign."

"How many do you think the portal will hold for?" Jordell asks.

"At best I would say six. It takes a lot of magic to transport a person such a long distance," Zariah explains.

"I will stay here with Gillam," Yaelor says. "I will also help the people here."

"As will I," Killian says. "I have no magic. I am sure the rest of you will put up a much better fight."

"Well, you didn't think you could have all the fun without us," a familiar voice reaches from behind me and sends a cold shiver down my spine. A voice that threatens me to lose my grasp on the dormant rage that sits within me.

"Esara!" I say in surprise. Why – how – is she here? I thought after our last exchange I would never see her again. "I told you what would happen if I ever laid eyes on you," I tell her.

She looks surprised by my heated words as the rest of the table falls into silence. I step out from the table, a swell of power threatening to rip from my hands, but then Ulrik steps through the clearing behind her. His soft expression makes him seem more of a stranger than the usually hardened face I am accustomed to.

"She insisted," he says. "Although I must admit, I did not realise where she was taking me." He casts his sister a scalding look.

There is too much that has passed simply for me to forget everything Esara has done. For it is Ulrik and Esara that stand here, while Darmour lies at the bottom of a grave.

"I can't do this," I say. "I need some air. When you are ready to leave, let me know."

"Erm, we're outside," Esara says. She is trying to be funny, but this is neither the time or place. This is just what I would expect from her – to act as though nothing has happened. To think she can simply waltz back into my life, despite everything that has happened between us.

Ulrik slams an elbow into her ribs as I finish my excuses and make my leave. More than anything in this moment, I need to escape, and I need some space.

I keep walking at a brisk pace, ranting and raving in my head, ruminating on Esara and Ulrik arriving in the forest. I have no clue how long I have been walking for, but I am taken aback when I stumble across the most beautiful lagoon I have ever seen. The waters are turquoise, and I can see the stones at the bottom of its surface. The sound of the waterfall at the far side soothes my tortured soul.

The thing that has brought me the most turmoil is that I've barely had time to grieve Darmour's death, barely had time to spare him so much as a thought.

Am I that shallow? This was the man that I gave my heart to. Is it that when I buried him, I also buried my heart, leaving me devoid of any emotion other than anger? Then I stifle a breath, bringing my hand up to my mouth at the realisation.

I am not so different from Esara. I channelled my grief with a rage, one that I only released once we reached the battlefield.

I sit at the water's edge and stare at the reflection of the full moon that sits atop its surface.

"I miss you," I say aloud, embracing the sadness. I speak as if I am talking to him, as if he can hear me, but he can't. I wonder what he would think of me behaving like this. He was devoted to me just as much as he was to his role as Esara's first mate. She was his captain, after all. It must have tormented him, seeing us at odds with each other. I sit in silence for a while, my knees tucked up to my chest.

When the bushes rustle behind me, I barely acknowledge it. I can feel their essence behind me and I know who it is before they utter a word.

"What do you want?" I ask, my tone flat and fed up. I am too exhausted to fight, I don't want to keep fighting anymore.

"Ulrik told me I should follow you, that you and I need to talk."

I continue to look out at the lagoon, hugging my legs tighter to myself.

Esara sits behind me and shuffles about uncomfortably. "I'm going to speak," she blurts out. "I am going to say some stuff, stuff that I don't normally talk about. Then you are going to have two options. Incinerate me with your fire magic, or allow me to try and make peace with everything that has passed between us. Then allow me to right the wrongs that have fallen upon you at my hand."

She waits for a moment for a reply from me, but I say nothing. I still find it strange to see her in her true form, to hear her true voice and realise it is the same person whom I have spent most of my adult life trying to protect. Whether or not I failed is another question I need to search for an answer to.

When I remain silent, Esara shuffles around uncomfortably for a moment, not quite sure how to place her legs before saying, "Well, I guess the fact I am not a pile of ash tells me you are willing to listen, so here goes. Just remember, I am not like you. I am not good with words. It's hard when I have been led by anger for such a long time."

I remain silent. For now, I will see what she has to say.

"I see that anger in you, Zerina, and I don't want you to lose yourself to it, not like I did. No matter who it is you blame for the things that happened. I gave in to the anger, and I allowed it to dictate who I was for so long that I truly forgot my own identity. I took the form of my brother as a way to cope. I didn't know what else to do, it was the only way that I could see him, to live as him. I truly couldn't accept that he was gone." Esara fumbles and stumbles over her words, but even I have to acknowledge that she has put them forward in an eloquent way.

"I did the only thing I knew to do, which was lash out. I lashed out at everyone and everything that got in my way, desperate to avenge my brother's death. When I pulled the trigger of Morvin's weapon and assassinated the king, I thought that I would be free from the burden that I had, that the anger I harboured would go away. I had avenged my brother's name, and as such, killed the person who had taken away everything from me. Then I only found myself further tormented when that anger continued to swell inside me. I couldn't shake it, no matter what I did, no matter how hard I tried or how much I wanted to move on. It became all-consuming. I knew that I couldn't rest. But I wanted to. I was so tired from it all, I hated who I had become, but I was too afraid to look at a reflection and see myself, see the monster that I had become. It made it easier staying as Ulrik. By the time I killed the king, we had built up a reputation, and that kept us safe, kept me safe."

Esara sighs loudly as she looks out at the lagoon. She takes a deep breath and leans towards the water's edge to look within it.

"I thought bringing Ulrik back would free me. But now when I see my reflection, all I see is a stranger." She brushes her hand over the surface and allows her reflection to become twisted and distorted. She sits back and sighs again, her breath shaking as she continues to talk through the void of silence. "Am I glad that Ulrik is back? Yes. Am I going to apologise for needing him here? No. But you have to know that I would take it back if Darmour could be here. He was a good man, and an even greater pirate. He taught me so much about captaining a ship, about sailing the seas. He gave everything to support me with what I endeavoured to do, even if it wasn't in line with his own wants and wishes."

She pauses for a moment. "And I will always remember and respect him for that. He was the bravest man I have ever met, and because of me, he is gone, and that tears me up inside. When he knocked me out of the way, I had made peace with my fate. I was happy to exchange my life for that of my brother. In some ways, it was my way of repenting for all the bad things I have done. A life for a life. I didn't want Darmour to sacrifice himself for me," she says, a slight raise in her voice with her own flash of frustration. "Do you not think that I valued his life over mine? He was worth ten of what I am."

"Yet, he made the decision, one that would see you live and his life end," I finish with the realisation that it was Darmour's decision to make, and one that he made freely. I have no doubt he would have done the same for anyone else in our crew.

"Please don't let anger win," Esara says as she makes to stand. "Please do not fall down the path that I have walked for so long. It is a lonely place. And I know that is not where your heart truly lies. You are destined for so much more." She turns to set off back to the camp. "Allow me to fight alongside you one final time. It is the only way I know I can make amends for the things I have put you through."

With this, she leaves me on my own, and I am left with nothing but the sound of the waterfall crashing into the lagoon, churning the water much like my thoughts churn my own mind. I am alone and confused and stricken with grief. I miss Darmour more than I can explain. Breathing without him near is painful. The air tastes thicker, the colours around me are less vibrant, my senses are dulled. But I am here because he has always helped guide me, and he is not here because he willed it. He saved his captain's life, sacrificing his own in the process. A decision I will never fully agree with, but one I have to respect, because it was his decision to make as a free man.

"I love you so much," I say aloud, and then I start sobbing uncontrollably. For the first time since he passed, because of Esara's words, I embrace the grief so that it does not consume me any longer.

30
LAITH

There are some families so obsessed with maintaining as much elven blood in their heritage that they will resort to incest. Their family histories going back hundreds of years, the consequences of such inbreeding can have a devastating effect on some newborns who are rejected at birth.

Anonymous, Note, KR Unknown

It is dark as we stand in the forest, yet the stars above combined with the moonlight cast an almost ethereal glow around us.

We have made our peace with the dead, carrying them into the Forest of Opiya and spending the day laying them to rest in the true tradition of Levanthria.

Orjan is different, however. He is Rashouyan, and despite having pledged his allegiance to these lands, he deserves a funeral befitting a knight who has redeemed the honour of his homelands. He redeemed it with me.

There is not a large group of us, only Jordell, Rior, Zariah, Killian, Zerina, Yaelor, and myself. We search to pay our respects as we send him into the afterlife. He lies above a pyre we have made in his honour. His body has been cleaned, his neck covered by the flag of Eltera placed over him, only revealing his face.

He seems peaceful, as though he is asleep. A gold coin has been placed on each of his eyes.

We stand in a half-circle at the foot of his body, our heads lowered as we pay our final respects to the man who taught me so much when I was younger.

"Would anyone like to speak?" Jordell asks. The flaming torch in his hand casts a warm glow over his pained face. He did not know Orjan that well in person, but I can see that he is pained, that he is grieving as I am grieving. He knew how important Orjan was to me, despite everything we had been through.

I look at Rior. He looks lost and in shock, and I understand how he feels.

"You go first," I say as Rior looks at me as though he seeks permission. He nods and steps forward to speak.

"Orjan did so much for me," he starts. "You did so much for me," he corrects himself, as if addressing Orjan directly. "Since the day I found you under that bridge, hungover and miserable, I knew that you were destined for much more than what you realised. You saved me from the Wyverns. You helped me to avenge my parents when they were murdered. You took me under your arm and trained me as a knight of the realm. You taught me what it takes to be a man, to put others before ourselves, to be a protector for those who cannot protect themselves." Rior's voice cracks. It is horrible to see such anguish in his voice, but a relief to see him embracing the pain that he feels, not holding it back, but instead putting it out into the world, raw and unforgiving. "Being your squire was the greatest honour you ever bestowed on me, Orjan, and despite the jokes we shared, despite the headaches I gave you all these years, I wanted to thank you for all that you have done for me. You were my brother in this life, and I have no doubt you will be waiting for me in the next." He bows his head, his sobs becoming too much for him to manage.

Jordell steps forward and places a solemn hand on his shoulder. "I have no doubt in my mind that he would be proud of the man you have become," he says. Rior steps back to stand beside Jordell, who passes him the torch.

"If I may," I say, looking for permission from Rior for me to speak. I would not blame him for not wanting me to. It must be so difficult for him to see the man who killed Orjan standing before him at his funeral.

Rior nods and I breathe a sigh of relief that I have been holding for some time. This in itself makes me feel like a weight is off my shoulders.

I clear my throat. My mouth is dry, but in this moment, I feel as though there is just Orjan and me. As if at any moment, he is going to laugh at me and reassure me that everything is okay.

But as I stand there alone, I feel nothing. There is no whisper on the wind, no reassurance that he is listening, no raucous laughter. And it hits me like a greathammer, threatening to cause my insides to implode.

"I am sorry, old friend," I start, struggling to form words, struggling to get out what I so desperately need to say. "Like Rior, our paths crossed when I was just a boy. A street urchin, stealing what I could from the markets in Askela, all so I could simply live. That merchant had captured me and was seeking to chop my hand off for stealing from him. He had every right to, such is the law. You may have stumbled into my path that day, but I am grateful that our paths crossed. Not just because you stopped me from being mutilated, but because you showed me what it took to be humble and to help others. I can't attest to your later years, but I know you had your demons that you always chose to face alone, searching for solace at the bottom of a never-ending tankard. Something that would often get you into trouble. It is, after all, what set us on our paths.

"We did not always see eye to eye, and over time, we grew further apart, but that does not mean I ever stopped thinking about you, Orjan. I owe you so much. I am the man I am today because of you. The values you taught me are chiselled into me like stone, and through that, I know you will live on. You are not truly gone. I know you sought redemption for the things that happened in your past, long before I met you, some of it during our time. But I assure you, old friend, that you have brought more good to this world than many other men ever will. I have a daughter that is alive because of you. The people of Eltera are free because of your bravery, and you cannot put a price on that. However, if there is a debt to be paid it will be, in Rhagor's blood." I step back, standing on the other side of Jordell.

"May you be at peace, old friend, until I see you again in the afterlife."

Rior moves forward slowly and holds the torch at Orjan's feet as the pyre takes light. It doesn't take long for the flames to lick up against the night sky, and his body burns, a true warrior's tribute.

I remain in place, collecting my thoughts as he disappears into the flames. All the memories we shared, the laughs we had, the good times, the bad. The only regret I have is that he is not here for us to discuss them. Part of me cannot truly believe that he is gone, and after this night, we must embrace the fact that these could also be our last days, that we may be reunited sooner rather than later. For now, though, we remember him as we all stand in silence until nothing remains but an ash-filled grave.

That night, I barely sleep. Yaelor knocks at my door as I ready myself for the morning's talks at the battle table.

But first, there is something I must do, something that is more important to me than anything else in this moment, and I do not care if that makes me selfish.

"Laith," Yaelor says, her body language telling me she is as nervous as I am. I stand there in a simple tunic, the fabric of which is rough against my skin, but it's better than the blackened, blood-stained armour I was wearing.

My heart beats faster then it has ever before, the weight of this meeting meaning more to me than I could have realised.

"Is she here?" I ask, my voice trembling.

"She is waiting in the clearings. I thought it would be best to do this away from everyone else." She smiles. "It is not every day you get to meet your daughter for the first time."

Taking an inhale of breath, I follow Yaelor through the village as wandering eyes fall on me. The village is even bigger than when I was here last. They all whisper to one another, some excited by my presence, others less so. For now, I simply ignore them. To me, there is no one else in the forest. The closer we get, the more I find my nerves taking over.

When we reach the clearing, I feel as though I can barely breathe. My throat is claggy, and I am in desperate need of a drink. I look around, but I cannot see her.

Jordell is standing by a large tree, smiling a tired, weary

smile. One that bears the weight of so many scars but for now is experiencing a joy that neither of us ever thought would greet us again.

"Is he here?" I hear a child's voice call out from behind the tree. It is so soft and sweet, like she is playing a game. There are nerves tinged on the end of her words, however. She feels the same as I do.

Jordell looks to his side and offers her a kind smile. "He is," he says. "As is your mother."

Yaelor moves towards the tree and whispers something that I can't hear. My whole body is trembling with anticipation, and I don't think that I take a breath. With a flurry of movement, Gillam darts behind her mum who now stands facing me. She raises her head and offers me a smile, and I admire her beauty.

"She wanted to do it this way," Yaelor laughs. "Laith, I would like you to meet someone." With this, a small figure steps out from behind Yaelor. She stands just above her mother's waist. She is thin, but she looks just like Yaelor, with her hair shaved at the sides and plaited back neatly down the centre of her head. She is wearing leathers like she is a miniature warrior, but she is clean and tidy. She doesn't seem to know where to look. I have no clue what Yaelor has told her of me, what she thinks of me, or even if she knew I existed.

"This is Gillam," Yaelor says. "Gillam, this is your father."

The two of us simply stand staring at each other. She tilts her head one way, then the other. I don't want to approach too quickly, I don't want to force her to acknowledge me when I have been absent all this time. I want to give her the freedom she deserves.

I am to her just a stranger, but for some reason, I feel

like I know Gillam. Her very name is borne from someone who meant so much to me. The fact that Yaelor chose it is a testament to her own feelings for Gillam. If not for her, Yaelor would not be alive, and our daughter would not be stood opposite me. She is the most beautiful thing I have ever laid eyes on, and in this moment, a fire stirs within me, a love that I did not know I was capable of. I would do anything for her, to ensure she is free and has a good life.

"Hi," I say, my voice trembling so badly that I can't tell if my simple hello was audible.

Gillam shuffles one of her feet in front of her, awkwardly rubbing her boot in the sand.

"Go on," Yaelor prompts her, and she seems to gain confidence from this.

"Hello," she says, her voice so soft that it melts the guards that I have in place.

"We have so much to catch up on. I have a lot of time to make up for," I say with a smile. I take a little step forward, but I do not wish to alarm her.

"It's okay," Yaelor adds, this time physically giving Gillam a nudge.

As if she had been waiting for permission, Gillam takes a deep breath and simply runs at me. "Papa!" she cries as her little feet scurry across the ground, and within a moment, she is upon me, diving through the air and wrapping herself around me. I squeeze her tightly, tighter than anything I ever have before, an embrace that lets her know that I am here, that I love her, and that I would do anything for her. Emotions swell in my belly as I spin her around in the air playfully, exploring each and every freckle on her face leading to her large green eyes. She is smiling at me, and in this moment, I feel acceptance, I feel as though I have one true purpose, and I wish that this could last forever. That time would stand still and allow us to be in this moment for as long as possible. I hug her again, and this time Gillam giggles.

How can a child endure the things that she has, seen the things that she has seen yet still be so happy and joyful?

"Thank you," I say, looking at Yaelor. She and Jordell stand side by side, completely overcome with the same emotions that I find myself shrouded in.

Joy, ecstasy, sadness, longing. It is all there.

Finally, I place Gillam on the ground, slowly allowing her feet to reach the floor, and she takes over my hand.

I know we don't have long, but for now, at least, I will share a small moment with my daughter, my one true meaning in life. As her soft hands pull me to look at the trees, all my worries fade. The weight I wear on my shoulders, the burden of the final fight that is coming, it all slips to the back of my mind. In this tender moment, we are free, and no matter how brief our time here may be, I understand that this is truly what happiness feels like.

31

RHAGOR

As I find myself in an old surrounding, I try and explore the strange tendrils of magic that I can feel gripped around my core. I feel something different, more power, coursing through me beyond that of which a spell caster should be capable of. At the same time, I feel strange, sentient, almost like I am not of this world but yet here I stand, like having one foot firmly in separate realms, between worlds.

The feeling is incredible. The life source surging through me is so much more than what I am used to with my previous host. I could get used to this.

I am standing at the base of a crumbled ruin, surrounded by collapsed stone walls. Vines creep up over them, masking them in their greens and browns. The sound of wildlife tells me that there are plenty of animals that now make their home here, a far cry from what the Kingdom of Zakron once was.

It takes me longer than I should to notice the bodies that are splayed around me. I must have inadvertently dragged them here with me when I opened the portal. A mixture of Elteran and Askelan soldiers are strewn about. One body that I recognise lies by a wall further ahead, his body covered in scorched, blackened marks. Pockets of pink and red mark where his skin has blistered and popped.

"How unfortunate," I say coldly, momentarily surprised by my new feminine voice. "This will take some getting used to." I saunter through the ruins, dragging my fingers against the rough, cracked surface of the stone.

Something feels strange, and not just because I have a newfound power. I am being drawn to something, but I don't know what. It is only when I pass one of the dead soldiers that I feel a pull towards them, a strange urge that I can't quite put my finger on.

When I look at the dead soldier, a strange, spectral glow emits from him. A green tendril of my own magic reaches out and grabs him, moving like the arm of a kraken as it drags the spectre free from the body.

"Hmph." I think for a moment, no clue how these powers work.

"How can I serve my queen?" the Askelan soldier asks, his voice loud and echoing, yet pained.

"How interesting," I muse as I study the other soldiers around me. My magic reaches out to their bodies in tandem and starts dragging their spirits free from their crisp corpses. Each of them stands to attention, awaiting instruction from me. Codrin is the last one to rise, his colossal frame dwarfing the others even as a spectre.

"My queen," he growls, "I am here to serve."

I clap my hands together and squeal in delight. My own undead army. Who would have thought it would be so simple? I curse myself that the thought of possessing

Morgana had not crossed my mind earlier, and I revel at how powerful I could have been.

"We have enemies that will be advancing on us soon," I say. "I need you and the other spirits to protect me at all costs."

"As you wish," Codrin says. He is every amount of the brooding hulk that he was in life. "You heard the queen, protect her at all costs."

The spectres spread out, moving into different formations around the ruined keep, not that the others are any match for me now. At least with my new abilities, it will give them even less of a chance.

"Where are you going?" Codrin asks. "Do you need me to stay with you?"

"No," I say, "keep watch, kill anything that steps foot on these lands."

"As you wish," he growls. He is even more menacing in this form than he was before.

I gather my bearings, looking out at the ocean that lies between where I stand and the mainland of Levanthria. It is a mesmerising view, one that I remember from back when I was younger. Knowing I am where the upper chambers of the Royal Family once were, I have only a short walk to find the ancient shrine that belongs to Opiya.

I can't help but smile when I see a figure standing at the base of the destroyed statue that was built in her honour. Her back is turned on me, her head bowed, and she is wearing a vibrant blue cloak.

"Mother," I say, a smile reaching every part of my face.

She does not turn.

"What have you done, Rhagor?" she asks. She knows it is me, despite my voice being completely different. Her voice is cold, not a hint of emotion towards me.

"What you forced me to do when you chose my sister over me," I say, a snide tone in my voice.

"I did what I had to. You were causing too much chaos, I had to stop you." She lowers her hood as she turns to face me.

She looks as though she is young enough to be my sibling, rather than older than time itself. Her hair is short and wavy, her skin soft and without blemish, unworn, untortured as if she has lived the most serene, peaceful of lives. She hasn't changed at all. Her face is a picture of kindness, of new life and beginnings. It is a shame she never afforded me any of those principles.

"I didn't want to, Rhagor," she says, taking a step forward before stopping herself, seemingly conflicted by her own thoughts. "You left me no choice, you tried to kill Zariah."

"Even now, when the world threatens to burn around you because of the things you did, you still choose her." Spit leaves my mouth as I slowly walk towards her. "Do you have any idea what it feels like, to be trapped in a prison where you can see the world around you grow, one day at a time, all while remaining motionless, no one to talk to, nothing to keep your sanity other than your own thoughts? It gave me a lot of time to think. Two thousand years to come up with delightful ways to end your life."

"And what will that achieve, Rhagor? After me, who next? When will all of this end?"

"When not one of you pathetic gods exists anymore. Consider this a cleanse. I am freeing this world of your duties to align the stars and bring about a new balance, freeing it of your boring rules."

"Do what you must. I will find a way to return."

"Will you, though? You have never been trapped here as a mortal, have you?" I charge forward with bile, hatred, and vitriol pouring out of every pore of my being, placing one hand on her back and then driving my sword through her stomach without a second's hesitation. She leans into me, mouth open wide with shock. Did she actually think I wouldn't do this? I have thought of this moment for so long that I demand to savour every last second of it as her life ebbs away. The hilt of my sword becomes wet with her warm blood as it seeps over my hand. Blood starts to trickle from her open mouth before I twist the blade and push it into her even further with gritted teeth.

"You deserve this," I seethe as I lean into her ear. Her breath quickens, and she tries to speak but is unable to. When I pull the blade free from her, she collapses to the floor, blood pooling around her.

"Goodbye, Mother," I say, and then I drive my sword into her over and over again, each time roaring out in anger as her blood laps up against my clothes, sticking to my skin. And I devour every second until she no longer moves, no longer breathes, her life ended.

I tilt my head and examine her. There is no spike in joy or happiness. I feel nothing for her, it is like she is a stranger to me. Then while gripping my sword, I raise her spirit from her body like I did the soldiers just before I arrived.

"How?" she cries out.

"NO!" I yell. "There is no afterlife for you." I don't know how to control this power, but green tendrils grab my mother in a choke hold and her spectral form gasps as my newfound magic starts tearing this form apart until her essence is eviscerated and I feel her presence no longer. She is gone. At long last, I am free from her.

I turn around and take a seat, planting my sword in front of me and watching over my mother's corpse, more than anything to make sure she is definitely dead. And then I start laughing, uncontrollable maniacal laughter, while I wait for the would-be legends of Levanthria to arrive.

32

JORDELL

Zariah, Vireo, Zerina, Ulrik, Esara, Laith, and myself stand on the edges of the camp. Yaelor, Killian, and a few others from the camp have come to send us off to battle. They stand solemnly, their heads bowed as they silently watch us ready ourselves for the fight to come. Morvin, Gregor, and Leandra also stand nearby, each of them ready to give their all to our cause. Elara beats her wings, sending a gust of air at my feet that causes me to look down at her.

Who would have thought that a little growlite – a creature that will grow ten times her current size until she's as large as a boar – would make such a fine companion? Her scaled feathers catch the sun, giving a sheen to her coat as she rubs her head against the upper part of my leg. Lowering my hand, I rub the top of her head to return the affection. Her scales are coarse to the touch, almost snake-like. She lowers her ears and lets out a soft rumble as she pushes her head into my hand further.

"You help look after everyone here," I say, talking to her as if she understands every word I say.

Laith is with Yaelor, saying his goodbyes to her and to the daughter he has only just met. Even in this moment, even in this darkest hour, he continues to put others' needs before his own. He looks saddened, as does Yaelor, and the two of them embrace before he kneels to the ground and gives Gillam a warm hug. I will be damned if he does not return. He deserves the chance to live his life, happy and free.

The others stand around me, ready to head to Zakron's Keep.

"Are you ready, old friend?" Vireo says with a smile.

"Can we ever be ready for what is to come?" I say.

"Just know we will give our all," Zerina says, her voice soft. She looks to her right where Ulrik and Esara stand, and offers them a polite nod that tells me she has made her peace with them.

"How do I open the portal?" I look at Zariah.

Zariah stands beside me, adorned in the battle armour of the fae folk: thin mail armour that looks similar to mithril but I am told is as light as air. It cascades down her body, and her poleaxe is strapped to her back. "Your staff is tethered to you," she says, "it is now the last remnants of the Elder Tree. You can channel the power of the forest through it, and with this, open a gateway. I need you to focus your mind, channel everything you have into your staff. Become one with it until your magic flows through it like breathing."

What she says sounds easy enough, yet it is a skill I have never harnessed. When my staff opened a gateway to the forest, I felt like I was being led by it in a time of need. Now it is I who must call on it to harness its energy.

"You make it sound so easy," I say coyly, feeling the weight of the situation.

"I have every faith in you," Laith says as he joins us.

Zariah turns to address the rest of the group. "I cannot say how long the gateway will remain opened when Jordell taps into the power of the forest. You will need to step through as quickly as possible. The more people that pass through, the more unstable it will become. When that happens, we may find ourselves scattered. Jordell has not used this power before, so chances are when we reach Zakron, we will be separated. Have your wits about you, as Rhagor is no fool; he will be waiting for us." She looks over at Gregor and the others. "If the gateway appears stable, seize the opportunity to try and pass through. The gods know we need all the help we can get if we are to finally bring an end to Rhagor. Just be aware of the possible consequences."

Gregor, Leandra, and Morvin nod in understanding.

"I will keep this camp safe until you return," Killian says. He steps forward and shakes Vireo's hand, then gives a nod of respect to the rest of the group.

The rest of us look at each other standing in a circle, and I notice that Esara reaches out to Ulrik's hand, then Zerina's. Zerina seems hesitant at first, but she grabs hold of Esara's hand and squeezes it before offering her a nervous smile. Zerina then reaches out for Vireo who in turn grabs hold of Laith's hand, and he does the same for Zariah until she eventually reaches out and squeezes my free hand. Her hand is colder than I expected, but her skin is soft and tender. She gives me a reassuring smile, and I close my eyes for a moment to channel my power as best I can, just as Zariah explained to me.

My energy courses through me, up through my feet and into my legs as if I draw on energy from the ground where we stand. The sensation is incredible, and I feel as though I could take the world on. The staff has changed the way in which I perceive magic. It no longer feels like a curse that will break my skin when I use it, and I am no longer crippled by the addiction that can take hold of all other magic users, save for Zerina.

A bluish white glow surrounds me, and my power emits a force of energy that swirls around me. I continue to focus as Zariah said, picturing Zakron, the place that I have called home since I exiled myself, my mind not able to comprehend that we could be there in a matter of moments as opposed to weeks of travel.

My magic surges through my stomach into my chest, causing me to feel like I have inhaled a sprig of mint leaves. The air suddenly becomes crisp and refreshing, like cold water runs through me. The feeling trails down my arm until it finally reaches my staff, at which point my staff starts to glow the familiar ice blue that its power emanates. The staff vibrates in my hand, and I try my hardest to keep my connection, the strength of my power only growing stronger with every passing moment, to a point where I think I could not let go of my staff even if I wanted to. I feel connected to it as though it is an extension of my body.

"Now, Jordell!" Zariah shouts through the storm of power. "Focus on Zakron, open the gateway."

I do as she says, and I think of the crumbled ruins, the broken shrine, the tower at the far side. I try and picture the sand-like stone that lies in ruin, walls collapsed, the chamber that was my room where I continued to research and carry out experiments, the etchings on the walls that I scribed as I descended into madness that only solitude can bring.

A brush of air forces its way in front of me, pressing so

hard against me that I almost lose grip of my magic, as though the strongest man pushes hard against my chest.

"That's it, Jordell!" Vireo says.

"Holy fuck!" Esara beams with wide eyes, mesmerised by the spectacle.

"GO!" I cry out. "I don't know how long I can hold on."

One by one, the others start to dive into the gateway without a moment's hesitation, save for Laith, who casts one final look at Yaelor and Gillam before charging forward.

"I'll see you on the other side," Zariah says before vanishing through the gateway.

It is my turn, and I step forward, feeling as if with each step I take, my feet are made of stone and metal. My body aches as I draw on so much energy, but finally I step through, just as Gregor, Morvin, and Leandra charge towards it.

I have no clue if they made it, as I am spat out of the other side of the gateway like I have been tossed out of a maelstrom. The world spins around me as I crash to a stop only when I slam into a wall.

Chaos has already broken out around us. I am alone, but I can hear the sound of battle already, as though a longer time has passed. When I gather my bearings, I realise I am in my old room. My desk lies overturned, and my papers lie across the floor, torn and trampled. I rush to the doorway, and when I exit the room, I see the carnage myself.

Spectral soldiers are everywhere, far more than our numbers. I run to the edge of the crumbled corridor and look down to see Vireo on one side of what used to be the great hall. He is firing arrow after arrow at the spectres. They fall like mortal men, at least, but I have no clue where they are coming from. The spectres wear the colours of

Eltera and Askelan warriors, and I know this must be linked somehow to the necromancy magic that Rhagor now possesses through taking control of Morgana's body.

Vireo continues to fire his arrows as Laith charges forward with the cover that Vireo allows him. He quickly enters into combat with a spectre, and the two break out into a fight.

"KILL HIM!" a pained voice calls out from behind me. When I turn, three spectral soldiers are bearing down on me, neither dead or alive, trapped between two realms. Instinctively, I smash my staff across the face of the first one that reaches me before reaching for my sword and pressing it into the second spectre. They wail in agonising pain, their cries reverberating in my mind. I channel my staff and emit a blast of energy that fires the three of them away from me. The remaining spectre slams against the wall at the opposite side of the crumbling corridor.

Before he has a chance to do anything else, I slam my sword into his chest, and with a groan, he starts to dissipate back to wherever it is he came from. As I look down the broken ruins around me, scores of more spectres rain down on me like rats. I am alarmed at how many there are, but at least they do not appear to be as strong as mortal men. I hold my ground as more spectres approach me, slicing them down from where I stand while simultaneously firing out blasts of energy, moving with an agility that my body should not allow as I draw strength through my staff. I continue my way towards the steps to the lower levels, driving back more and more spectres as they continue to charge, undeterred by their presence. No matter how many I slay, more seem to appear. They scream out their ethereal battle cries as I frantically look around for the others. I can hear blasts of magic, and flashes of fire in the distance tell me that Zerina is not too far.

By the time I reach the bottom of the stairs, my body is tired, but I must continue. I push through, I must find Rhagor, but I can't take him on alone.

I continue to push forward when an explosion sends me sprawling. The world around me rings like church bells in my mind, a high-pitched squeal ringing in my head. Plumes of dust and ash surround me as I watch at least five or six spectres disappear, their bodies destroyed even in reanimation.

I look around desperately for what caused the blast, and see that Morvin lies motionless on the ground. He is holding the cylindrical contraption that I saw before. The metal of it is shredded, like a force has torn through it. Morvin's body is slumped into an unnatural position. Blood trickles out of his mouth that's still curved in a maniacal grin, and his eyes are wide, yet vacant, and I know that he is no longer with us.

I can't see clearly, and it is difficult to breathe as I cough and heave with the dust that continues to settle around me.

"Is everyone okay?" I call out desperately, hoping there is a reply. No one calls back, but I can hear the sound of the battle nearby. As I take a step forward, I hear another groan.

"Who's there?" I ask, searching desperately through the settling explosion.

"Over here." It is Leandra. She is sat against a wall, mortar and stone covering her.

"What happened?" I ask.

"There were so many," she says. "We told the others to push forward, that we would hold them off as best we could. When there were too many, Morvin used whatever his magic is. He warned me to run, I tried." She coughs up blood, and the rattle in her chest betrays the severity of her injuries. "I just hope the others managed to get enough distance between us and the blast."

I place my hand on her shoulder, and with a glow of my staff, I do what I can to ease her pain, but I worry that her injuries are too grave.

"Thank you," she says as she exhales, her last breath prolonged. I brush my hand over her eyes and allow her to finally rest. Her bravery was commendable.

When I turn to leave, a dripping noise causes me to look down, and I see my own blood splashing onto the floor. Some form of metal is sticking out of my side, likely from the blast. I channel my magic to try and heal myself as best I can while pulling the metal from my skin. It is as though I have been pierced by white-hot fire as I pull it from my body. As I channel my magic, more spectres start descending onto my position.

Slamming my staff into the ground, I ready myself to continue the fight, my concern growing; we have already lost two of our warriors, and I worry what has befallen the others.

There are so many, they just keep filling the room. The more that surround me, the less chance I feel I have of surviving this.

With a roar, Gregor charges into the room, his greatsword coated in a green flame that is as fierce as his fury. He runs free of the plumes of smoke and dust, barrelling into one of the spectres and swinging his blade, covering a enormous amount of space in front of him. He cleaves at least four spectres in half with one strike as he continues to roar. He grabs another spectre by the throat and picks him up into the air before driving his flaming sword through its chest and tossing it at the feet of the others. The spectres change the focus of their attention to Gregor as he continues to cleave his way through the fallen soldiers. He is like a berserker, enraged and unforgiving as he doles out his own form of retribution. He is every bit of the monster hunter I have studied for so long, and so much more.

The spectres start to swarm him, grabbing hold of him in sheer desperation as more and more of them start to latch on.

"Go!" Gregor bellows, his eyes meeting my own as he draws them towards himself. He emits a blast of green energy that is akin to Morgana's necromancy powers, and it causes me to wonder where he draws his magic from. The spectres that cling on are eviscerated where they touch him, their hollow screams echoing throughout the destroyed former great hall.

"Now!" Gregor demands as he continues to wave his greatsword, cleaving spectre after spectre.

I continue through the ruins until I can no longer hear the sound of Gregor fighting behind me. Explosions and magical blasts continue to cause rumbles in the earth. The walls shake, and debris falls from above. Sections of the keep start to collapse, causing more traps for me to be wary about.

As I follow the ruined path, I know where it is where I must head, where we must make our final stand. It is where the shrine to Opiya was on the far side of the keep.

My chest heaves as I descend on the position. I have the advantage of knowing where it is. As for the others, I can only hope I see them on my way so that they can follow me to Rhagor's location.

When I arrive on the ruined shrine, I am mortified by what I see.

"NO!" I cry out. A body lies on the ground by Rhagor, who is still in possession of Morgana's body. His sword is outstretched, protruding out of his sister's back.

"Zariah!" I cry out as he pulls his blade from her.

"This is the last time I am going to kill you," Rhagor says as Zariah collapses at his feet.

I charge down on him. One way or another, this battle ends now. I charge up my staff and let out my own battle cry as I see Morgana's face warp into a sinister smile.

33

VIREO

Healing magic is considered one of the most dangerous, for the spell caster at least. The more grave the injury the greater essence of magic that will need to be drawn on, draining the caster of their own life source.

Frederica Jorai, Healers Guild, KR 199

Nausea grips the pits of my stomach as I land in what I assume is Zakron. It takes me a few moments before I recognise the crumbling ruin where I came in search of Jordell. That feels like a lifetime ago now.

"Fuck!" I call out. No sooner do I look out than one of those blasted spectres is taking a swing at my head.

The blow is blocked by a blade dangerously close to my face.

Laith pushes back the spirit before slicing his sword through its chest. It vanishes into the air like a wisp on the wind, and Laith helps me up.

"They knew we were coming, they were prepared," he

says as I get to my feet. He looks around the ruins where we stand.

"Where are the others?" I ask. I can't see any sign of them, and that worries me.

Before Laith can answer, there is a commotion ahead of us, and more of these blasted spirits start charging towards us, weapons drawn, teeth bared. It is as though we are in the grip of a nightmare. This whole scenario does not feel real.

"Push forward," I say. "We can't afford to let them flank us." I draw on my bow and reach for an arrow, firing it into the chest of one of the spectres. I half expect it to pass right through, but I am pleasantly surprised when it beds into its chest and slams it to the ground. The spectre disappears like a flame flickering into the air. I continue to reach for my arrows, taking cover behind a pillar that still stands after all this time. My arrows allow Laith to press forward, and he quickly strikes down some more spectres.

I follow him to the far side of the room, keeping my bow drawn, and when another spirit steps from beyond the doorway, I send it back to the afterlife when my arrow burrows into its head. The deathly screams they emit when they pass is haunting and terrifying in equal measure.

We continue forward, killing every spectre that crosses our path. I am impressed with how Laith wields his blade, as though he hasn't been away at all. But it is strange seeing him so much more mature than the last time we met. So much has happened since then.

"We need to find the others," Laith says. "Rhagor will be too powerful for us, we need numbers to defeat him."

"We must continue our path, we do not know if the others have made it this far yet. We don't even know if they are here."

"I pray they are. Rhagor was a monster when he took over my body. I dread to think what he is now that he has Morgana's powers. You only have to look on the spirits that he now has control over."

We reach an opening which I assume used to be some form of garden space. Laith destroys another spectre with relative ease while I take down a few more that are on the upper levels surrounding us.

"Going somewhere?" The deep rumbling voice causes me to stop, sliding in the dirt. His voice echoes, pained and broken as I turn to face a familiar enemy.

"Codrin," I say. He stands with a blade in one hand and his whip in the other. His skin is decayed, charcoaled and burned, the familiar ethereal glow surrounding him. "Just how many times do I have to do this!"

Codrin simply growls. If anger was a liquid, it would be dripping from him as he breathes heavily, psyching himself up.

"I have to ask, is that air you're breathing?"

Laith turns to face him too. "There are scars on my back that I think we need to have a conversation about."

"I've got this, Laith. You continue on your path, you must find the others."

"This is not just your fight, Vireo. Besides, at your age, I am guessing you will need all the help you can get," he says, a flash of the young confidence reminding me of our past conversations in the forest.

Codrin charges down on us, a theme that is becoming common with him. I quickly fire arrows at him, and all but one hit him, bedding into him like he is some kind of spiked creature. It does not stop him. Something is different about him than the other spectres.

"Shit!" I curse. "He drank an elixir moments before he died."

Codrin slams into me, taking with me any air that I held in my chest as I crash into the ground. He lashes out at Laith, and though Laith tries to block him, Codrin's power is incredible. With a crunch, Laith slams into the wall.

Codrin's attention returns to me as I crawl backwards on the ground, using my feet to push me away from him as fast as I can.

As he approaches, I continue to fire arrows into his chest before he barrels down on me. He raises his blade in the air and slams it down, and I roll to the side as the earth flies up beside me. As I move away, he coils his whip and cracks it towards me, catching me square in the back as I try to make some distance between us. Blistering pain sears through my skin, and I cry out in agony until I roll to a stop. The pain is intense, and I arch my back as I grit my teeth. Codrin is already on me, a wide grin in the corners of his Elven mouth.

Laith crashes into him shoulder first. It throws Codrin off only slightly, however, and he spins with his sword just as Laith is bringing his own blade up to defend himself. I muster what resolve I have to climb to my feet. I will be damned if I die on my back. The skin in the centre of my back feels as though it is on fire, like a white-hot poker has been held there. I double down on Codrin as he pushes Laith back and takes another swing. This time, it is my turn to defend my friend, and I block Codrin's strike, but he's even stronger than our last fight, no doubt charged by the magic drawn from the elixir he drank. It has some how corrupted him, even in this spectral form.

The three of us continue fighting in the gardens, dodging and blocking Codrin's sword strikes while simultaneously avoiding his whip as it viciously cracks the air around us. His speed is alarming, each strike reminiscent of the hatred we share for one another.

He unfurls another crack of his whip and I barely avoid it, but Laith is less lucky as it lashes against his shoulder. He cries out in pain as he drops to the ground. Codrin laughs abruptly.

He swings his sword at me, building up his momentum as I lead him away from Laith.

Sword strikes fly at me, followed by the cracks of his brutal whip as I continue to spin and dart back from him, dodging what I can. I cannot afford to let that whip hit me again. I don't think my body could cope with the force of it. My back feels wet and warm where my blood trickles down from the last blow. Codrin's face is contorted with anger and rage. He is determined to bring me to an end.

My arms are beginning to tire, heavy from the blows that I keep needing to defend against, when Codin changes his tactic. With a roar of unadulterated fury, he boots me square in the chest. I hit a wall behind me, and he pushes against me with his sword. I fetch mine up and stop him from pressing his blade into my neck, but I cannot maintain this position for long. His putrid, spectral breath lingers on my face as he snarls at me like a wild animal, chomping and biting at the air as if he is feral. His breath is cold, like the death that has touched him, yet he smells vile, like decomposition has already taken over.

With a roar, he cries out, loosening his force against me. He turns, and over his shoulder, I can see Laith stood with my bow in hand. Codrin claws at the arrow that is protruding out of his shoulder, and taking my opportunity, I drive my sword into Codrin's chest, pushing him backwards. He staggers, still flailing, somehow not vanishing like the other spirits have. Fuelled by his rage, he is not ready to go. It doesn't injure him as an arrow should, but he is no longer of this world, he is something else, and I have no idea how the laws of spirits raised from the dead work.

Laith leaps through the air and grabs hold of him from behind, straining against Codrin's weakened strength, gripping hold of his arms as best he can. I drive my sword down, slicing through his forearm and detaching it. His whip falls on the ground, and Codrin snarls as I grab hold of it and wrap it around his neck.

"GO!" I call out to Laith, who jumps out of the way as I swing back while Codrin desperately claws at his throat. We have the upper hand, but it still takes every ounce of my strength even in his weakened state as he bucks around like a wild bull. I yank back as hard as I can again, and he drops to one knee. Laith charges at him, and his sword meets Codrin's neck as he detaches the Elf's head in one strike. It bounces off the ground, contorted features and blackened eyes staring at me as his body erupts into wisps of flames. He vanishes into the air.

The two of us stand panting, both injured from the fight but somehow still standing.

"Even the afterlife doesn't want him!" Laith says, straightening himself and arching his back. "Vireo, your back?"

I try to look over my shoulder, but I can't see it. All I can feel is the warmth that my blood brings as it oozes down my spine.

"It's only a scratch," I say with a wince. "How is your shoulder?"

"I will live," he says. "Come, we must continue our path. We need to end this once and for all."

34
ULRIK

There are guildmembers who have become too forthcoming with the sharing of information of our ways. Valeras Xeck is one such fool. He knows too much and he is saying too much. You know what to do. His whereabouts are thought to be around the city of Eltera. Make sure you burn this after reading.

Annonymous, Burnt Note, KR Unknown.

White-hot flames lick up around us as Zerina casts her magic against the undead soldiers that were waiting for us when we stepped through the gateway. Thankfully, I found myself alongside Zerina and Esara, who immediately set about fighting. Zerina seemed to know that they could be killed as if they were mortal, their souls vanishing no sooner than they are greeted by her power. Taking confidence from this, Esara dances around back-to-back with Zerina, and although she has no magic power as fierce as what Zerina holds, she is just as deadly with a blade.

The two protect each other as they continue to fight wave upon wave of the ghosts, and I wonder if the same would happen to me if my life were to be taken. I feel similar, yet somehow different. There are scores of dead soldiers' bodies scattered around Zakron's Keep. No doubt this is where their spirits have been raised from by the damned Rhagor, who is somehow controlling them. He was ready for us when we got here.

Cutlass in hand, I do what I can to strike down the spectres over and over again. They seem weaker than humans, but there are simply too many of them. No matter how many we strike down, more appear, the wailing, the screaming getting louder and louder as though they are in agonising pain just by simply being here.

"What do we do?" I ask. We can't simply wait here, we are walking into a trap here. It is only a matter of time before we are overrun.

"We need to find the shrine. Where are the others?" Zerina says as, with a flick of her wrist, she sends a ball of molten fire into the chest of a spirit. She grimaces and drops to one knee.

"What's wrong?" Esara says, killing the spirit in front of her before placing a hand tenderly on Zerina's back.

"I have used a lot of magic, it is taking its toll on me," Zerina says, her face already weary.

"What about the water? Surely that will help you?" Esara asks, quite matter-of-fact in her approach as if she is talking to a child.

"I ran out before the battle. I am afraid I can only draw on my own lifeforce now."

"Fuck!" Esara says. "Why didn't you say? You need to conserve your power."

More spirits descend on our position, and with a cry of

pain, Zerina fires a large blast of fire, blocking the entranceway where they pour through.

"Zerina!" Esara scolds her. "What are you doing, I just said!"

They have no time to argue as the spirits continue to push through Zerina's magic and swarm us. Esara and I hack and slash our way through them as Zerina gathers her composure.

"Use your sword, conserve your magic for when you need it most," I demand. She does as I say and draws on her own cutlass, and then the three of us continue to stand against the spectres, but there are simply too many of them.

"What do we do?" I ask as I finish another spectre, its essence disappearing as I stab it through its heart.

"I'm thinking, I'm thinking," Esara says as she acrobatically rolls out of the way of a strike before slicing through a spectre of her own.

"Perhaps we can lend aid?" a thick accent that I do not recognise calls upon us. It is the Dwarf from the camp, I think his name was Morvin. He has managed to make it through the portal, alongside another woman whose name I do not recall. She carries two hatchets in her hands as she starts spinning through the spectral warriors like a storm of violence, slicing through multiple enemies and allowing us some much-needed breathing space.

"Morvin!" Esara beams with delight. "You are here!"

Morvin looks at her strangely, then looks at me and Zerina quizzically.

"There is a lot to explain," Zerina says. "I am so glad you are alive, old friend."

Morvin steps forward, gripping the strangest contraption I have ever seen in my life.

"Come, Herelda, let's do what we can," the Dwarf says

before unfurling a powerful blast of energy from his weapon. The force is incredible as it tears through multiple spectres, and he starts laughing with a crazed expression on his face.

We continue to defend our position, but more and more of them keep appearing, their strikes getting dangerously close.

"There are too many!" Esara calls. "We need to fall back."

"Go," Morvin says. "I have got this."

"No, not again, not after last time," Esara says. Morvin draws a confused expression as if he isn't quite sure who Esara is. Then it dawns on me that he thinks I am her. The thought gives me a headache.

"Lass, fall back. I can give you the time you need."

There is a doorway behind us; perhaps through there we can find another way to reach the shrine.

"GO!" Morvin demands.

"I will stay with you," the other woman says as she buries both of her hatchets into another spirit.

The rest of us make for the door as more spirits than I can count enter the chamber. I can hear Morvin's laughter over the blasts of his cannon.

"See you soon, my love," he says, and then he reaches into his pocket and pulls something out. "Go!" he repeats. He then focuses on the other woman. "Get as much distance as you can, there are too many."

Grabbing hold of Esara's arm, I drag her kicking and screaming through the doorway, followed by Zerina. The door shuts behind us and we barely take a few steps before an almighty explosion sends us all hurtling through the air.

I cough and splutter as I drag myself back to my feet.

Esara is on her hands and knees, as is Zerina. I help them up. "Come, we must find the shrine."

"Ulrik," Zerina says with shock on her face. She is staring at my abdomen.

I look down at a piece of a blade that is protruding from me. I should be in pain, I should be greeting death. But I feel nothing. No pain, no agony. The blood that seeps from me is thicker and darker than it should be, and I am greeted by a putrid smell. Instinctively, I grab hold of the broken blade and pull it from my body, still feeling nothing other than the sensation of it leaving me. It doesn't hurt at all.

"Are you okay?" Zerina asks.

"I am fine," I say. "Come, we must make haste, otherwise Morvin's sacrifice is in vain."

Esara and Zerina both look saddened as if they have lost a friend and ally. His shall be a name that I etch into my memory. I owe him that.

"How are you not dead?" Esara asks. "I can't lose you again, not after everything we have been through."

"I already am," I remind her.

Cries and howls from the spectres erupt behind us as they start to chase us.

"RUN!" I bellow.

Esara sprints ahead and takes a left, and Zerina hobbles after her, her mobility hindered by the blast.

We continue running as fast as we can, hurtling through the ruins as blasts of magic cause dust and debris to fall from the roof.

"Keep going!" I stride behind them, and as fast as I run, I do not feel my reserve of energy depleting, the other two clearly lagging compared to me.

"Look out!" I cry, seeing the wall collapsing in front of us. I charge forward as fast as I can, slamming into Esara and knocking her out of the way as the crumbling wall falls on top of me.

Zerina, where is Zerina? I think as stone knocks me to the ground.

"Ulrik!" Esara calls out.

Darkness overcomes me, but there is no pain.

I think back to nicer times, a life spent at sea as part of the King's Navy, then my thoughts go back even further. To pushing Esara on a rope swing when she was just a child, prior to me enlisting. It was a simpler time, and I wish more than anything that I could take my sister back to that moment, away from all of this.

I refuse for this to end here. With all my might, I push up against the intense weight that sits on my back.

I can hear Esara and Zerina both calling my name. It sounds like they are trying to pull the stone from me, but it is hard to tell as I am surrounded by darkness. I continue to press up, growling and roaring as I use all my strength. To my surprise, the stones start to move, and I push myself free. It is inhuman. I display more strength than I should, and I wonder what else the Resurrection Stone has done to me until, with one final push, I am able to stand tall within the centre of the rubble.

Esara and Zerina watch on in disbelief.

"I thought you were gone, again." Esara smiles, joyous in her expression. She looks wild, as if she is actually enjoying this fight, as though she only feels alive when we find ourselves in imminent danger.

Ahead of us, a bright blue light forces itself out from a nearby chamber. I can feel the intensity of the magic from where I stand as debris flies through the air.

"Jordell," Zerina says, and the three of us charge towards him to lend him our aid.

35

LAITH

When we reach the chamber, I skid to a stop, weapon drawn, exhausted but ready to continue the fight. Jordell stands opposite Morgana's body, but it is Rhagor who he faces.

Jordell's staff is bedded into the ground as he draws on his power. Rhagor simply stands smiling at him as he waits to make his move.

"It's over, Rhagor," I call out.

He snaps his head up to me in disgust. "However strange it is seeing a face I have called my own, you are foolish if you think you can actually stop me. I am more powerful than you can possibly imagine. I am no longer bound by the magic contained within my sword. Yes, that is where my essence lives, but this –" he looks down at his arms and they start to glow with the green magic of Morgana's necromancy. "Well this makes me a god amongst men."

The ground tremors underfoot as everything around us starts to rumble and shake with Rhagor's power.

"You will not win," Jordell says, standing firm despite

the sheer power of magic that Rhagor is emitting. It truly is incredible and I have never felt power like it.

"Oh, but I will. I already have." Rhagor takes a step forward. "I stand by the bodies of my mother and my sister." He looks down at their corpses that lie by his feet. "This is only the beginning. The gods have returned, they walk amongst us now."

With a roar, Rhagor pushes forward bright green tendrils of power that whip out from multiple directions at Jordell.

Jordell manages to contain this as best he can, using his staff to create a barrier between him and the strikes. Bright flashes of light spray out as if the stars themselves fight one another. Jordell holds his own against the onslaught of magic.

Behind me there is a flash of heat.

Zerina and the others are bearing down on our location. She has used her magic to dispel a group of spectres that were advancing on our position.

I charge forward, advancing on Rhagor, drawing back on my sword as I reach him. His magic flicks up and grabs hold of me before tossing me to the side like a ragdoll, and then he does the same with Vireo. Meanwhile, Jordell continues to stand firm, using his barrier magic to deflect the tendrils of power that threaten to grip him in a stranglehold.

I jump back to my feet, dodging the tendrils that move more like tentacles. It is as though we are fighting against a kraken. I manage to weave myself close enough, but Rhagor does not hesitate to pull up his sword from the ground, and I block his strike. I hate him for what he did to me, for everything I had to endure him doing while in possession of my body. He has taken so many lives, he cannot be allowed to continue.

"You will pay for what you have done!" I shout. While I distract him, Vireo and Jordell grow closer. Jordell forces forward a blast of power with a blinding light, which crashes into Rhagor, forcing him back with a furious snarl. He collapses onto one knee, and Vireo leaps through the air, firing an arrow. Rhagor's magic is too strong, however, and one of the tendrils stops the arrow mid-flight, spins it, and flicks it back at Vireo.

"NO!" I call out as Vireo collapses to the ground. When he lands, he clasps his hands to his stomach where the arrow has buried deep into his flesh.

I raise my sword and strike again and again, each blow unfurling all my anger on Rhagor, who simply laughs as he blocks each and every blow.

It is as though he is savouring every moment of the fight, his power unlike anything we have faced before. He pushes his hand out at Jordell, and one of the tendrils flicks out and catches his feet, knocking him over, too.

"You are all pathetic!" Rhagor snarls. "Did you actually think you could best me?"

Rounding my sword through the air, I lose my balance, and he grabs hold of the back of my head before driving his pommel over and over again into my face until I see nothing other than a flash of light as my vision is replaced with stars in a vast and infinite universe.

He only stops when another blast of magic crashes into his chest. I just about manage to keep my balance as I gather myself from the blow. My face is throbbing, but I cannot stop, I will not stop.

Zerina continues to fire blast after blast at Rhagor, which he continues to block with his magic, each time being forced to take a step back, closer to the edge of the crumbling ruin.

Zerina continues her volley until she has no magic left. She cries out in pain as she collapses, Ulrik catching her before she falls. There is only myself and Esara left standing.

The pirate sprints forward, her sword in hand.

"What are you doing?" I call out to her.

She looks at me with an almost accepting smile. She seeks to distract Rhagor, she has seen what I have seen, and as she swings her cutlass at him, his attention falls on her.

"Pathetic," Rhagor says as another green tendril darts forward, this time not in a grabbing motion but like a blade itself.

"Esara!" Ulrik shouts her name but it is too late. The magic has passed through her and she is suspended in the air as if she has run into a spike. She spits out blood as her head snaps back, but Esara doesn't cry out. She simply smiles, staring Rhagor in the eyes.

Siezing my opportunity, I dive at Rhagor, catching him off guard and grabbing hold of his shoulder with one hand before driving my sword through him with the other.

In an instant, his magic vanishes, and I hear Esara crumple onto the ground.

I lean in close to Rhagor's ear and I say to him, "For Orjan." Then I push him back to the edge of the footing, overhanging the cliffs below.

"This can't be. You still won't win. Don't you see? I win, I have brought chaos," Rhagor says as he frantically tries to keep his balance. He almost does as well, until a blast of arcane power slams into his chest, sending him hurtling over the edge of the keep and tumbling to the jagged rocks below.

We did it. We defeated Rhagor. His reign is over.

Rhagor's sword lies on the ground as I listen to Morgana's voice scream as Rhagor plummets to his death. Bound by a mortal body, there is no way he can survive that fall.

"Keep away," Jordell demands, knocking me away from the sword. "Do not touch the blade, to do so only gives Rhagor chance to return once again."

"You did it, Laith, you did it! Perhaps your prophecy wasn't wrong after all, Jordell." Vireo says through pained, laboured breathe.

My attention at once returns to Vireo who sits with his hands clasped over his stomach, holding the arrow that has struck him.

"Jordell, do something," I demand, kneeling at Vireo's side.

"Esara!" Ulrik shouts out as he and Zerina rush to her. As vocal as Vireo is, Esara is the opposite. Ulrik scoops her up and brushes her hair free from her face.

"It's okay, brother, it's okay," she says.

"Jordell, is there anything you can do?" Zerina asks. "Help them."

Ulrik frantically looks over Esara, desperately looking for a way to help her. "DO SOMETHING!" he demands, a similar growl like the spectres comes from his voice that is terrifying.

"It's my time, Ulrik. I have done a lot of things in this life. The world may be free now, but I have made my peace, and it is not a world that I should be free to walk."

The sword beyond Jordell starts to glow, brightly.

"We do not have time," he says. "You need to leave now. We have to destroy the sword. It is the only way we will prevent Rhagor from ever returning." He looks at the staff.

"There is only one item powerful enough to do this, and only one able to wield it."

"No," I tell him, "there must be another way, we can find another way."

"This is the way it needs to be," he says simply. "When this is done, you must take the staff and return it to the forest, do you understand?"

"No, Jordell, you need to come with us."

"There is no other way,"

Molten tears fall from my face. "Jordell –"

"Take the others, get as far away as you can." He turns his back before looking over his shoulder directly at me. "I am proud of you, my son."

He raises his staff high into the air and starts channelling his power. His magic splays around the room, projecting flashes of icy blue and white magic that swirls round him. He is grimacing, but focusing everything he has into one last strike.

I pick up Vireo and set off running, and Ulrik does the same with Esara. With no option, we make our escape, Zerina alongside us.

I glance over my shoulder as Jordell brings down his staff onto the blade and an almighty flash of light passes us. It is almost blinding, and within seconds, the energy starts destroying the keep behind us as we run. The ruin disintegrates as though it falls into the earth, and still we run as fast as we can, through the crumbling ruins, my legs burning. We have to make it.

When we reach a clearing, a force of energy crashes into our backs and we are launched forward as the explosion takes grip of the keep.

36
MORGANA

I t is a strange sensation being dead, one that I cannot quite explain. It is just as those visions played out all those years ago as I stare up at the cliffs above, an explosion causing all manner of stone and masonry to collapse the cliff edge down on top of us.

I can't move, my body is broken, no longer of use. After all, I am dead. I know I am.

As the stones fall onto me, everything goes black. Darkness surrounds me until I see a familiar ethereal glow of a figure walking towards me.

"It is done, Morgana," the voice says.

"What now?" I ask.

"What you promised me," the figure says, finding simplicity in his answer. "Now rise, and do as what we agreed. Reap." The figure glows brighter and brighter as his light reaches out towards me at an incredible speed until all I can see is vast, never-ending whiteness.

"Rise, my harbinger of death." The words echo loudly in my head, a sharp stinging pain forcing me to close my eyes tight. "You are neither alive nor dead, blood-bound to serve as a guide between this world and the afterlife, for all eternity."

When my eyes snap open, I am looking down on my own body. My mouth is wide, and blood crawls from the corners of my mouth. My arms and legs are snapped and bent in unnatural positions, bones protruding from my body. The back of my head is nothing more than pulp.

I draw on the original visions of me being kicked off the side of a tower. It was Laith who dealt my final blow, he spoke the words that I heard over and over, every time that I dreamt this moment:

"*For Orjan.*"

It happened how it was meant to, though in my visions, I did not understand I was being possessed by Rhagor.

I feel strange. The wind blows but I feel no breeze against my skin, just the faint flicker of my magic. I move my arms to inspect them, just to make sure it is me in control of them.

From my body, a glowing form stands, and it only takes me a moment to realise who it is.

"Rhagor," I say as he looks at me with bewilderment.

He is tall, strong, with a powerful physique. He has a middle-aged appearance, and his hair is slicked back. His very demeanour is odious even in this form.

"Morgana," he says in surprise, "you look different." He looks up at the cliffs as if searching for a way back.

"There is no way back for you, your sword is destroyed."

"Then I will find another way."

"There is no way back from where you are going," I say coldly as I harness my powers, understanding what I must do. Green tendril hands burst from the ground where he stands and grab hold of his ankles, followed by more and more.

"These are the souls of those that you damned. I think they have something they want to tell you."

"No, no!" He panics, trying to prise his legs free but his efforts are futile, he cannot control this fate, not when I have control of the pathway between this world and the afterlife. There is a balance to be restored. One that was destroyed by the actions of this man and my own to a certain extent, something I will gladly spend an eternity making up for. It is no more than what I deserve.

"Morgana, please."

I turn and ignore him as he screams loudly, the gnarled hands clawing at him, tearing his spectral flesh from bone as he is torn limb from limb.

Until his essence is completely destroyed.

37

LAITH

I have heard tales on Rivah of a band of unlikely heroes, forging a path that is bringing forth its own legends. A rogue, a cleric, a fighter and a bard. This band of rag tag heroes are said to be causing quite the stir, foiling werewolves, witches and more.

Alderic Smith, Personal Note, 259KR

We stand in the forest after a long journey home. I cannot believe that Jordell is gone, but I am proud to have known him. To be able to call him my father. We have laid to rest those that fell in the final battle against Rhagor, those that we were able to, anyway. My heart is broken and I am bereft with grief. How am I supposed to cope with what has happened? How can I expect those of Levanthria to simply accept that my appearance may not have changed, but I am not Rhagor? Surely people will not believe us. There are so many who have sacrificed everything. They gave everything in that final fight, and they will be remembered for eternity, for they are the true legends of Levanthria, the ones who will forever be immortalised for the things that they have done.

I look down at the ground and watch as a tear falls from my face and splashes in the soil. When I look up, I notice how the trees have withered as the magic slowly fades from the soil with the death of the Elder Tree. It is why I am here, to finish what Jordell asked of me.

"Are you ready?" Yaelor asks. She stands by my side, comforting me in my grief. I take a deep inhale of breath and pay my respects to the grave we have fashioned in Jordell's honour: stones piled together with a wooden carving that Gillam made for him. Beside him are the stone graves we have fashioned for the bodies we were able to bring back.

"He was a good man," I say. "Because of him, we are all safe, we can all step into a new world."

"They all were," Yaelor says. "They gave everything for all of us, and we will honour them in this life and beyond."

"That we will." Vireo's hand clasps my shoulder as he hobbles next to me, still not recovered from his injuries. I am grateful that he is still here.

"We will remember them," I say, my heart breaking for the losses that we have faced, guilt gripping me to my core that we have survived, that we get to live our lives.

"Are you sure this will work?" I ask, turning to look at Zerina.

"We can only try. My Elven knowledge of magic only goes so far." She stands beside Ulrik and Esara. They have all come to pay their respects. Esara was so close to death, but somehow made it back, somehow she is still here.

Surrounded by my friends and allies, I step forward with Jordell's staff and walk in front of his grave.

"We will make sure the world knows your name," I say

before driving his staff into the top of the grave. As it buries into the soil, the tip of the staff glows blue as it nestles in its new position, its new home. White veins reach out from the base of the staff into the soil towards the trees, and we all watch on in wonder as new life breathes into the decaying forest. Vibrant greens and luscious, exotic flowers grow from the soil, and I know in an instant that from this spot, a new Elder Tree will grow with the last remnants of the tree that gave new life. It is a symbol of what we stand for, of what is to come, and I stand proudly beside my friends as we continue to pay our respects to the fallen.

"This marks a new dawn for Levanthria," Vireo says. "The world will not be the same, but with you here to lead it into a new era, Laith, we can only prosper. Jordell would be proud." He pats me on the shoulder again and turns to leave along with the others, leaving me to my thoughts with only Gillam and Yaelor by my side.

"I can't do this," I say to Yaelor.

"You can. You can do it for your father, do it for your daughter."

"How can I lead?"

"Because it was your destiny."

There is so much to do, so much to process. I have watched Levanthria crumble while Rhagor took control of my body for so many years that sometimes I feel like it was me who was responsible. After all, it was me that freed him, it was me that enabled him to walk this world and cause the chaos that he did.

"We will erect statues across Levanthria to honour those who gave their lives," I say. The grief I am feeling causes me pain in the centre of my chest. It is a heavy pressure, but one I want to endure as I do not want to forget them, I can't forget them. They have made me the man I am, moulded me in the white-hot flames of life, and despite everything that may have passed, I will be forever grateful to them. I bow my head once more, solemn and withdrawn. "How will I rule? How can I expect the people to follow me after everything Rhagor did while in my body?"

"Because you are a good man and you will be a fine leader," Vireo says. He moves in front of me and kneels, bowing his head. "You are not Rhagor. The people will see that. We will help them see that by righting all the wrongs that he has inflicted on everyone."

"How do you mean?" I ask.

"We will return to Askela with you. Those that want to return home now can. I give you my word and my honour that I will stand by your side throughout this next chapter of Levanthria's story. No doubt this will be filled with tales of valour and prosperity." There is a steely conviction to Vireo's words. "Long live King Laith."

Everyone takes a knee around me, and I am overcome with emotion.

Zerina, Ulrik, an injured Esara, Gregor, Killian, members of the community here, they all kneel before me.

"Long live King Laith," they all say in unison.

"Please, there is no need to bow to me, even out of respect. I am your equal. Please stand." I wave my hands, gesturing for them to rise. I do not want to rule like this.

As they stand, it is I who takes a knee in front of them. My voice trembles as I speak, but I know the message that I wish to convey.

"Know this, as king" – I look across to Gillam, who clasps Yaelor's hand tightly – "as king regent, by the new remnants of the Elder Tree, I swear to you all that it is I that will serve you and the people of Levanthria. For too long have we lived in fear, been impoverished by the greed and vanity of others. It ends today. We will work together, we will rebuild, and we will prosper. We will form a council, one that stops one single ruler having absolute power. I will spend the rest of my life righting the wrongs that Rhagor inflicted on you all, in my body. I want the world to see that Levanthria can be a beacon of hope. This is my vow."

"Long live the king!"

"Long live the king!"

"Long live the king!"

The cheers vibrate through the trees, the thunderous chorus slamming into my chest so hard my heart hammers like a drum.

I bow my head to them all.

A warm hand takes hold of mine, soft and gentle. I look down to see Gillam looking up at me, less hesitant as she accepts me as her father. In Gillam, I see flashes of my friend who she is named after in her big hazel eyes. She is the future, she is who will lead Levanthria into a new age. She will bring forward a new age of prosperity, one never seen in these lands.

And it is my duty to make sure that she becomes that leader, that she learns how to rule, how to help, how to support, how to thrive. Because it is her and all the other children of these lands that are the future. As Jordell once taught me, the seeds we sow now will bring new prosperity in the future.

After all, legends are not born, they are forged.

EPILOGUE

M*organa*

Reaping souls, helping them pass from this life to the next, that is my life now. I have aided those that helped us free this world from Rhagor's grip pass the bridge across from this world to the afterlife, and I hope in that life, they can find the peace that they so deserve.

I wander the land between Askela and the Forest of Opiya, where the Battle for Levanthria took place. So many souls were lost here. Most of them, I have already helped cross over to the afterlife as they deserve. That is my duty now.

But there is one soul more than any other that I have been in desperate search of all this time.

The ground is still scarred from the fight, but the bodies are gone, consecrated and buried.

"Morgana?"

His voice brings a shiver down my spine and in an instant, I know it is him. I turn to see his spirit, a face that I thought I would never see again, and my legs grow weak as I nearly collapse.

"Orjan," I say as he rushes to catch me.

"I am here to help you, I am here to free you," I say as I raise my head to look up at him, and the two of us share a kiss.

"How do you mean?" he asks, his voice more tender than I remember. His touch is delicate as he holds me, and I place a hand on his chest. I feel no heartbeat.

"You died," I said, "as did I."

"What happens now?"

"Now I must serve the being that granted me this power. I did what I had to do to help stop Rhagor. This is my way of repenting for everything that I have done." Shame gnaws at me and I lower my head. "My duty now is to guide lost spirits to the afterlife."

Orjan cups my chin and raises my face to meet his. His face is beautiful, his jawline hardened, a thick, greying stubble lining his face. His dark, tired eyes are weary, but even in this spectral form, they sparkle as they search deeper into me than I have ever allowed anyone to do.

"And I will wait an eternity in the afterlife if it means I will one day be with you."

I take his hand and set off walking to guide him to the afterlife, so he can be free of the cruelty and torment that he faced in this world.

At least in this life, we can finally be together.

Vireo

Standing in the courtyard of the castle, I take a deep breath of air, and for the first time, it smells fresh, the putrid stench of death and decay finally evaporated. People buzz around me, getting ready to trade wares. A cart of grain is heading out of the castle gates, a gift from Laith to the people of Askela, for them to take and plant new seeds on the lands they have been given, not just within Askela but on the boundaries beyond.

It has not been an easy few months in the aftermath of the Battle for Levanthria, but slowly, we are rebuilding.

Gillam is in the training pit, but she bears no weapons, nor is she practicing her fighting. Instead, she sits on a bale of straw next to her mother, both holding books as they practice their reading together.

I look down at the broach that is pinned to my chest: a lion, clasped around a sword, the new sigil of Askela. One not to signal a family crest, but to represent the kingdom. It was bestowed to me by Laith when he asked me to become his steward, to help support him as he bids to fix Askela and the rest of Levanthria.

"How are you two getting on?" I ask as I walk over to Gillam and Yaelor. Yaelor is more enthusiastic than Gillam, who wears a fed up expression, almost sulking.

"How much longer do I have to read, Vireo? I want to train with Mama's hatchets. When I am older, I want to be a fierce warrior like her."

Yaelor rolls her eyes and laughs.

I kneel in front of her and ruffle her hair, and she scowls at me in return. "Not all battles are won with brawn," I say. "In time, you will train to fight, but for now, you will read, and you will learn the history of Levanthria. You will discover how crops are grown, how magic can be used to help others."

"But that bit is boring."

"One day you are going to serve Levanthria, as your

father is, as your mother is, and as all these people are doing. Not as its ruler, but as something else. Your father has entrusted me with helping you get there, which unfortunately means more reading and less fighting."

"Gillam, your papa has entrusted Vireo with watching over your education. I promised I would learn these things alongside you, but I need you to show faith in your teacher like I do."

"Okay, Mama," Gillam says with a sigh before returning to her book.

"You are wearing a cloak, are you going somewhere today?" Yaelor asks.

"How observant of you." I smile. "I just have something I need to do. Laith is aware I will be gone for a while, but I will be back before long."

I wave them off and head towards my horse. It feels strange wearing clothes that are not tattered and worn, the soft leathers groaning with every step that I take. I hop onto my horse and take a short journey through Askela towards the main gates.

I pass through the markets, where the hustle and bustle of trade is returning with the sound of barter and people deep in conversation. The smell of bread fills my lungs and brings a warm smile to my face. I bow my head to people as I pass, and they do in turn. The sound of hammer against wood and stone chimes as I pass through what used to be the slums. Work has already begun on fixing the homes in this area and building new ones, with scores of men and women hard at work as they continue to rebuild what was broken. When I pass the Great Temple, the boarded windows and doors have been removed and the glass is being replaced by more people hard at work. It will no longer be used as a place of worship, but will be dedicated to healing those in need, as Jordell would have wanted. Askela is already prospering. It will continue to take time, but we will get there, of that I am sure.

When I leave Askela, I head to a small oak tree that sits on the bend of the river. It is a place where I often come to gather my thoughts and remember. On this occasion, however, I have fetched something with me. After I dismount my horse, I reach into my satchel and remove the withered green cloak that once belonged to Allana. I wore it for so many years as I clung onto her memory and dealt with my own grief of losing her and our unborn child.

I kneel down in front of the tree and hug the cloak one final time, tears filling my eyes. My throat burns. It is a grief that has consumed me for so many years. I place the cloak by the tree and rest my hand on it.

"It is time for me to move on, my love," I say. "I will not forget you or our child, what we could have had. Know that I am a better person than I was. That is down to you." I stand in silence for a few moments before turning to look at Askela from afar. The grime has been removed from the walls, and the stone walls and turrets are brighter than ever before.

"Something tells me that everything is going to be okay."

Zerina

The fresh breeze of the Pendaran Hills presses against my skin as I take in the sight of Levanthria. Hot drink in hand, I sit cross-legged with a blanket wrapped around me as I think about my sisters. I do this every morning now, and it has helped me find some semblance of peace, if such a thing exists.

It helps me to gather my thoughts. Sometimes I laugh, sometimes I cry, but most importantly, it allows me the time to share emotion that for too long I kept bottled up.

The sound of clucking chickens reminds me that they have not had their morning feed, and I get up from my sisters' graves and head over to the pen.

As I scatter the chicken feed, I can't help but think about Darmour. This was the life we should have had together, he should be here with me. At least this way I can honour what we wanted to build together, starting with these chickens.

I have been learning how to care for them from scratch, having never managed livestock before, but it has been a welcome change to sailing the high seas. There are times that the world around me rocks and sways as if I am still on a boat, and I hope that in time this will pass, for I will never set foot on a ship again. There are too may memories, too many that remind me of Darmour. It is too painful to live through.

The villages at the foot of the hill are more accepting of me now, with tales of the final battle against Rhagor having spread through the lands like wildfire. It is nice to have people looking at me with pride rather than fear, and they are the ones that have helped me get set up here. They helped me repair the house I once shared with my sisters and build the chicken coop.

I look across at the pen I am in the middle of building for the next lot of livestock. This will be for sheep when it is finished. As I finish feeding the chickens, I smile to myself and place the bucket by the gate before making my way back to my home.

Standing in the doorway, I wrap the blanket around my shoulders and let the coarse fabric rub against my cheek. It was Darmour's, and it brings me comfort every single day. I look out at the vibrant green lands around me and I know that I am going to be okay with this life. It is all I dreamt of, and with the memories of my sisters and Darmour to spur me on, I am proud of my home and the new life that I am building. One away from battles, one that doesn't require me to use magic. The king offered me resources, but I want to build this myself, I want to do this myself.

Hopefully, my sisters and Darmour are looking down on me from the afterlife with pride.

Esara

"Can you smell that, Ulrik?" I say with a smile, leaning against the side of the ship as we make port. It has been a long journey, but the smell of the fresh sea breeze along with a vibrant port brings a smile to my face.

"Remember, no killing," Ulrik says dryly as the crew set about their duties of docking the ship.

"Now now, brother, it is like you don't know me."

"We have had a lot to catch up on, sister."

The air itself is warm here, the climate somewhat different to that of Levanthria, but it does not stop people going about their business here.

As Ulrik and I disembark, the port master greets us. He is wearing a thin tunic that hangs just below his knee, with gold embroidery lining the outer edges of his short sleeves. He wears a hat that sits close to his head, like a bandana, no doubt to shield himself from the sun.

"Welcome to Bruyt," he says, his accent different from any I have heard before.

"It is good to be in the capital of Argosia," Ulrik says, offering a small purse filled with gold coins.

The port master raises the purse next to his head and gives it a light shake before nodding his head in satisfaction.

All around me, a riot of sights and sounds assails my senses. Merchant sailors in loose linen tunics and sandals haul crates from the bellies of great wooden ships with carved figureheads depicting fearsome sea monsters. The air is thick with the aroma of exotic spices, sweet fruits, and the unmistakable tang of fresh fish.

The port itself is a vast expanse of smooth stone quays and piers jutting out into the sparkling azure waters of the bay. Mighty columns of white marble support lofty archways decorated with friezes depicting heroic battles and the exploits of legendary heroes. Banners of bright crimson and indigo flutter from the masts of the vessels.

In the distance, I can see the famed acropolis of Bruyt rising up on a craggy hill, its temples and grand civic buildings a breathtaking panorama of fluted columns, sculptural pediments, and steeply pitched tile roofs. The whole city seems to glow like a gem in the brilliant morning sunlight.

All around the port, market stalls are set up, their owners loudly hawking their wares – plump olives and crusty bread, jars of golden olive oil and honey, bolts of vibrantly dyed fabrics, and all manner of craftwork from delicate pottery to finely wrought jewellery. The people seem a lively, cosmopolitan bunch dressed in colourful robes and tunics, with dark curls bound by coral-studded headbands or left flowing free.

The sounds of haggling and laughter compete with the

raucous calls of gulls wheeling overhead and the rhythmic slap of waves against the dock's pilings. For a moment, I feel utterly transported to another world, one steeped in ancient glories yet still vibrantly alive. The port of Bruyt promises adventures untold.

It is here where we will make a new name for ourselves, on a continent where we have no sullied reputation to tar us. We can make an honest living here, and bring a new meaning to the title of pirates.

"Think of the treasure that we could find here," I say with a beaming smile.

"Did you say treasure?" the port master says, leaning into us with a hushed tongue.

"I apologise, my sister meant no offence. She can be a bit overeager and excitable at times."

"None taken," the port master says. "It just so happens that I know someone in need of help. You see, things have got a little strange across the lands in Argosia. Cursed beings, gods walking the earth and procreating like never before, and long-hidden treasures unsurfaced."

"Really," I say with a widened smile, my curiosity piqued. "Are you to tell us any of these stories?"

The port master's smile matches my own. "Let me tell you about a young warrior named Eras, the minotaur and the labyrinth where it now hides."

AFTERWORD

Well, I never thought we would get to this moment. The Levanthria Series is finished. Trust me when I tell you that I needed a rest after completing it. With this afterword for once I find myself lost for words but I will do my best. The last few years have been a whirlwind, never in a million years did I think that this series would reach the parts of the world that it has and garner such dedicated readers. This whole series started out as me wanting to write my very own version of Robin Hood and developed into something far bigger than I could have ever imagined.

The future is an exciting and terrifying place, stepping into new story worlds and series for you to dive into, with a whole new cast of characters which I hope you will come to love. I sincerely hope that you will join me in this next stage and I hope that you have enjoyed The Levanthria Series.